Connecting in Iceland

Mark Archer

Dedication

To my legs that carried me unflinchingly, well nearly, across the unrelenting lava and tarmac.

To those who connected: Margrét, Benedikta, Laura, Hilary, Katharine, Nonni, Martina and Hrefna.

To my family who followed me on my emotional journey.

To Ted Edwards, explorer, who planted the seed...

Acknowledgements

Thank you to Kath, my sister, for reading my draft and giving
advice generally; to Helen, another sister, for proof-reading;
thank you to my son Joel for permission to use
his cover photographs, as well as other photos at the Solfar; to
Björgvin at Egilsstadir Airport for looking after my pack; to Icelandic
Farm Holidays for valuable information concerning accommodation;
to everyone associated with my former primary school who followed
my trek on my Spot Tracker. Finally thank you to the many people
who really helped and encouraged me while I was in Iceland.
I could not have endured without you.

Revised

ISBN:
ISBN-10:151469171X
ISBN-13:978-1514691717

Calm before the Storm

Walking across the coulee,
Conjures an immense sense of trepidation.
Will it be rough or crumbly, gravelly or crunchy?
A footslog along vast swathes of scoria.

A perception of foreboding and unease,
Allied to the thrill of adventure, excitement and novelty.
An odyssey into the unknown, a journey of surprises.
Backpacking for the long haul of four hundred miles
A fundamental challenge.

And now, with a few weeks to go,
The barometer of apprehension rises,
Inextricably rises,
Like floodwater after heavy downpour….

Will I handle a vista of basalt and obsidian?
A magma-enriched topography,
A panorama of volcanoes
Split solely by tense footprints of exploration.

Eleventh hour approaching,
The greatest peregrination of my life.
My brain is Icelandic!
A mind of ice and fire,
Volcanic anxiety and dread.

But my resolve is stronger, greater,
More potent and efficacious.
I am going to do it!
Seydisfjordur to Reykjavik!
A tramp! A trek!
A lifetime aspiration,
Satisfied

Each chapter is preceded by a saying derived from various sources including the Hávamál – words that provided Vikings with solace, advice and guidance on their voyages to new lands, including Iceland. Other sayings are basic Icelandic proverbs or are attributed to leading authors or writers.

Distances travelled over the course of a chapter are indicated in miles.

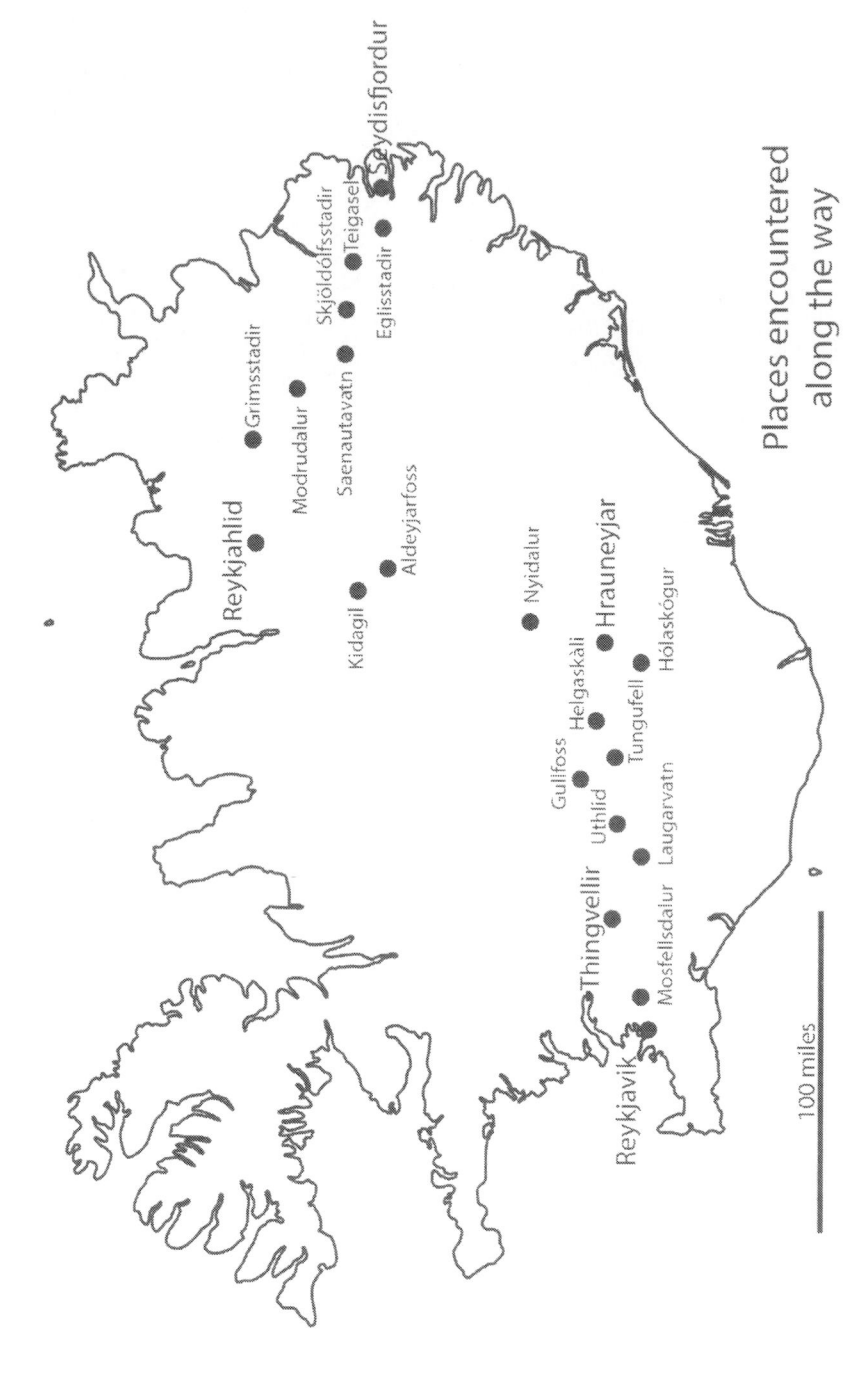

Places encountered
along the way

Skaydisfjordur

Teigaseis

Skjöldólfsstadir

Grimsstadir

Modrudalur

Reykjahlid

Saenautavatn

Egilsstadir

Aldeyjarfoss

Kidagil

Nyidalur

Hrauneyjar

Helgaskáli

Hólaskógur

Gullfoss

Tungufell

Thingvellir

Uthlid

Laugarvatn

Reykjavik

Mosfellsdalur

100 miles

Contents

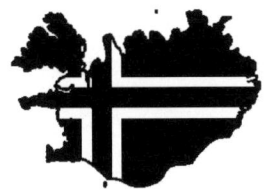

1. Handshakes all round

You don't forget an Icelandic handshake. A firm, resolute grip as strong fingers wrap around yours; an intensity and warmth that suffuses through your skin. Then there is the length of time your hand remains locked in a vice-like grasp, moulded between the jaws of a newly purchased Mole Wrench or a frenzied man-eating crocodile. Your hand ain't going nowhere for the next few moments, as your phalanges and metacarpals are subjected to a force of violent compression akin to a stroppy car-crushing machine. It must be an Icelandic trait – a strong handshake, because everyone whose hand I shook, from this small, unassuming country, lying just on the periphery of the Arctic Circle, affected me with an immense handlock, that at times made me wary as to what physical abuse I was about to become subjected. From the wiry hotel waiter in Reykjavik, to the swarthy horse farmer outside Gullfoss; all had a steelish grip that said, "Welcome!" or, "Thank you for coming to our country!" or, "Don't even think about stealing our cod!" No limp lettuce handshakes here. This country, Iceland, is made of stronger stuff, and its people like you to know it.

And why do they countenance you with such forceful, titanic arm-rattling? Well, their display of strength reflects the lifestyle they lead, five hundred miles off the top of Scotland, and then left a bit. The harshness of their environment, the unpredictable and ever-changing face of their weather, reputedly the worst in Europe, the youthfulness and unpredictability of their geology, their absurd fondness for eating sheep heads and puffin develops within them a purposeful and undaunted resolution not to be fazed by whatever meteorological or volcanic nasties the Norse gods throw at them. They are not a wimpish nation of pinafores and fondue meals; winceyette sheets and flower arrangers. No, instead they are an imperturbable, stolid and level-headed unit: calm, self-composed and phlegmatic, prepared to face the notorieties of their extreme Arctic nature, or the fickleness of their modern economy, with a roll-up-their-sleeves attitude that says, "Don't bloody mess with us!"

And when I shook hands with Ingi Steinn, receptionist at the Hotel Natura, situated next to Reykjavik's busy domestic airport, I knew exactly what these kind, considerate and stoical people were all about. His handshake said everything, reinforced with a reassuring smile and the sincerity in his voice told me I was in a good place, with good people. And then, there was the look. His eyes fixed mine during our handshake and, in that brief moment, well the best part of half a minute actually, we both understood each other;

a sort of miniaturised telepathy in which we shared a tiny part of ourselves. This was something repeated, with other Icelanders, many, many times. Weird, but nice. But now I was leaving, after a whole month of Icelandic company and hospitality. I had shared, for thirty three days, their lifestyle, their culture, their geography, their weather (definitely their weather), but above all, their kindness. And I would miss them because they had influenced me greatly. I had been surprised, almost startled, how much they had wanted to assist me personally, to help me in my quest to carry out the most difficult, the most physical and the most challenging task of my life.

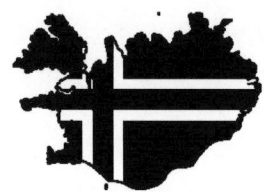

2. Fight the Wild Island

In Iceland, you can see the contours of the mountains wherever you go, and the swell of the hills, and always beyond that the horizon. And there's this strange thing: you're never sort of hidden; you always feel exposed in that landscape. But it makes it very beautiful as well. - Hannah Kent

It was all Ted Edward's fault of course. Over fifteen years previously I had borrowed a book from my local library. I often read books about polar explorers and adventurers, and this day was no exception. A particular book caught my eye, by an author called Ted Edwards. The cover displayed an intrepid looking character weighed down with a cumbersome looking rucksack. He was equipped with an ice axe, a camouflage jacket and a pair of red gaiters. He wore a pair of dark glasses, as he looked far into the icy distance. Opening the pages of his book, I was quickly enthralled to learn about his pioneering exploits in crossing Iceland, from one side to the other.

4

On foot. Unaccompanied. His travelogue included not only details of Icelandic sagas and legends, but also a very personal account of his travails into the wilderness of this exceptional and remote country. And I was captivated. I couldn't put the book down. It became my security blanket. I soon became immersed in all things volcanic – lava deserts, black sand, magma, fumaroles and mud pools. Ted described his expedition in vivid detail, relating his trials and tribulations, his successes and near disasters as he journeyed from remote Seydisfjordur, in north-east Iceland across the highland interior of Sprengisandur to the friendlier, but still impressive and exciting environs of Reykjavik, a journey of several hundred miles and, all of it, under his own steam. "Fight the Wild Island" he called his book. What a title! What an adventure!

When I finally finished reading, having stopped only momentarily for life-sustaining meal breaks, I made the decision that, one day, I too, would attempt to complete this walk. I would explore the Icelandic wilderness for myself. I would join the throng of explorers now and then; become a modern day Shackleton, my childhood hero, but hopefully, without the dramas and mishaps associated with this celebrated Polar adventurer.

I shoved the idea to the back of my mind, resurrecting it from time to time, in occasional discussions with family and friends, about bucket lists, aspirations et al, but otherwise there the idea remained, on the back burner, as I lived a very conventional life as a married primary school teacher with a single son. The most exciting things I ever became involved in were modest holidays to vaguely exotic places such as Cyprus, Tuscany and the Balearics, along with mobile home holidays in the Vendee and the romantic Loire Valley. As I got older, I found myself sinking into middle-aged lethargy caused by a sedentary lifestyle, watching Strictly on the television, completing the crossword on the back of the daily rag, feeding the guinea pig, bringing in the washing, planning lessons for my schoolchildren and stuffing Jaffa cakes down my fat neck at every opportunity. Knee joints started to complain due to inactivity, and lassitude, associated with most overweight fifty-somethings, became the order of my day, until the day of realisation at my aunt's funeral, that important choices and changes needed to be made.

My aunt, an intelligent but stubborn lady in her mid-eighties, was the last of the older generation within my family. A long illness culminated in her sad demise, and we all gathered for her funeral in Wood Green, North London. After her cremation, we returned to her terraced house and ate blown-dried ham sandwiches, stale vol-au-vents with dubious fillings, all involving coagulums of distressed mushroom and other unidentifiable black bits, along with sorry-looking pizza slices that seemingly originated in the previous century. As we mournfully munched our food and exchanged platitudes, I suddenly became very aware of man's impermanence on this earth, especially mine. The older generation had gone, next up was my generation and this hit me like a fizzing thunderbolt. Lord, I could be next! I gripped the Parker-Knoll chair tightly, sweating profusely, maintaining my tenuous hold on life as best I could.

After the funeral, my mortality gnawed away at me like a dodgy tooth or a persistent migraine. I was becoming rather dissatisfied with the way my life was going. I did not feel fulfilled. I enjoyed my primary teaching job but it had completely taken over my life. Each day seemed like the last one; a relentless tide of planning lessons and marking books, writing reports, and being overly nice to people all day long. I particularly found it difficult to cope with the constant changes and interference from the powers that be, in my teaching role at school, as know-it-all governmental authorities kept re-inventing the wheel and telling me what I already knew. For the first time in my life, I started to look beyond teaching and considered what the future actually held for me. What was I going to do with the rest of my life? After all, my analogue time clock was now ticking.

I looked at my family – my son was almost college age and he would soon be embarking on a career, more than likely, away from home, off into the big wide world. My wife was working herself to the bone as a sister in a local hospital. We vaguely saw each other every other month and at Christmas for just half a day and appeared to be leading increasingly separate lives. We exchanged birthday cards now and then and took it in turns to pay the papers and the grocery bills. I looked at my job – did I really want to be teaching right up to the age of 65? I considered this a truly dreadful proposition. I remember kneeling at a child's desk, helping him with contraction apostrophes, in particular distinguishing between the use of "its" and "it's", when I went to stand up, but could not. My joints had seized and I was severely in need of some Castrol GTX or WD40 to remedy the problem. My teaching assistant, noting my discomfort, came over and offered to help the creaking old fool up. No, teaching youngsters was for a younger generation, and I was, as I had shockingly discovered at my aunt's funeral, now a geriatric, a coffin dodger, distinctly past my prime.

 For the first time in my life, I considered doing something radical; I started to consider my Iceland dream to be something more than just a fanciful whim. Could I actually make an Iceland trek a reality? Could I, grey haired and rotund, embark on something ever so slightly insane?

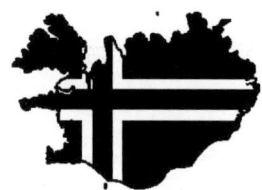

3. Vita non est vivere sed valere vita est

These things are thought the best: Fire, the sight of the sun, good health with the gift to keep it - The Hávamál

I remember broaching the subject about retiring with my wife one evening. Generally our evenings were spent with her watching the television downstairs while I was ensconced in my office doing schooly things upstairs. Who said romance was dead? My son was conveniently out so I took the opportunity to put forward thoughts about my future, just as the adverts began, half way through Corry Norry. Normally an interruption of a TV soap opera was greeted with snarls of aggression akin to a rabid Rottweiler, however I took my life in both hands, puffed out my cheeks and muttered my ideas about my future at a volume so quiet, only a mouse could have heard it. I tried again, somewhat louder intimating that my life needed a fresh impetus. This bombshell provoked the comment, "What are you on about?" so I nervously repeated my idea that my teaching career may be nearer the end than I had previously thought. I mentioned hassles I was having at work, the constant never-ending workload, the demands made on my time every hour of the day, the fact we only ever went out together on our son's parents' evenings and other people's weddings. Surely there should be more to life than this? She listened quietly as I moaned and whinged and then I suddenly threw a spanner in the works and mentioned that I might retire from teaching early.

 I waited for a reaction, expecting possibly a hostile "You can't do that! We can't afford it!" But instead, what I got was a more measured response, as she flat-batted my proposition back to me, so I outlined my ideas and went through the options where we discussed how I felt, the implications of me finishing, as well as our finances and pensions. I outlined possibilities for the future, but, most importantly, *she did not disagree with me.* She looked across the room at me almost as if she knew that it would be pointless trying to convince me otherwise. I think she realised that the demands of my job were making life exceedingly onerous and she knew that I was basically quite unhappy with my lot at this time. I mentioned briefly what I wanted to do instead and, for the first time in a long while, I reiterated my intention to walk across Iceland. This was not news to her. She'd heard me obsessing about Iceland eons before, in fact we'd spent two enjoyable holidays in Iceland many years previously. What was different this time was the fact that my intent, for the first time ever, was deadly serious. I wanted to walk across Iceland and I wanted to do it soon. Our conversation ceased with nothing really settled or decided, but the seeds had been sown…

I decided to attend a pre-retirement course set up by my teaching union just before Christmas 2013. The course was designed to help people just like me, who were considering throwing their hand in. Could I really bring my illustrious (as viewed through my very own rose-tinted spectacles) teaching career to an end, after many years of dutiful dedication and commitment?

I ventured out, early one sunny December morning to attend the course at a rather pleasant location in a charming clubhouse on a golf course in North Manchester. I was slightly apprehensive when I arrived there with other hesitant, confused and uncertain individuals of similar age and outlook to me. We all had a strained look on our faces that said, "I've had enough of the rat race and I want out." We talked quietly in small groups, almost apologetic for being there, staring uncertainly into our cups of filter coffee, far too strong for my liking.

The course started and the introductory session was to establish the arguments for and against retirement, but within just two minutes of listening to the opening speeches, I knew instinctively there and then, that I *had* to retire. I *had* to follow my intuition; to make the most of the opportunities in the time left for me. They say that teaching is a very selfless career, but I had finally decided that no longer was I going to put my self-interests on the back-burner. For the first time in my life, as a member of the older generation, on the gangplank to an inevitable eternity of subterranean existence and dust, I was going all out to achieve something, just for me and me alone. I was going to retire and, within a realistic and reasonable time frame, get fit and prepared, in order to take on the hardest physical challenge of my life!

After the day's course I drove home to north-east Lancashire. I felt serene and calm and somewhat relieved. I now knew exactly what I wanted to do and as soon as I saw my wife, I said simply:

"That's it. I'm going to retire." I explained how the day had gone, how I'd met many people on the course, in a similar situation to me, with wonky knees and burnt out body parts, however none of them was contemplating a major trek across a polar wilderness. Instead they were considering more passive pastimes such as fiction writing, coarse fishing and wild flower photography. My wife simply looked at me but said nothing. I think she was scared of the uncertainty that lay ahead, of the changes that would be enforced on us, but I think she realised too, that this was something I was really serious about, and trying to change my mind would be futile.

Over Christmas, my mind changed gear as I considered how to actually kick start the retirement process and how to plan for my Arctic adventure. I informed family members of my intentions. They were somewhat surprised about my proposed retirement because they knew how much my teaching career, particularly my involvement and interaction with my school children, had meant to me, but they also understood and sympathised, because they also knew the intense pressures teaching brought. What they did not understand was why on earth I would want to walk across an out-of-the-way place like Iceland? Wasn't it, after all, near the North Pole and rather cold?

This slightly flummoxed me because I thought I had told them all years before about my proposed venture, however they must have considered my nomadic aspirations to be mere pipedreams. O how wrong they were! I had never been more serious in my life. I had always intended to walk across Iceland, it was just that the time to actually do it was now fast approaching.

Two and a half months later I gave my notice to quit in resignation letters to my head teacher and Chair of Governors. Both letters started with the Latin phrase –

"Vita non est vivere sed valere vita est" which means: "Life is not being alive but being well." I intended this to indicate that wellness includes having the time and opportunity to do things which fulfil and satisfy you, whereby aspirations are finally achieved and realised. Just being alive was no longer sufficient to sustain me, and at the age of fifty seven, I had to make sure I got a move on!

Initially, people were surprised, even astounded.

"You! Walk across Iceland? What for? You'll break the ice, carrying all your weight! Plus, it's full of polar bears." That, I felt, was a little unfair, a tad unkind and zoologically, way off beam. True I was overweight and out of condition, however at a younger age, I had, after much careful training and preparation, cycled one thousand miles from John o' Groats to Land's End. I simply had to do exactly the same amount of planning, fitness training and exercise once again. My sisters were actually quite worried for me. My welfare became their primary concern but when I informed them I wanted to do it solo, a sense of dismay filled their hearts. But I was comfortable with my ability. I just had to train up and lose weight. I had to improve my navigational know-how and basically go through an extended and rigorous period of preparation and logistical planning. One thing I had always prided myself on, was my ability to prepare, to cover every eventuality. I would quite simply apply my organisational skills to my Icelandic challenge. It was hardly rocket science. It did slightly irk me that I seemed to have more confidence in myself than my family, immediate and extended. After all, they had seen me get lost and become disorientated right outside my front door on numerous occasions in my youth. But I was a distinctly different creature from that fresh-faced teenager who readily got lost in the aisles of Tesco and Woolworth's, after all, I now understood contours, the vagaries of magnetic variation and I had a sound knowledge of the 1975 Cod War between Britain and Iceland. In fact, I could not really think of anyone *more* qualified to embark on a trans-Iceland trek, I mused rather absurdly, with a smattering of arrogance.

One afternoon, in a quiet moment, I told the children in my class at school I was going to retire. Initially there was a noticeable silence and an atmosphere hung heavy over the classroom. They were very shocked and upset, which was quite humbling. Several thought however that I was far too young to retire, which I thought very kind and flattering. I would, I inwardly concluded, give them extra team points for their fawning compliments of ingratiation. Wonderful children! Several others no doubt thought quietly, "About time too, old bugger. Should have gone years ago." I would see their mums later! I knew who they were. The whole ambiance in my classroom and the relationship I had with the children, changed instantly as they came to terms with this unexpected curved ball.

"Don't worry," I told them reassuringly. "I'll only be around the corner. (The school was just four minutes from my front door). "I'll be keeping an eye on you all, to make sure you turn out all right." The trouble was, I was not even sure if *I* would turn out all right.

"What are you going to do when you retire?" was one of the questions asked. I informed them that I was going to be an explorer! That response went down really well with the more adventurous children, while one or two more imaginative and pragmatic ones simply shut their eyes tight with dread.

"He'll be dead within a week!" they thought, with a confidence in me bordering on zero. Henrietta, a nervous, sensitive soul, nearly fainted with worry, so traumatised was she at my unexpected bombshell. Thank goodness I had more self-belief than they did!

Within hours, parents were accosting me to discover more about my Icelandic adventure. They too were, on the whole, suitably impressed and congratulated me on my resolve in attempting to achieve my life's ambition. One or two thought I was mad, with a death-wish and shook their heads sagely. One particular parent just laughed, an annoying, long extended laugh that started off as a slight chuckle and descended rapidly into outright hysteria, which I considered rather rude and obtuse. I think he thought I had as much chance of surviving, as a walrus in a Turkish Bath, but generally, the feedback was positive and encouraging. Comments of "Mad fool," were outweighed with "Captain Scott of Pendle," (Pendle being the local area). Again, my school parents' knowledge of all things polar, was distinctly poor, Scott having gone to the South Pole, not the North. I blame the teachers.

After all the hullaballoo, things quietened down somewhat. There was just one snag. It's one thing to tell people you are going to walk a long way across some remote country like Iceland. It's totally another thing to actually do it!

For a start, there is a great deal of physical self-preparedness required and I hadn't done anything vaguely physical for at least fifteen years, unless you count wallpapering the downstairs and carrying in the bags of groceries from the local supermarket once a week. My weight had ballooned to sixteen stones which marked me in the obese category. I could still go on walks but where I particularly felt my excess weight, was in my groaning knees and they complained constantly whenever I climbed a set of stairs. I had put this down to ageing joints, however I soon realised it was caused by carrying around too many pounds, not the monetary type, unfortunately.

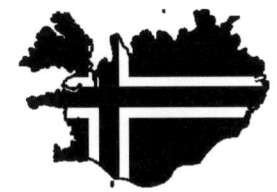

4. Marti's Kit

A wayfarer should not walk unarmed, but have his weapons to hand: He knows not when he may need a spear, or what menace meet on the road - The Hávamál

nitially I decided to go on a series of walks around my local area to get back in shape. But where? I armed myself with the local OS Map, invested in a Silva Compass, promptly placed it too near a metallic object and consequently reversed its poles, much to my intense annoyance, so I had to go out and purchase another bloody one. I bought a pair of over-trousers, from Milletts, dusted down my trusty kagoule and shook the cobwebs from my rucksack, secreted away in the garage, and in which, one of my hens - I had two - had laid an egg in the top pocket the best part of a year ago, which now, as I gingerly removed it, appeared very slightly coddled and off. And so, a very faint sulphurous smell accompanied me on day one of my training, but I gallantly chose to ignore it. I remember bravely venturing out to complete a four mile walk around the village of Chatburn, when I tried out my GPS for the very first time. This device had been bought by my wife as a Christmas present three years earlier and had hardly made it out of the box. It came with a rather complicated set of instructions, with sub-sections entitled: "Waypoints" and "Highway Page" and "Track Log". This threw me completely to begin with. Not only was I trying to get fit, I was also having to learn a foreign language at the same time. The jargon of GPS was quite complex, indeed baffling, and required as much concentration to learn and understand, as conjugating irregular verbs in the first declension, or whatever arcane grammar device I was taught in Latin many years previously. I persisted however and got to grips with all the literary and technical complexities Garmin could throw at me. Before long I was tackling modest circuits around the local area of Pendle, the Ribble Valley and the Forest of Bowland. Small steps was the way to do it, both literally and metaphorically, and I realised that five mile walks – lots of them – was basically the way to go.

However, there were anatomical problems from the outset. My rusty pins had not been exercised for a considerable period of time and so immediately they suggested that repetitive strain and endeavour was not to their liking whatsoever and could they simply stop please? Various rickety stiles I encountered on my walks presented themselves as tricky obstacles that I had to climb over in slightly doddery fashion, whilst I attempted to retain a sense of decorum, modesty and dignity, for I had all the flexibility of a reinforcing rod set in concrete. My body was not for bending. Some of the ladder stiles I came across were patently ridiculous, if not downright dangerous, with rungs set an absurd distance apart for someone who generally struggled to ascend a set of ladders into the loft. I could not remember the last time I had raised a leg more than two feet off the ground except when climbing into a bath of hot, foamy water and even then I sometimes slipped and fell, creating a bow wave of tsunamical proportions, followed by anguished howls of pain as my tender posterior landed heavily on something hard and ceramic.

After a couple of hours walking, I also had problems with bruising on the sensitive soles of my feet, which worried me slightly because I wasn't that sure if my feet were up to the task. They protested regularly, when faced with cross-country walks, having spent years doing bugger-all, snuggled inside a pair of Marks and Sparks slippers in front of a blazing coal fire developing raging athletes' foot. I persevered however, putting up with bruised feet, throbbing soles, knotted muscles, a hobbling gait and gradually increased my distances. Five mile walks became seven milers. I threw in the occasional reckless ten miler and felt extremely pleased with myself, but then suffered considerably the following day, when I could barely shuffle down the stairs. The neighbours used to watch me, in quiet bewilderment, from behind their curtains as I limped off on yet another walk, even though I could barely reach the end of my driveway without resembling someone who looked like they had just survived the consequences of an exploding bomb close by. This walking malarkey, for a late fifty year old, took a hell of a lot of getting used to. It wasn't like this in my youth when I used to canter sprightly across the fells of the Lake District, bagging peaks for fun. No, my springs had worn and my levers were, quite frankly, fit for the knacker's yard. Plenty of work to do! Bending over to pull on my trousers and socks, the day after an average walk, was an impossibility, such was my stiffness, soreness and lack of flexibility. My wife looked at me with scornful disdain, as if to say I had as much chance as walking across Iceland as I had of flying to the moon. In fact, the whole Iceland thing left her stone cold, emotionally speaking if not literally. My son just thought I was mad; pure and simple. I was sure he pitied me for trying to regain my youthfulness. At one point I think he thought it would have been better if I had bought myself a high powered motor bike to ease my way through my mid-life crisis. But a mid-life crisis it most definitely was not; this was about me discovering myself while I still had the energy and capability to do so. I could buy my motor bike when I got back.

All this training however, was all part of my long term plan to get fit. Rome wasn't built in a day and it was going to take a while to get my ailing body back in condition, one villa, nay one tessera, at a time.

I carried on my schedule of walks throughout the first half of 2013. At the same time, my life as a teacher was coming to a close. I worked just as hard, teaching, assessing, reprimanding, supporting, cajoling, being nice all the time, saying "Wow!" on a regular daily basis, but every time I went out for a walk, I remember thinking:

"Ah, walking! *This* is going to be my new job soon!" Good weather meant that I spent many a pleasurable day exploring the contours and villages of the Ribble Valley: Chipping, Dunsop Bridge and Chatburn, just three of its delightful rural gems. My knowledge of local geography improved out of all proportion, as I explored all the near and not-so-near highways and by-ways. Rambling across the hills and the countryside was becoming an exciting new way of life.

It's strange when you tell people that you are going to walk across Iceland, what their perception of it actually is. They imagine it to be a vast, hostile polar country similar to the Arctic and the North Pole. They imagine it to be an austere land of white; of remote igloos and truculent polar bears; of brave Arctic explorers battling their way through blizzards with the occasional penguin or walrus for company. In fact, polar bears can occasionally be found in Iceland, but only after hitching a lift on a southbound iceberg, then swimming to shore. Most polar bears are discreetly shot by farmers and eaten, well, there isn't any documentary proof they are eaten, but if I had shot a polar bear I don't think I'd forsake a meal or fifty of polar bear steaks, chops and burgers, with relish and fries, of course. As for penguins, they inhabit the other end of the world, preferring more elegant southern climes rather than gritty northern ones. Walrus too are not native to Iceland's shores either, reaching only as far as leafy Greenland. I was actually quite disheartened with most people's complete ignorance of Icelandic geography and zoology. I know it's not usually found in travel agents' brochures as are Malaga, Turkey, Benidorm or Lanzarote, but honestly! They didn't have a clue. All they had was a stereotypical knowledge of this vague faraway country based on comics and cartoons that was completely and utterly wrong.

Iceland is actually very unique and different. For a start, it is not especially icy, just 11% of its landmass is covered in glaciers. Secondly its summer climate can be remarkably mild, although somewhat changeable. When I visited Iceland for the first time in 1990, it was as warm as Spain, making my fluffy long johns and four season sleeping bag rather redundant. The landscape is bleak and barren, especially in the interior where lava fields and nothingness extend for miles in every direction, punctuated by occasional, impressive conical volcanoes standing like traffic cones along a motorway. Rivers flare off in all directions like the gossamer produce of a deranged spider. Waterfalls drip and dribble to excess like Saturday night binge drinkers, but with rather more sophistication and dignity. From time to time, you come across steaming hillsides: outdoor saunas of superheated steam as a reminder of that huge volatile mass of energy lurking just beneath the surface. There are precious few houses to break up the interminable sameness of the landscape, however it is this very sameness that draws you in, like a mesmerised moth to an alluring lamplight. Then there is the smell of the place, ranging from a sulphurous pong emitted from geothermal pools to rancid fishy odours emanating from rows of racks of drying fish corpses. Noxious, but completely true.

My sisters were still very concerned about my mad adventure and insisted that I take a walking buddy, in case I got into difficulty, a bit like Dr Who, travelling the Universe in his Tardis, with his rather pretty travelling companion. I *had* thought about walking with somebody else, but none of my buddies were particularly pretty; most were as ugly as sin, as unfit as hell, with the social graces of a diarrhoetic baboon, however this was supposed to be *my* walk and *my* dream. If I was accompanied, it would somehow dilute what I was trying to do. It would also give me someone else to consider and worry about. At least when you walk on your own, all you have to think about is yourself. You can get up when you want, set off when you want, stop when you want, eat when you want and smell as you want.

The problem with walking solo is there is no one to bail you out if you get into difficulty. You have to rely on yourself to get you out of any problems that arise. For instance, you may get hopelessly lost, which is why I was determined to become very proficient in the use of my GPS in order to prevent this. I was also going to arm myself with the very best up-to-date maps I could find and a swish looking compass to establish the easiest route from A to B. Another issue I had was I may get injured, tripping over an inconvenient piece of lava, scalding my hand in a boiling mud pool or fending off an enraged polar bear. In which case, I was going to ensure I bought the best pair of vari-focal spectacles my teachers' pension could buy, acquire a pair of flame-proof gloves and, of course, learn self-defence techniques of the Ecky-Thump variety, wafting a black pudding wildly in the general direction of any ursine assailant. The important thing to consider for a solo trekker was to set an agenda for walking that did not involve going too fast or taking risks crossing awkward and risky terrain. I had decided, where possible, to follow established tracks and roads, steering clear of obvious dangers such as steep slopes, boggy marshland, quicksand and itinerant polar bears. There was no way I was going to consider crossing any glacier unaccompanied, so Vatnajökull and Hofsjökull would be off limits. I was also not going to consider venturing up any of the volcanoes en route. I would be fired up quite enough already in my quest to reach the finish. No, volcanoes I could climb on another more dormant occasion. My focus was simply to get from the north-east side of Iceland to the south-west side, starting from Seydisfjordur, along parts of Route One, then following Route 26 through Sprengisandur before heading off to the touristy areas of Gullfoss and Thingvellir and then finally onto Reykjavik. My sisters still remained to be convinced however. They so wished I'd take a friend, just in case. I thought, to placate them, I might take a sonic screwdriver, *just in case*.

But I was relaxed and at ease with the cynics and disbelievers. I did not mind that some friends and family thought I was slightly deranged with a misplaced faith in my physical prowess and ability. I knew that I was going to do it. I knew that, if I prepared sufficiently and got myself physically fit, I could do this. I could indeed walk solo across Iceland.

During July and August 2013 I completed many local walks up to ten miles in length. A slight concern I had was my legs were getting fitter, however the rest of me was not. I had Seb Coe legs on a Billy Bunter body. I was still sixteen stones – way too heavy and inflexible for a long distance walk. Into September, having now officially retired, it felt slightly strange, for my life was now lacking the constant multi-tasking of teaching that I had been used to. Every day I now felt a sense of isolation; no longer harassed by children wanting to sharpen pencils or wanting to go to the toilet in the middle of a lesson on square numbers. I was now child-free and segregated from the hustle and bustle of the real world. My wife used to set off early in the morning for work, reappearing in the dark of the evening. My son similarly hurried off to school, leaving me with many hours to fill on my own. I thought sometimes as if I were playing a bit part in the film of life in general, detached from the daily hullaballoo of the twenty-first century. Conversely, I also possessed within me, a strong quality of renewal, of freshness and energy allied to a single sense of purpose and anticipation. I knew that instead of just sitting there thinking about getting fit, I had to seriously get on with it! So in September, I joined a local gym. I needed to get much fitter and lose at least two stones if I was to have any realistic chance of completing my objective.

Attending a gym for the first time is quite a shock to the system. One: it's cold. They seem to not have discovered radiators in these places of sinewy development. Two: stripping off down to your oversized shorts and baggy T-shirt, in front of a group of people you do not know, revealing bright white wobbly parts of your body that usually only see the light of day on a remote and barely populated beach in northern Spain, is a considerable achievement. It is only when you realise that many of the people at the gym are flabbier and weightier than you, some exceedingly so, that you take solace and worry rather less. You then submit your body to a rigorous examination that makes you sweat profusely and pant considerably, all in the name of fitness, on various ill-conceived instruments of torture that seem designed to take you to the very brink of death. It took me one pain-inflicted assault on the treadmill, pitched at an ever so slight upward angle of five degrees, facing a bare, painted breeze block wall, to discover what Hell is really like. Five minutes in and my body was on the verge of collapse. Ten minutes in and I felt I needed a benevolent vet to put me out of my insufferable misery like a condemned dog.

As for sweating, what is that all about? Hardly two minutes of feverish striding up and down on the cross walker would induce litres of perspiration to leach and percolate from my permeable skin like a very efficient colander, soaking other unfortunate would-be fitness freaks, within a two metre radius, with a modest Niagara-like spray of water, slightly salted of course.

The rowing machine I hated with a passion. Whatever possessed Steven Redgrave to spend his formative years sliding his formidable sweaty bottom up and down a sharp, oily metal beam, on a barely comfortable seat beats me. This medieval piece of equipment just seemed intent on wrenching my labouring shoulders from my exhausted frame, whilst at the same time sending my back into temporary seizure. Three times a week I suffered considerably on this evil contraption, sliding in and out like a demented piston on a Fred Dibner steam engine, all shiny and greasy, groaning with a bronchial gasp, like someone in the last stages of terminal TB, whilst breaking wind quietly, somewhat slyly but intermittently, as my digestive tract and sweaty trunk were subjected to being folded and unfolded like a piece of frenzied origami. All the while my eyeballs-out gaze was focused dementedly on an annoying digital meter above the groaning pulley wheel that wound in the taut wire, recording my meagre distance travelled, as it stubbornly refused to count as quickly as my maniacal efforts deserved. As ten minutes eventually elapsed, having rowed a frenetic 2268 metres, I expired to a sound of absolute anguish; a last-ditch plea for mercy; a dying lament followed by a desperate laconic wheeze of depletion, limbs akimbo, disgracefully so, salivating wildly like a rabid dog, with demon eyes blazing, sitting in my very own puddle of perspiration as large as a dinner plate. For the next twenty minutes I was not fit for purpose of any kind; a tormented shell of a human being – spent, wiped out, wasted.

All this self-inflicted physical abuse and torment paid dividends however, and within weeks, I was shedding the pounds; the first week, five pounds, the third week, four. I was also sticking to a strict diet based on 1500 calories a day. I was discovering the nutritious delights of proteins and vitamins, vegetables, fibre and fruit. Out of the window went chocolate biscuits, cream cakes and Cheddar cheese, and in came green tea, cherry tomatoes, Ryvita and sardines. The only food treat I allowed myself was an indulgent

Cornetto for dessert on a Wednesday evening. How I savoured, nay desired, this. I still salivate rudely, to this day, at the thought of such extravagance.

Allied to gym work I was walking every other day and swimming a mile at weekends. I felt the need to vary my exercise, so toning different sets of muscles. Now, I am only an average swimmer, but pretty good at breast stroke, in fact it is the only complete stroke I can technically manage, but I do like to know where I'm going and front crawl does not really allow you to do that. So I used to plough up and down, head bobbing, frog leg kicking, swimming sixty lengths, trying to avoid such unpleasantries such as itinerant strands of human hair, usually blonde, a foot in length, that tended to get wrapped around my face and nostrils and, more disturbingly, pink waterproof used sticking plasters of the Band-Aid variety, that had detached themselves from some septic knee or scabby chin and now floated uncomfortably close to my gaping mouth. Occasionally I'd get out of rhythm and ingest copious amounts of chlorinated water, but I sought solace in the fact that my insides would be bacterially protected from whatever sewage or waste products had been deposited in the pool that past week or so. When swimming, I used to suffer from "swimming pool rage" as I paddled up and down at breakneck speed, when small children and frail pensioners who got in my way, were elbowed and kicked with rather excessive spite. What particularly annoyed me were the two or three pensioners who would congregate in the shallow end to pass the time of day and discuss their various ailments and afflictions, preventing me touching the side of the pool and starting my next length. I muttered profanities beneath my breath, splashing them as inconsiderately as I could, kicking them in the groin or any other squishy sensitive place whilst maintaining a vestige of total innocence. I was not a pleasant person to know in the pool. A tyrant indeed.

My motivation for all this effort, sweat and strain was standing on a set of scales each week and finding out that the excesses of the last few years were peeling away like onion layers. In just over a month I had shed a stone and within two and a half months, over two stones. And all the while, I was becoming stronger, feeling better in myself and, walking up the stairs, was no longer akin to climbing the Matterhorn. Strangely, my wife did not mention my change in physique. I think she was becoming increasingly bored with my Icelandic obsession. I simply focused and persevered...

The new year of 2014 was important psychologically. No longer was I telling people I was going to walk across Iceland *next* year, because, overnight, it was now *this* year. A brief period of mild panic was followed by more rational and reasoned thought and appraisal. I still had an awful lot of work to do to become the shape and fitness of a polar explorer. Gradually I increased my distance, my pack load and the frequency of my walks. I maintained my dietary regime, however I remained a stubborn 13 ¾ stones for a while, so I endeavoured to do something about it. I picked up training after a Christmas break and set about completing longer, more demanding walks above ten miles. Many of these took me up into the Yorkshire Dales around Wharfedale, centred on Kettlewell and Malham, of karst scenery notoriety. It made a change to broaden my horizons and this undoubtedly renewed my spirit and motivation. I carried a brick or two in my pack, to add to my load, to replicate rather more the burden I would have to carry upon my back in Iceland. Thinking about it, I would have been better off with a bricklayers' hod really, rather than a rucksack.

Aside from the physical preparations, one major consideration was the logistics of such a trip. First of all, when to go? I had decided months previously that the window of opportunity for such a trek was either in the months of June or July. Any earlier and the highland interior might still be snowbound but I had no intention of trekking hundreds of miles across snow-covered lava desert and any later would mean shortening days, when the sun would start to set. What I really needed were long walking days when the sun never disappeared below the horizon, however briefly. Another problem with walking in summer however, is meltwater. The glaciers of Iceland thaw rapidly in hot weather and meltwater pours off the glaciers into fast-flowing streams that lace the landscape. This meltwater can be very dangerous indeed, particularly for a solo walker. I knew that attempting to cross a river just at the moment when a silent tsunami of meltwater was passing by, could prove fatal. I also knew that any significant rivers needed to be crossed before the heat of midday, otherwise I would have to wait until the following morning before venturing through the freezing glacial overflows. I don't mind admitting I was worried about the rivers, more than any other aspect of the walk.

I also spent a good deal of time looking at the type and amount of food I could take and I rapidly realised that my food provision was one of the heaviest, if not *the* heaviest, item I would carry with me. I pored over food labels looking at calorific energy content and came to the regrettable decision that, in order to cross Iceland, I would need a strange concoction of chocolate raisins, cashew nuts, granola and noodles in order to arrive at my destination fully sustained and bloated, if not a trifle constipated.

A set of 1:100000 maps of my route were obtained, six in all. I would be a walking atlas but not of the he-who-held-the-world-on-his-shoulders variety. My Garmin GPS was loaded with routes compiled on google earth and I purchased a neat piece of kit called a Spot 3 Satellite Tracker that would inform friends and family of my whereabouts each day. It also included a handy emergency button, to summon the rescue helicopter if I broke my leg in a remote area. Remote area? That included about 90% of Iceland then. I made sure my technical equipment was the best I could afford.

I spent a morning at an outdoor wear shop in Long Preston, near Settle in the Yorkshire Dales, because I had heard their merchandise was top quality. A friend of mine had purchased a pair of trousers from this store over twenty years previously and had not a bad word to say about them. With that in mind, I decided to have a look for myself, because choosing the proper kit was something I had to get right, after all, I could not afford my clothing to let me down in the middle of nowhere. But where do you start? I had no idea what the difference between "shells" and "mid layers" was. Did I need a "base layer?" All I knew was all the kit looked very impressive with prices to match. I also knew you got what you paid for. I spent a vague ten minutes searching the racks not really knowing what I was doing, when a young lady sidled up to me, obviously sensing my total ignorance and my anxious air of desperation. Her name badge indicated she was called Marti, and I told her about my mission to walk across Iceland and how I had come to kit myself out. Marti seemed impressed with my intended Arctic sojourn and appeared confident that the kit I needed was right here. She also didn't doubt my ability to carry out this trek, which boosted my frail ego enormously. In fact, her faith in me far outweighed my own family's. Perhaps she saw in me a competent explorer for whom nothing was too much. Anyway, I quickly warmed to her and her unerring belief in me, in fact I was distinctly flattered. She showed me various items of lightweight, durable gear that would do exactly what it said on the tin. I knew I needed clothes I could completely rely on. Marti showed me a particular pair of "Explorers" trekking trousers, remarkably light and guaranteed not to let water through. I, the biggest cynic of them all, doubted this claim, however Marti, with her striking blue-grey eyes smiled sagely and said in a soft confident voice that carried total conviction, that the trousers were indeed waterproof and of course, they would keep out Iceland's worst. Of that, there was no doubt. She fixed me with a stare of total conviction and smiled disarmingly. She also knew she had me hook, line and sinker. Maybe it was the eyes, maybe the tenet of what she said, I just truly believed in her.

"Trust me," she soothed. "These trousers will not let you down." She would, I felt, have staked her house on the trousers staying waterproof in an Icelandic storm. So, Dry Explorers trousers became a part of my kit, along with various other items that weighed almost nothing, took up no space and yet promised to keep me warm. I thanked Marti and she wished me well in my venture, reiterating the fact that I would be absolutely fine. Her eyes told me she actually believed that, and she was not saying that just to be polite. The connection was immense. I had finally found someone apart from me who actually thought I could do this! Empowered, I left the shop; wallet somewhat lighter but my confidence boosted sky high.

My shopping also took me to a variety of other well-equipped outdoor shops where I also bought some reinforced socks, various pairs of inner socks, along with merino wool base layers and mid-layers. Strange, the terminology of walking wear. It used to be string vest, T shirt and woolly jumper; now it was all high-tech "active diffusion technology"; "micro baffle anatomical construction" and "aqua dry membranes". I needed a degree in fabric technology to fully understand what the dickens everyone was on about.

The following week, I broke the bank and purchased the most expensive jacket I have ever bought of the Paramo variety and spent a whole day and a half admiring it. It even cost more than my wedding suit. It nearly cost more than the whole flipping wedding actually. I almost didn't want to bespoil it by putting it on. I also purchased a pair of walking poles. Black Diamond they were and both had a compression spring below the handles, perhaps to help me bounce my way over the lava. I had never walked with walking poles before but I was assured that they would be a great help when walking long distances, acting as a brake when tottering downhill and as a stable support when fording rivers. These walking poles were to prove to be a crucial piece of kit on more than one occasion.

My Swedish tent, a one man Hilleberg, cost me a small fortune, however my research suggested it was by far and away the strongest one on the market, and I surmised that solo trekking merited a house made of bricks rather than one of straw, so if the Icelandic wolf did his very best to blow my house down with a huff and a puff, then he'd fail miserably. I also obtained a lightweight sleeping bag, weighing in at a modest 630 grams filled with down. All told my equipment cost in the region of £1500. I was as well-equipped as Ted Edwards. All I had to do now was become as fit as him.

5. Toilet Training

Pissing in your shoes won't keep your feet warm for long – Viking Proverb

I spent a good deal of time finding out how solo trekkers perform their ablutions in the wilderness. It worried me rather, that I may have to spend an inordinate amount of time squatting whilst performing my No 2s, amidst the lava fields of Iceland, because at home, I seemed to spend an excessive amount of time in the lavatory on a daily basis, sometimes twice a day. I had come to realise that once you enter your fifties, you become more preoccupied with all things lavatorial, so my solo trek preparations had to take this important function into account.

I checked out youtube and various informed and suitably qualified American outdoor gurus suggested squatting and grabbing hold of a tree whilst performing, then burying the distasteful mess with your special spade in a hole of correct depth and size, then covering it over neatly with a prim layer of soil and leaves. Another consideration was: how do you cleanse yourself in a howling gale in the middle of a lava desert, having performed one of your more…considerable, possibly rather pleasantly enjoyable, lavish excretions? Apparently toilet paper was no good in the wild, because of its tendency to shred into a million useless pieces if it happened to get wet, and wet it would undoubtedly be in Iceland. Some informed sources suggested kitchen roll – a tougher version of loo roll, but I discarded this idea because of its bulk, and to have a kitchen roll holder hanging decorously down the back of my rucksack would rather bespoil my attempts to be taken seriously as a hardened trekker or explorer. The experts, you know, Bear Grylls clones, however, suggested cleaning yourself with a convenient stick, or flat stone or a handful of moss. This intrigued me initially, having spent a lifetime associated with Izal, with its inappropriate glossy surface and Andrex, of cute puppy dog fame, but then alarmed me, because I could not think of any other foreign body having got anywhere near my delicate, gentle posterior in my life time, save my friendly intimate nylon bathroom sponge and my fluffy Persian blue bath towel, both decidedly soft and comfortingly reassuring. A piece of hardened granite, coarse millstone grit or flaky quartz, or a slippery branch of silver birch or knotty horse chestnut being introduced to my tender rear end would take some getting used to. I therefore contemplated for a while having a tentative practice at cleaning my posterior al fresco, in my back garden, armed with samples of various flints and withes, however I was dissuaded from doing so, firstly: by my dismayed wife who could not have faced the sight of me, as she innocently looked out of the kitchen window whilst making herself morning coffee, denuded from the waist down, me not her, clinging desperately to our gnarled and cankered apple tree, gurning in a frightening and apoplectic way, squeezing my eyes tight shut and shouting "Thar she blows!" and secondly: by myself, who could not bear the thought of being viewed by vaguely voyeuristic, (not really) neighbours next door, whilst I was in paroxysms of anal ecstasy. Furthermore, I was worried that the particular stick or stone I chose to clean myself with, might inflict major internal damage to my rear, causing me more injury than my persistent haemorrhoids. Also, catching Dutch Elm disease in the rear end from a piece of rogue timber did not bear thinking about. No, I needed an alternative. I realised too, that in Iceland, trees are in short supply, so there would be precious little to hold on to while squatting. Now I don't know about you, but I haven't been able to squat on my haunches without holding on to a supporting object, since I was about seven. After that, whenever I squatted, without support, I simply fell over on to my back or my front. Not a clever, or particularly pleasant or hygienic thing to do, when performing a full blown and thunderous No 2.

The alternative manifested itself in a roundabout way. I had thought about getting hold of a fisherman's fold-up stool and cutting a neat round hole in the canvas fabric of the seat. I then thought I would place a thin plastic bag of the type freely available at the checkout of your local supermarket, underneath the hole, and voilà, I could perform my necessary functions while sitting down! Gravity and careful aiming would result in a steamy, gently warm, handsome pile contained artistically and rather nicely within one of Morrisons very own. BOGOF, the supermarket maxim, would now take on a totally new and appropriate meaning. It was a little while later however, I realised that there already existed a commercially available version of my BOGOF, called quite graphically, and rather discourteously, "Bog in a Bag." The only difference being, the bag is placed through the hole in a fold-up seat, so it is suspended conveniently and strategically underneath one's rather ample rear. The sight of this must probably appear quite ludicrous, however if it worked, then who was I to complain? The bag also contained absorbent material, similar to that found in a baby's nappy and special chemicals to break down human waste. How scientific! Without further ado, I purchased a blue triangular seat complete with neat hole, about fifteen centimetres in diameter. Large enough to allow the nasty stuff to pass through, small enough to stop my delicate rear following it! I also purchased five packets of bog in a bag bags. Enough I surmised for my month's trip, provided I did not go down with the Nordic equivalent of Delhi belly.

When I told friends and family what I had purchased, their reactions ranged from acute dismay to rather vulgar laughter, completely at my expense. They'd heard of the Appalachian Trail, mine was to be the Defæcation Trail. I was not amused by this, rather slightly annoyed. I was actually quite pleased that I had solved the problem of squatting in the wilderness. "Put it this way," I said matter-of-factly. "The seat is just a seat. Why, I could be sitting there, eating my breakfast of granola and drinking a refreshing cup of coffee, whilst performing my ablutions at the same time! Think of the time I'll save!" The image this created and the reaction this produced, was one of shock, disdain and disgust. O well, Scott and Shackleton must have had similar discussions once. For me though, somewhere to sit was a luxury I needed. Not just for the loo, but generally. When camping, I would need to spend a lot of time sorting out my food and my feet. If I could sit down to do this, it would make my Iceland challenge much easier. And so it was to prove. As for the choosing between the stone or the stick? Well neither, in the end. There was no guarantee I could find a suitable implement of the right shape to get into the more intimate creases or contours of my unique backside so in the end I wimped out and went for good ol' Andrex and prayed to high heaven it didn't disintegrate in my fingers…

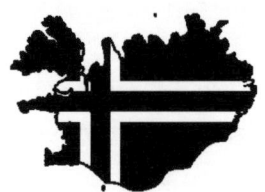

6. Inner Core

An ounce of prevention is worth a pound of cure – Benjamin Franklin

My training was interrupted in early April by a rather painful and debilitating back spasm. I quite simply stepped out of my car one day and felt a twinge and stiffness in my spine as the muscles contracted. Within a day I could barely climb out of my chair without excruciating pains searing through my lower back. It did not look good. From a relatively fit 58 year old, I had been reduced to a frail and pathetic invalid of about 90. Iceland suddenly looked a long way off. An urgent visit to the physiotherapy department at Burnley Hospital reassured me. Charlotte, a wise owl, informed me that most back conditions dissipated in six weeks, with the right sort of exercise and conditioning. She said I would have to develop my inner core, which was very weak.

This concerned me a lot, because I didn't know I had an inner core, and if I did, I was not sure I could put my finger on it to locate it. I didn't recall seeing the term "inner core" in anatomy diagrams of the human body at school. Was my inner core the latest fad to come to the attention of the medical world, or had it been newly discovered? Could I manage without an inner core, a bit like your appendix? Why was my inner core weak? Did my inner core have pips? Should I have eaten more vegetables as a child? I really did not know. Could your inner core grumble and have to be removed in an emergency procedure? Suppose my inner core started complaining in the wilds of Iceland's lava deserts? Would it be covered under the health insurance of my E111 card? All these inner core concerns of mine needed addressing and I made a mental note to google "inner core" when I got home.

Anyway, I put my faith in Charlotte and began a programme of physical exercises to improve my inner core, which basically meant getting up close and personal with my living room carpet for twenty minutes, twice a day. To start with, some of the exercises seemed to be just hurting me, quite spitefully so actually and making me feel worse, which was not especially good, so in the end I altered them, so that I didn't hurt quite so much. I informed Charlotte, who seemed to think my modifications were fine, in which case, why had she asked me to perform these masochistic and agonising activities on myself in the first place? Perhaps she herself was of rather dubious persuasion with strange, perverse sadistic fetishes. They say never trust physios or nurses in the NHS.

As the weeks went on, I learned to control my back spasms and I reduced my walking regime to half the usual mileage to aid my rehabilitation.

Strangely, I found that carrying a heavy load appeared to do my back more good than bad, by compressing my vertebrae tightly, so I persisted with carrying at least 13kg on my back, uphill and down dale.

April came and went and into May, I was back to long distance walks. My back problems had all but subsided; just the occasional twinge and ache, but I knew which movements troubled me, so I avoided them. No sharp twisting and bending. I had now bought practically all the walking equipment and clothing I needed, the problem was I had bought far too much, and the decision what to leave behind, would have to be made.

I knew that food not only weighs heavy on your stomach, it also weighs heavy on your backpack too. Ruthless decisions therefore had to be made about how much food I could carry. I knew I could manage four days food maximum on my back, so I set about establishing a series of food parcels that I could pick up on my way, usually a few days apart, so I would never actually go hungry. These parcels were to be located at Skjöldólfsstadir, Modrudalur, Reykjahlid, Kidagil, Nyidalur and Gullfoss and contained hopefully, enough food to see me by. After Gullfoss, I hoped to find sufficient food stores to allow me to reach Reykjavik. This supposition almost backfired as I was to find out.

I then looked at what else I was hoping to take with me. My expensive solar battery charger was placed in the "not to go" pile. It simply weighed too much. Instead I would include spare batteries in each food parcel, to provide power for my GPS, my camera and my word processor. I considered a Psion word processor would be a useful tool on which to record my daily ramblings, instead of a diary. If it was wet, a diary could become soaked and tatty. A word processor appeared to suit my needs much better; furthermore, it only weighed 325g. To accommodate the word processor, my safety rope for crossing rivers, also about 325g, was placed, perhaps rather unwisely, in the "not to go" pile too. I changed my sleeping bag to a 2 season one from a 3 season one, so to make up for that, I purchased a silk liner for my sleeping bag, to improve its insulative properties. This was a wrong decision, as my first wild camp was to prove on only day three of my trek, however back then in May, this decision appeared quite reasonable and sensible. Mind, all my May decisions appeared this way too. I reduced the number of clothes I was taking, so basically it was one item to wear, one item spare. One on, one off. Over the passage of time I might come to hum a bit, but I was going to the middle of nowhere. What did it matter?

I trimmed the covers off my maps and cut them down to size including only the precise route and the immediate areas where I was going to walk. Surprisingly, this paper trimming exercise saved me 200g in weight.

I had purchased a single blade knife, for defensive purposes as well as for light whittling duties. As already stated, I had heard that polar bears occasionally swim across to Iceland after hitching a ride over on southerly drifting icebergs. Apparently they would swim ashore and maraud around the coast, looking for food of the fleshy variety. Any bear unfortunate enough to be spotted, would usually be shot by a belligerent farmer with high powered rifle. Myself, I didn't possess a rifle, so instead I bought myself a polar bear knife, a modest item, quite sharp, with a non-serrated blade, no more than nine centimetres in length. Ample defence I convinced myself against a ravenous top predator with claws so honed it could slice straws vertically. Yes, I was happy with my polar bear knife, weighing in at 290g.

My cooking stove was a petrol powered one. I had been practising with this item for a while. At home, I cook using gas, so to boil a pan of water, one simply turns the knob, a few ignition clicks and the flame alights and away you go. A petrol powered stove is a different matter. Firstly, you have to prime the thing by allowing a dribble of petrol to seep into a convenient reservoir beneath the flame ring. A storm match is then tossed onto the petrol, which ignites with such gusto as to make a yellow mass of flame, the size of a medicine ball, a bit like the inferno unleashed from a flame thrower. The flame then tries to engulf or swallow insatiably, anything and everything within two metres, for what seems forever, before becoming soothed and becalmed, resulting in a neat blue ring of flame that boils a pan of water in exactly three minutes. I became quite adept at controlling the medicine ball. I knew how near I could sit to it, without singeing my eyebrows or charring my finger ends. In fact I could judge the distance to a matter of millimetres, causing anxiety and consternation to all those around me. However, I was confident in my fire-making ability and, after all, three minutes for brewing a cup of coffee is not bad, especially when you have slogged miles across the Arctic tundra all day. The only problem I foresaw with this stove, was to find a convenient source of petrol, for replenishing my supplies when my half litre canister of fuel ran dry. As it was to prove however, my timing would be impeccable, and friendly motorists conveniently topping up their fuel would come to my aid on at least two occasions.

I prepared a comprehensive first aid kit. I was concerned that an injury, however slight, could cause me serious disruption when trekking alone, so I stocked up with plasters, bandages, pain killers, anti-inflammatories and anti-chafing cream.

The last item I considered very important. Chafing can rear its ugly, and painful head, so to speak, when you least expect it, and when it does, progress is very restricted, in fact all but impossible. Chafing, the posh word for scrubbing or rubbing, normally occurs in the personal sweaty, intimate regions between your upper thighs, It does with me anyway. Once it starts, it sets to work with such relish, any movement of your legs is like scraping a rasp over a peach. Damaging, bloody and highly sensitive.

I remember completing the last leg of the Pennine Way many moons ago, when the rasp set to, and I was reduced to walking in very pathetic minute steps the final five miles to remote Kirk Yetholm. I think it took me the best part of four hours, such was the agony and my degree of sensitivity. My colleague was highly amused to see me tentatively attempting to walk with my thighs apparently clamped together, bending ever so slightly at the knee, a bit like Max Wall.

I remember too, a visit to Lake Garda in Italy, where my chafing was so serious, having sweated profusely beneath the Italian sun all day, an evening stroll around the lakeside shops became like a never-ending expedition of purgatory, so much so, it took me all night to return to my holiday apartment around dawn, when the towels were already on the sunbeds around the hotel pool. So, I bought for Iceland an expensive anti-chafing cream from Boots the Chemist that was highly recommended by none other an authoritative body, as the Daily Mail. I always believed everything in the Daily Mail to be the gospel truth, after all, my father was a staunch Conservative. As a reserve, I also bought a tub of Sudocrem, the sort used on babies' bottoms when they have nappy rash. No way was I getting nappy rash on my trek! (I know that sounds rude but I decided to leave it in!)

I cut my bar of soap into three, taking with me just a third. I reckoned I could make this fraction last me the month if I was careful, frugal and ever-so-slightly unhygienic. I also measured out shampoo and toothpaste in miniature plastic containers, all in the name of saving weight. I was therefore pleased, after all my weight reducing measures, that my pack weighed around 17kg. This I felt, I could cope with, when traversing Iceland's lava deserts.

I was now fully kitted and prepared. My inner core was as firm as it was ever likely to be… imagine a half-inflated lilo and you get the idea. I was reasonably happy with the weight I expected to carry, but I sincerely hoped my back would be able to cope with the rigours of day after day trekking. An unknown quantity, but I remained positive and hopeful it would.

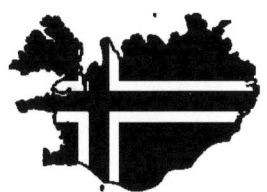

7. Self-doubts

A fall bodes a lucky journey from the house but not toward it – Icelandic Proverb

A few weeks before my departure for Iceland, I decided to go for an easy stroll along the River Ribble around Winckley Hall, near Whalley in Lancashire. My months of training meant I had now developed and evolved into a moderately fit fifty eight year old. Whilst I was nowhere near being a honed and athletic specimen, at least I had improved my muscle tone, as well as vastly improving my stamina and mental resolve. My navigation skills meant I could confidently get from A to B without ending up at C and I generally felt comfortable traipsing along unmade paths in the pouring rain in the middle of nowhere without panicking and worrying that I might never see civilisation ever again. Generally I considered myself to be durable and up to the task of wandering about outside for hours at a time.

On a pleasant spring morning I found myself following the river on the opposite side to the Ribble Way pathway, heading downstream, when the path entered a shadowy woodland. The camber of the path increased considerably, as did the density of the wood, to the extent walking became almost impossible. If you imagine a drunken skier trying to make his way home on a Saturday night through a forest on the precipitous slopes of Mont Blanc, you get some idea of my predicament. I stopped to balance and steady myself before continuing, placing my hand on an old tree stump. Unfortunately for me, the blasted stump was completely rotten and gave way beneath my grasp, catapulting me head over heels, in a display of compelling artistry, fifteen feet down an embankment almost into the river. I remember distinctly, a kaleidoscope of greenery and sky revolving prettily and creatively about me, when I came to an abrupt halt, after three aesthetically pleasing revolutions that an Olympic gymnast would have been proud of. I landed at the bottom of the slope, slightly groggy and bewildered, in an undignified heap.

After a few moments to regain my composure and bearings, and with the wind knocked out of me completely, I immediately checked my ankles and wrists.

"No breakages there," I muttered aloud with some relief. Then I checked my arms and legs. "No damage there either." I quickly came to the conclusion that I had survived the fall without serious mishap. It would have been somewhat ironic if I had chosen this moment, whilst on a gentle ramble, a mere few weeks before my Iceland departure, to suffer an injury putting my whole trip in jeopardy. I floundered around for a few minutes, seeking out my glasses, my GPS – still at the top of the slope - and my walking poles, scattered apart by several metres, both in distance and altitude. It also took a while to retrieve my drinking bottle which had detached itself from my rucksack pocket and had buried itself inconveniently in the undergrowth.

Slightly gingerly, I made my way back up the bank, along the treacherous riverside path and headed for Brockhall Village. Although I was not hurt, the fall had made me decide enough for one day and I headed back to my car outside Whalley, sensibly keeping to the paved roadside and away from slippery slopes. When I reported back home that I had gone for an almighty tumble, whilst performing three near perfect forward somersaults with one and a half twists, the comment came back:

"How are you going to cope with the extreme terrain in Iceland?" I simply commented that this had been a freak accident on a path that had not been maintained. "Well, do they maintain the paths in Iceland, then?" was the response. I was a tiny bit worried.

Indeed, my fall had made me rather concerned. I was actually more vulnerable than I had recently considered myself to be. My back, although it had not been giving me any grief for a while, could easily flare up again when I was in the middle of an Arctic nowhere. My fall by the River Ribble indicated that a moment's bad luck could result in me being injured or worse. Sobering thoughts indeed. Then again, had I bitten off more than I could chew with the whole expedition? All right, I had planned and organised everything down to the nth degree for over a year now. The bottom line was, "Was I up to it?"

Physically, I felt fairly well prepared, although whether I could walk sixteen miles a day, every day, had yet to be proved. Did I possess sufficient outdoor skills of navigation and map work? Well, I had negotiated my way along all manner of walks in Lancashire and Yorkshire now for months and months without getting seriously lost. I also had my reliable tried and tested Garmin GPS, which I now trusted implicitly.

How would I cope with extreme conditions outdoors? I possessed all the right equipment for camping, but my experience of wild camping was almost zero. I knew however, when wild camping, I needed to seek as sheltered a spot as I could, not far from a water source but away from any physical dangers such as falling rocks or flooding rivers. How would I cope with the solitude, where I had to rely exclusively on myself, to make correct judgement calls when under stress? I simply had no idea. I was reasonably happy with my own company. I was renowned for talking to myself and I trusted myself to get it right in difficult circumstances, however I had not yet truly tested myself in challenging conditions. Perhaps I should have completed one or two solo walks before now, up in the wilds of Scotland. Too late for that now.

I was extremely worried about the rivers. Iceland is bursting with rivers. Rivers fuelled by rainwater or meltwater from Iceland's dribbling glaciers. I had no experience of river crossings. I knew how dangerous they were to cross after watching numerous youtube videos, where 4x4 vehicles were simply lifted up and carried downstream. If that could happen to a car, what could happen to me?

I read all I could about traversing rivers safely, and most instructions carried the rider, "Cross as part of a group. On no account try to cross a river on your own." Advice I was choosing to ignore. In my mind, if I applied the river crossing technique properly and chose my fording points carefully, armed with my reliable walking poles, then I should be all right, I but I was still greatly worried. Whenever I was having a quiet moment, my anxiety always surfaced and my innermost survival expert said to me, "What about the rivers?" The answer was, I did not have one. I really did not have a solution to allay my concerns. It was something I would have to deal with, in the fullness of time, when the occasion arose. And arise it would most certainly do.

I had considered at length, the dangers involved in a solo trek such as this one. So too had my family. My wife was worried, as was my son. My sisters were convinced I was going to die, and one sister Ruth did not see me lasting beyond a week, which was distinctly unnerving and somewhat disappointing. Whenever I saw her, she would stare at me for a minute, then flee the room crying, in mental anguish. I never realised I meant so much to her! Of course I shrugged off such concerns with a pseudo-blasé attitude of: "Don't worry, I'll be fine." But underneath I knew that there was a possibility things could go wrong and I might not return. For that reason I had spent several days completing my last will and testament, which was held securely by my bank. I had also composed a last letter to my wife that I had secreted in a desk at home, without her knowledge. Upon my demise, various designated persons were to instruct her where to find the letter, which contained my final thoughts and sentiments, as well as my preferred funeral arrangements. All serious stuff, quite morbid really.

The last two weeks before my departure, I eased up on my walking, partly not to injure myself on any other innocuous pathway, but also to save my energy and instead, direct my attention to the logistics of travelling overseas. I checked my travel details, flying out from Manchester to Keflavik, then transferring to Reykjavik, before catching an internal flight to Egilsstadir. From there it was a connecting bus over the mountain to Seydisfjordur, where I would spend the last night before setting out on my trek, at a convenient hostel. A night of luxury, with en-suite thrown in!

The days before embarking on a possibly life-changing experience are filled with many moments of soul-searching and self-examination. For months, in fact well over a year now, I had been absorbed in a regime or routine with one direct focus – to prepare for Iceland. Now that time to leave was almost here, I began to wonder exactly what lay ahead of me. I knew I may struggle with the weight of my rucksack. Issues with my weak back might resurface and the thought of crossing the rivers filled me constantly with a heightened sense of dread. I think I gave off a slight air of uncertainty despite my attempts to appear nonchalent and in control. As a consequence there was a degree of tension, a sense of unease between me and my wife. Strangely, Iceland was not really discussed by the two of us at all. I prepared in isolation and she carried on her working life as usual. The pair of us seemed reluctant to talk about what lay ahead – in the short and long-term. She had never really shared my Iceland dream, in fact she never opened up to me about it in the months previously. Iceland did not excite her like it did me, in fact I think she regarded it to be somewhat of an imposition on our lives, which I suppose it was, after all, I was going to be away from home for a month. She never shared my barmy sense of adventure and purpose. Basically I got on with my training and she got on with her life. She did not ask if I was scared or excited or whether I was actually ready for such an experience; she did not ask about what I was going to do when it was all over. I too did not ask how she felt about me leaving her for so long; I did not ask if she was scared that something nasty might happen to me. We had simply stopped communicating. In fact, thinking about it properly, we had stopped communicating a considerable period of time before.

Now that zero hour was approaching, there seemed to be a sense that things would never again seem the same. Iceland could change me, in fact I felt sure it would. This Iceland thing was going to be so hard! I tried to play down my sense of misgiving and dispel any feelings of self-doubt I may have had. Instead I busied myself with my itinerary and my clothing list, my maps and my equipment.

I knew Iceland was going to prove so much more to me than a physical challenge. It was going to test me mentally and emotionally. It would allow me to discover exactly the type of person I was. It would also test the strength of my marital relationship and my aspirations for the future. It seemed that everything was coming to a head. All I could do was prepare as best I could, despite the uncertainties on so many levels that lay before me.

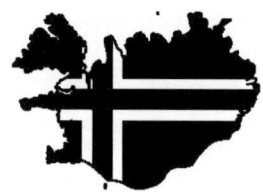

8. Keflavik Bound

Strong legs are needed to carry good days – Icelandic Proverb

With a large bucketful of fear and trepidation, my A320 easyjet flight accelerated across the runway at Manchester Airport at the start of a two and a half hour flight to Keflavik. It was 7am. My nerves were jangling and although I had eaten a little breakfast, my stomach was registering a good deal of discomfort and apprehension.

To describe how I felt, I would probably equate it with sitting an important exam knowing I had not revised properly, or performing in a play without having learned my lines. The stresses were incredible. I am normally a fairly phlegmatic character but this experience was testing my unflappability to the limit. I now knew the meaning of the term, "living nightmare". It was also fear of the unknown – a trek across unfamiliar territory in a possibly, very likely, hostile environment, all on my own. It was now sinking in exactly what I was undertaking, and I drew a sharp intake of breath at the size of the task.

Twelve hours previously I was sitting waiting nervously for the taxi to the airport, not really knowing with to do with myself, not settling to anything in particular. My son was prowling quietly in the background, pacing up and down, jaguar-like, counting down the seconds to my departure. When the taxi eventually appeared, it proved to be a rather quick, almost overly hasty, goodbye. No one really knew what to say; me, my wife and son standing there uncomfortably with scrambled emotions, although our eyes suggested that there was a slight dread in the air, a possibility that this departure might be rather more final than we would wish. My son attempted a feeble joke that elicited false laughter and he over-casually told me to be careful and to look after myself. He grinned at me with tight lips, and a somewhat haunted look. I blinked back a few tears. Sometimes not saying something is more powerful than any words. I stared back at him and our eyes said everything there was to say.

"Don't cock it up, you bloody fool," was the message he silently implied, although he would never have dreamt saying such words to his dad. He had *never* understood why I was embarking on this insane junket, and even at this eleventh hour, I still don't think he got it. Mind, as I looked back at him, I was not sure I really knew why I was doing this hare-brained thing either.

"Don't forget to feed the pets and make sure you do your fair share of the washing up," I burbled irrelevantly, just for something to say, to ease the intensity of the moment.

I gave my wife a hug and a hold. We said nothing but our eyes suggested that this was going to be a defining moment for both of us. Perhaps our connection would be enhanced; perhaps it would be irretrievably broken. We did not know, but then again, perhaps we *did* know but did not say anything. My head was in total turmoil and I simply had to get going. I looked back at my son, desperately sorry to be leaving him. I then looked at my wife with a forced smile and, in a moment, the taxi headed down the road and I was gone. The start of the most challenging and emotional experience of my life.

On a muted summer's day, my plane left the runway with an intense roar, Arctic-bound. I had spent a disturbed few hours at one of Manchester Airport's budget hotels before getting up slightly earlier than the crack of dawn. I can tell you now, the crack of dawn is a misty, sombre place where everything tends to happen in slow motion and people walk around like zombies in catatonic trances, including me. All my senses were dulled, almost as if someone had thrown a dark blanket over me and I was peering out on the world through tiny gaps in the weave. In what seemed to be moments, I was waving farewell to Scotland and I settled back in my seat, emotionally dulled, my stomach growling like an irritable Labrador. But as the minutes progressed and the plane headed ever northwards, I started to feel vaguely anxious. Initially I just felt slightly uneasy, you know, the sort of feeling you get when you miss the opportunity to visit the loo and then afterwards rather wish you had. I closed my eyes and tried to catch up on some sleep, however this was futile because my brain was now working overtime. Way out over the North Atlantic, west of the Faroes, that vagueness evolved into quite a bout of serious misgiving as I finally realised what I had let myself in for. My brow furrowed, my hands became clammy and visible beads of perspiration ran down my temples. I felt distinctly queasy and unnerved for the enormity of my rapidly approaching task was really hitting home. I had forgotten to take a book to read on the flight, and because I had nothing to occupy my thoughts, I just began to fret continually. The simple truth was: I was now committed; there was no turning back.

After nearly two long hours of what is euphemistically known as squeaky bum time, the southern Icelandic coastline came into view. There was a good deal of cloud around, but I imagined the areas below and to my right, to be east of Vik, a town right at the southern-most tip of Iceland, but then again, we could have been even further east, towards the glaciers around Skaftafell; I could not tell. We skirted the southern coast and I recognised a place that I thought was Grindavik on the Reykjanes Peninsular, with neat white buildings surrounded by dark lava fields, a quiet harbour containing resting trawlers and a sinewy road heading deep inland in the direction of Reykjavik. I saw a misty steam plume rising from the Blue Lagoon, a popular geothermal region complete with heated outdoor swimming pool and a large percentage of Iceland's tourists.

Minutes later, the plane dropped lower, houses and buildings became clearer and larger, and with a mild thump on the runway and a loud blast of airbrakes, we were down. I was so glad to be on terra firma and a let out an audible grunt of approval. Sitting still for so long, with waves of apprehension washing over me, was not really doing me much good at all, to put it mildly. I felt rather annoyed with myself for feeling like this. I had thought I was made of stronger stuff but unfortunately the glue holding my composure together was under far too much strain and needed remedial treatment – fast! What I really needed was a stiff drink of something distinctly alcoholic, however Icelandic prices for anything stronger than a still mineral water would have made a severe dent in my wallet, something at this early juncture I was not prepared to do.

Keflavik Airport is about thirty miles away from the capital. It lies in the south-west corner of Iceland on the Reykjanes Peninsular that juts out into the North Atlantic. Built by the British and the Americans at the start of World War Two, Keflavik had been important strategically for all the latter half of the 20th century providing a convenient stop-off midway between America and Europe. Strange to think that a world crisis back in the 1940s had been the making of Iceland. A decent road system now connects the airport to the capital, and, shortly later, I was hurtling along R41 parallel to the northern shoreline bound for the city centre.

Within the hour, I had arrived. I soon recognised some of the more familiar sights of Reykjavik I had last set eyes on, twenty two years earlier: the Pearl Restaurant perched high above the domestic airport - a gleaming silver hemisphere; the elegant churches of the white Hallgrímskirkja and the Moorish-styled Háteigskirkja standing imposingly against the skyline. I hoped to visit both during my time here. Yellow buses darted about this clean city, like bees around a flower bed and sea birds wheeled lazily overhead. There was much evidence across the city of frenetic construction work and lofty tower cranes, a sign of continuing evolution and rapid modern development. I felt slightly calmer in myself now, because I was returning to familiar territory. My sleek transfer bus turned left, then right and the iconic and somewhat dated BSI Bus Terminal came into view; my destination. It was now nearly ten o'clock, in adjusted Icelandic time, so I had plenty of time to spare before my connecting flight across Iceland to Egilsstadir, which was due to leave at 1545. Time to kill, but unfortunately, time to get nervous and tense once more.

I found a seat in a café and bought myself a sandwich and a coffee, priced rather exorbitantly at around £9. I knew already that Iceland's prices were probably the highest in Europe. I would just have to grit my teeth and get accustomed to them. One custom that I thoroughly approved of was, if you buy a coffee, you get a free refill or two. Some places let you refill your coffee cup as many times as you like, thus seriously reducing the overall average cost. At the BSI, I gratefully downed three coffees, desperate for my caffeine fix to allay my nerves.

I felt really tired, because of my early departure and everything was finally catching up with me. I sipped my drink and became engrossed in the ancient art of people-watching; it fascinates me to see folk from different cultures conduct themselves differently, wear different clothes, greet each other differently and, of course, speak differently. I detected a rich cosmopolitan mix of accents – Northern European, German, French, American, Italian, but no English. Where were the English?

As I sat there, I looked round the café and saw large, colourful, dramatic posters lining the walls, depicting the very extreme and raw nature of Iceland – glaciers, volcanoes, waterfalls, rivers and fumaroles and suddenly, I once again became distinctly afraid. I gulped two or three deep breaths and felt slightly nauseous. What on earth was I doing here? This country was way out of my league. I was in the lowly Vauxhall Conference Division and Iceland was definitely Barclays Premier League. The whole country now started to intimidate me in a way I had not thought possible. My forehead started to tighten and my hands again felt smooth and uncomfortably moist. I shifted uneasily in my chair for I knew I was facing a great adversity and that face was menacing and aggressive, unfriendly and distinctly alarming. If you have ever walked singly through a gang of violent drunken revellers, you will understand my deep sense of unease.

The problem with being on your own is you do not have anyone else to placate you and calm you down. There is no one to whom you can say, "I feel scared. I don't like this." You have to sort it all out yourself. Now I had always considered myself to be fairly good in stressful situations, but right then, I was not coping with my vulnerability at all. My resolve was being shattered and my spirit was inexorably ebbing away. In those circumstances, I decided to walk about, to do something active and energetic, anything, instead of just sitting around feeling sorry for myself. I had over four hours to kill before my flight; the trouble was, my heavy rucksack meant I was somewhat restricted in where I could go and what I could do. I could not just head off anywhere, so I decided to seek out the domestic flight terminal, from where I would catch my next flight, which I reckoned was about fifteen minutes away.

Forty five misguided minutes later, having mistakenly gone left instead of right – not a convincing prelude for an unaccompanied walk across Iceland - I arrived at a compact, prefabricated building full of laden travellers, some flying to other parts of Iceland and some even going on as far as Greenland. I appeared to be the only solo traveller: everyone else had a reassuring companion to talk to and laugh with. Me? I just had my own miserable company. Things were not looking good. My check in desk was closed and did not open for at least another three long hours, so I was stuck with my rucksack, which was not inclined to talk to me, and settled down in the café and drank many more refills of coffee, at least ten, I think, just to while away the time. How I wished I had brought an English newspaper with me. At least I could have attempted the various crossword puzzles and sudokus – anything to distract my mind from my impending sense of doom. My caffeine levels must have been going through the roof, but basically, there was nothing else to do. Occasionally a plane would land and the sound of the propellers would reverberate and resonate throughout the terminal building. Cohorts of passengers would suddenly become active and excited and disappear through a gate and onto their plane, the last time I would ever see them. I just sat around drinking coffee, filling my veins with concentrated caffeine, getting bored and anxious in equal measure.

Eventually 1545 came round. I was almost beside myself with tedium and anxiety, however, having something to do at last, meant my bubble of despond burst, thank God. I climbed up the aluminium steps onto a small twin propelled plane and sat near the front, with about forty others squeezed tightly behind me. This small plane, a Fokker 50, was not designed with the more rotund members of the public in mind. Luckily I was sitting next to a rather svelte female passenger of minimal proportions, however there still wasn't a great deal of room and with a mighty roar, the plane took off steeply and headed eastwards. Views of Reykjavik, with its multi-coloured buildings, quickly vanished as we climbed rather noisily up through the clouds. All I could see below was a vast, dense, white blanket. It was at this point, about short five minutes after take-off, that I suffered what I thought retrospectively, to be a major panic attack. I felt totally helpless and completely overwhelmed by my dire situation. I was totally intimidated by the plane, the passengers, the noise of the engines, the cramped overhead baggage compartments, the small porthole windows, the inadequate fold-down tray in front of me, the blinding white-out below, in fact, everything. What the hell was going on? I shut my eyes tight and screwed up my face, trying to alleviate my emotional turmoil. I felt hemmed in, constricted, tight. I tried to change my thought processes and thought about anything, anything but where I was, to reduce my sense of desperation and panic, but I could not. I just could not. What was happening? Squeezing my leg. Picking at my face. Scratching my head. Closing my eyes tight. Wishing I was anywhere but here. I felt the world pressing relentlessly against me and I could not restrain this burden, so suffocating, so oppressive. My heart was racing and my skin was hot and clammy. I was shuffling and squirming about in my seat constantly and how the woman seated next to me didn't complain I have no idea. I swallowed hard, over and over, trying to reassure myself, but I was not for reassuring. I held my face in my hand, grasping my cheeks tightly into a tense pout. Things were going ever so wrong and I did not know what I could do to help myself. I looked across at the woman next to me and caught her eye. She looked back, but failed to comprehend my intense anguish and instead averted her gaze. I then faced forward, eyes shut, just wanting to get off the plane.

The journey seemed to take for ever and I suffered considerably. I felt hollow, constricted, overwhelmed, suffocated; too much emotion, too intense to handle. This was way beyond anything I had ever experienced. I simply was not coping at all, and still the blasted plane flew relentlessly on. The cloud remained thick, bright, white, constant. My mind was blown and I was quite exhausted. I was silently screaming but no one was listening.

The flight was scheduled for one hour. The pilot intermittently informed us of our progress, but what struck me was how long this single hour actually took to elapse. It was flying, I estimated, at about 250 mph, way too slow for me in my current predicament. Below me was the great vastness I was going to have to cross in the coming weeks, but it simply appeared to be much too far for me. How could I cover all that distance in less than a month? It seemed absurd; totally implausible. The passengers were offered coffee, but I had drunk too many coffees already, absorbed too much caffeine back at the airport terminal. Instead I sat there, twitching and imploding.

After a god-awful eternity, the pilot informed us we were on our descent and within seconds, I could discern the terrain below. Thank God! Thank God for that! My panic-stricken world was now coming to end and and my attention could now be diverted to the landing. Finally, I had something concrete, quite literally, to focus upon, and then I could get off this god-awful, damned plane. As I looked out at the fast approaching landscape, what struck me initially, was the sheer amount of snow everywhere. I had assumed this being July, it would have practically all melted by now. Wrong! It was there in abundance.

A sharp turn, first banking one way then the other and we were down, skidding along the runway rather hastily but then settling down to a steady taxi. I breathed a sigh of relief that that particular episode of my journey was over. My back was sodden with perspiration; my face and forehead creased with consternation. I had never felt myself quietly go to pieces before and it was an experience I hoped never ever to repeat. I was actually quite cross with myself. I have dealt with many situations over the years, with family who had got upset; dealt with crises at school with emotional children, and I have had the dubious distinction of helping severely injured car accident victims at the roadside; all of which I had dealt with in a calm, compassionate and logical manner. On a simple domestic flight across Iceland, I had fallen way short of the rational standards I expected of myself and I chastised myself repeatedly as the plane drew to a halt outside the quaint, rather compact terminal building at Egilsstadir. After a few deep, concentrated breaths to compose myself, I brushed myself down, reverted to type and a calmer, more resolute and dignified person climbed steadfastly out of the plane. Panic attack? What panic attack?

I now needed to get to Seydisfjordur, a quiet town and port on the east coast, fifteen miles, over the mountains, east of here, but first, I had arranged to meet a man called Björgvin, the operations manager, who worked in the control tower atop the terminal building, probably personally handling and directing a dozen flights or so a day into and out of Egilsstadir. He had agreed, via email, to look after my rucksack for one day. I had deemed it unwise, almost unnecessary, to carry a heavy rucksack over a high mountain pass, when I was headed back this way within the next twenty four hours. Instead, I would leave my rucksack with Björgvin, catch the bus to Seydisfjordur, where I would spend one night. The following day I would travel light over the mountains from the coast, the starting point of my trek, and return to Egilsstadir to reclaim my rucksack, stowed safely away in the airport control tower. What could be simpler? I soon spotted Björgvin, but he looked rather apologetic as he approached.

"I'm sorry," he said. "I tried to hold the bus, but the driver wouldn't wait." I immediately knew that Plan A had gone out of the window. "Don't worry," I replied, thinking rapidly. "I'll hitch instead." Within moments I had given him my heavy rucksack and put on my extra smaller one, brought just for this first leg of my journey.

"What time do you expect to pick your pack up tomorrow?" he asked.

"What's the latest you will be here to?" I asked of him.

"Four o' clock," he stated.

"Don't worry. I'll be here, by then," I said in my customary business-like manner. If only he'd seen me, a gibbering wreck, a blob of jelly, minutes earlier. I was not the same person. If I have something to do, or something to organise, I'm normally quite all right. Responsibility tends to sit well with me, so if there's a decision to be made or a job to do, I generally handle the pressure well. My problem seems to lie if I partake of too much caffeine or have too much time on my hands. Then, I tend to fret and worry. "Keep busy!" would seem to be my motto. Björgvin then shook my hand, quite firmly I remember. I winced in surprise. My first Icelandic hand cruncher. I could almost hear my bones disintegrate, so I retaliated in kind, with a stout Anglo-Saxon handshake of my own. He grinned at me and stared strongly with his deep blue eyes, typically Icelandic in colour, perceptive and calculating. Then, I was gone, on my way across the small airport car park towards Route One that led into town a mile away. I was now on my own. In Iceland. Time to get focused.

The issue now was to get to Seydisfjordur, the best part of twenty miles away to the east, over the mountains. I knew there were no more buses that day, so the solution would be hitching a ride over the tops. Now, I consider myself to be quite a good hitchhiker, based on many years practice as a student, hitching all over England with my "golden thumb". Generally my thumb is so persuasive, I can snaffle a lift, on average, after ten minutes. Why should Iceland be any different? I'd read that Iceland was fairly easy to hitch around, so I was not that worried.

After a fifteen minutes comfortable walk along the roadside, I arrived in Egilsstadir centre, a modest town with neatly laid out houses, a couple of supermarkets, a commercial area, a church and some petrol stations. I was looking for R93 to Seydisfjordur, my hitching point, and quickly found it. So far, so good. But then it started to rain.

Not just any old rain; a complete deluge lashing down. Within seconds my jacket was soaked and my light rucksack was drenched. I felt as though it had been through a car wash several times over. This was bad news, because no one likes to pick up a soaking wet hitch hiker. One wet passenger means steamed up windows and damp seats. Not good.

I retreated to the drier sanctuary of a bus shelter, but all that happened was the rain outside got heavier and the sky much darker. Considering Iceland was supposed to have perpetual daylight at this time of year, I can confidently state that this is a complete misnomer. Iceland gets dark whenever it rains hard. I waited a while for it to abate, but then momentarily considered the possibility of walking all the way to Seydisfjordur. A silly idea, but then I'd only had two hours sleep in the past thirty six hours, so it was not surprising I was drawing irrational conclusions really. After a few minutes, I walked onwards and upwards, waving my sodden golden thumb pleadingly at any passing car. Of course, no one stopped. I wouldn't have, but then rather surprisingly, someone did. Rather suddenly, as it happens, and a small car pulled right across in front of me, so

I nearly disappeared over his bonnet. The driver wound down the window and, through the rain, in two different languages, we just about ascertained we were both going to Seydisfjordur.

I gratefully jumped in the back seat of the car driven by a Spanish man, who was accompanied by his wife. I explained I had missed the last bus and was very pleased to be picked up. His English was quite weak so there was a degree of uncertainty and confusion in our conversations, but we managed – just! We talked vaguely about the weather and where we both lived. The rain meanwhile, came down even more heavily. The visibility diminished to about twenty metres as the road meandered haphazardly, this way and that up the mountain. It dawned on me fairly rapidly that the Spaniard had only recently hired this car and he was almost incapable of driving in wet conditions over a high mountain pass. In fact it seemed to me that he had only recently passed his driving test. The car lurched violently from side to side as he made last minute adjustments in his steering, marginally keeping the car on an inadequate strip of slippery tarmac. I grabbed hold tightly onto the seat, ripping the stuffing out of the upholstery, in the process. It was like a wild roller coaster ride at Blackpool.

When we attained the top of the pass, things just got worse. The driver now imagined he was Ayton Senna as he threw the car over the crest and down the descent. I could almost hear him whooping suicidally rodeo-style as he cavalierly hurtled through the rainstorm. Late braking then became the norm as he desperately tried to keep the wretched vehicle on the metalled surface. Several times we appeared to be veering off the road over the edge into some unknown Icelandic abyss. My heart had palpitations of coronary proportions. Conversation between us now completely stopped. It was just a matter of survival now and we all knew it. Not for the first time today, I shut my eyes tight and prayed. The Spaniard's wife appeared to be desperately writing her will on the back of a cigarette packet, while the

Spaniard himself just looked possessed, exorcist-like, the reflection of his bulging, bloodshot eyes shining maniacally in the rear view mirror. The road dipped further swerving left and right, until at last, a glorious, welcoming sign saying "Seydisfjordur" appeared out of the spray and the misty gloom. I almost sighed out aloud, nay, cheered my head off. Instead I laughed a wild, frenzied hysterical laugh like a hyena on speed. It is not often I venture down the corridors of insanity with magnolia walls, bulky iron radiators and Georgian wired polished plate glass windows; fluffy teddy bears floating hither and thither to the sound of Helen Reddy blasting through the tannoy…

I pulled myself back from the brink of madness to the relative normality of north-east Iceland.

"I'm alive!" I screamed inwardly. Corrugated buildings appeared from nowhere and I immediately suggested the couple could drop me off here. Anywhere. Just let me out of the sodding car!

With a quick thank you, mainly for being still alive, I stepped out of the car into the road and in a second, it had gone, probably straight into the deep water of the harbour that lay fifty metres further on up the road. I listened for the sound of mangled metal and a dying engine, but heard nothing. The dense, low mist muffled any sound of ongoing doom. I shivered in the unpleasantly cool air and looked around at the remote outpost that is Seydisfjordur. I soon got my bearings. I had had the forethought to look at streetview on google earth only two days earlier to find the location of my hostel, and so now, despite the murky conditions, the roads and buildings looked virtual-friendly and familiar.

With a slight smile of satisfaction, I headed the short distance to my hostel, which apparently used to be a hospital. The entrance was unusually, around the back and it opened into a wide foyer at the end of which was a small reception desk. One or two people were loitering in the dim lights of the entrance. A sign suggested I take off my boots and then I was greeted warmly by a lovely lady with short, brown hair and deep blue-grey eyes, whom I was later to learn was called Benedikta, the manager of this establishment. It took me all of three seconds to realise that Benedikta was a very special person. Her smile instantly made me feel I belonged here and her welcoming nature suggested that nothing was too much trouble. My room, just along the corridor on the ground floor was functional but clean and warm. It contained a double bed, simple bedside furniture and an empty, dark, wooden chest. The basic en-suite was in a separate room with a shower and rather strange, antiquated window latches. From this room I gazed up at the mountains on the opposite side of the fjord – dark, oppressive and intimidating, and once again I felt rather perturbed. Where was the dry weather July had promised? I dried off and then went outside in search of food establishments alongside the harbour.

Seydisfjordur is a busy port that accommodates ships travelling to Iceland from Norway, the Faroes and the Shetland Isles. There were no large ships in port while I was there, but I got the impression that this place yo-yoed from being a quiet, reclusive place to one of total bedlam when the ships were in harbour. At this evening hour, a misty stillness hung over the water and a general sense of calm and tranquillity pervaded the atmosphere, which somewhat settled my jangled nerves and feelings of vulnerability. A drizzly rain came in persistent gusts saturating everything.

A welcome supper of burger and chips, typical tourist fare in Iceland, and two coffees, was consumed in a roadside café adorned with formica tables and wooden chairs, that reminded me of Lyons Corner Houses of my childhood. I then wandered around the town, which lined the banks of the fjord here. My favourite building was the Bláa Kirkja or Blue Church, a turn of the century, light blue, corrugated clad building with half round, arched windows lined in white. Apparently a musical concert had been held here just the night before. A shame, because I would have liked to have been entertained with a slice of Icelandic musical culture, as an overture to my walk. There was also a diverse range of restaurants scattered about, however their menu prices would have broken my bank balance, all too quickly. Anyway, I had enjoyed my basic fast food supper. After half an hour's aimless wandering, I retraced my steps back to the hostel, where several people gathered in a common room that also doubled as the dining room.

I sought out a conversation with Benedikta, who was intrigued to find out that I was walking across Iceland. She asked me why I was doing it and I replied that I had wanted to do it after reading a book by an intrepid explorer, Ted Edwards, who had set forth from here, to walk across Iceland, back in 1984. It was something I was doing just for me, and me alone.

"Most things in my life," I intoned, "I have done for other people, particularly young children at my school. Well this walk is about me – me challenging myself and finding out who I am. It is simply something I have long wanted to do and now is the time I have to do it. " This resonated very strongly with her and she applauded me for tackling such a venture. I told her I was going to venture down Sprengisandur.

"How exciting!" she observed. "An adventure is good for you."

I think that given half a chance, she would have come with me. She seemed to be an impulsive type who appreciated the bold and adventurous. Life is definitely for living, her eyes seemed to be saying to me, as we conversed and empathy crackled between us. We talked further about the weather and my kit and my training. She certainly put me at my ease and I felt rather more confident than I had in the last day or so. Eventually I retired to my room; the soft lights penetrating the thin curtains to the gloom outside where the high mountains were leaning threateningly over the hostel.

Emotionally I was completely and utterly spent. I soon fell sound asleep, the breaking waves on the harbour wall a distant interruption, no more than that.

9. Mountain High

Unbearably long is the day when the sun is not to be seen – Icelandic Proverb

Seydisfjordur – Egilsstadir 16.6 miles

I woke around seven and immediately looked out of the window. Rain! And lots of it! I had hoped for a dry start to get me used to my alien environment, but it was not to be. Never mind! It would have been nice to have started my solo trek with clear and bright sunny skies; after all, that was how I had imagined it was going to be on my first day, but reality often confounds aspiration. I put on my merino base layer and waterproof trousers and headed for some breakfast across the corridor. The hostel oozed a 1950s feel of a historic bygone age. You could almost hear Johnnie Ray and Frankie Laine crooning their hits in the era which would, I suppose, back in time, have been background music for a dozen or so patients who recuperated in the efficient cottage hospital that once existed here. But right now, small groups of travellers quietly but busily prepared their own breakfasts amongst cooking rings and worktops in a well-equipped kitchen area, laden with pots, pans and utensils of every description. Adjoining this was another room containing sundry tables and chairs, occupied with residents eating their breakfasts, who obviously had awoken somewhat earlier than me.

At that moment Benedikta greeted me warmly and asked me to be seated at a reserved table near the corner. We had a brief discussion about my walk to Egilsstadir, over the mountain. I think she was quietly flattered that I had chosen to walk across her home country, out of all the countries of the world I could have chosen. She appeared to like my spirit of adventure and she seemed to believe in me, which I found quite morale-boosting, especially after the quite pathetically wimpy way I failed to believe in myself just a day earlier.

She told me a little about the building, now a hostel, built in 1898, but which began work actually as a hospital back in 1901, incorporating a surgery and a delivery room, so most of the local people started life here. As time went by, the herring industry in these parts declined and the population of Seydisfjordur moved on, so the hospital was instead used as a residential home for the elderly, until eventually it became a hotel, then finally, at the beginning of the twenty first century, a hostel in its current form. I just marvelled at its functionality, its woodenness, its minimalistic simplicity and how it possessed a charm and retro-ambience all of its own.

Breakfast was delightful. A concoction of various items of the continental variety but what topped everything was a glass of granola covered in a delicious Skyr yoghourt with the taste of baked apples and all completed with one juicy strawberry that tasted divine, appreciated not only by me but other breakfasters round about. Benedikta busied herself around the kitchen, a machine of great efficiency, ensuring everyone's breakfast was done on time and to perfection.

After breakfast, I sorted my pack, got ready to leave and passed on my heartfelt gratitude to Benedikta for her kind hospitality. I hoped everyone I met was as confident in me, as she was. She had definitely lifted my spirits. Now, I was refuelled, rejuvenated and ready to go, light rucksack in place. She wished me well on my journey and made me promise I would send her a postcard upon reaching Reykjavik. I stared into her eyes and assured her I would, but that pledge seemed an awfully long way down the line. There were four hundred long and difficult miles to the Reykjavik post box before then. We embraced and I turned, full of anticipation, immediately out into the grey, dismal rain and headed straight for the harbour, a mere five minutes away.

As I walked away from the hostel, I reflected on Benedikta's kindness, which surprised me somewhat. A total stranger who had made me feel so welcomed and, well, *valued*. If this was Icelandic hospitality, I craved more of it.

At the harbour, I reached down into the water and selected two stones to carry with me on my journey. One to keep as a memento and the other to throw symbolically back into the waters of the North Atlantic, when I finally reached the Reykjavik shoreline, on the far side of the country. I secreted these carefully in my jacket pocket and zipped it up tight. These pebbles were so important to me and under no circumstances was I going to lose them. I then headed for the supermarket to buy some food to sustain me over the mountain. I told the checkout girl of my intention to walk across Iceland and would she possibly mind taking my photo. She agreed but then asked,

"But why are you wanting to walk across Iceland?" I simply said,

"It's long been an ambition of mine and now is the right time to do it." She looked at me not really understanding and said prosaically:

"Why?" Another English lunatic she probably thought. I probably agreed with her.

With that, I turned left and headed on the only route out of town, R93, the road on which the Spanish couple had done their darnedest to kill me the day before. A digital road sign suggested the air temperature was ten degrees Celsius, but this was at sea level and the route I was travelling would reach a much chillier altitude, at least 2000 feet higher.

Initially the tarmac road was accompanied quite spectacularly by a river called the Fjardará, which tumbled and crashed over the rocks with fierce abandon. Impressive waterfalls cascaded over stubborn rocky ledges and all the while, the rain poured down with determined resolve. I felt that Iceland was doing this on purpose, testing me, seeing what I was made of. Well, at that moment I felt a bit like a damp mollusc, rather squidgy, leaving a wet trail behind me as I sloshed through the puddles.

The initial miles showed up some faults in my clothing. My very expensive jacket was leaking around the neck which rather irritated me and my boots too were letting in water, which was equally frustrating. I know it was raining heavily however my clothes were supposedly designed to withstand weather such as this, after all, they had never let me down before. This was not the start I was hoping for. Perhaps I should have re-waterproofed my boots before I came out, an oversight I was now regretting.

As I climbed relentlessly onwards and upwards, with the road bending slightly this way and that, the air became cooler and I was aware of an icy freshness on my cheeks, an Arctic chill to focus my mind. It was becoming distinctly wintery! I was walking steadily, head down into the wind, occasionally stopping to stare back at the gradually diminishing town of Seydisfjordur over my left shoulder, then a long curve of the road ahead to the right, and Seydisfjordur was completely gone from view. I wondered if I would ever go back there again, after all, Benedikta's breakfasts surely needed more than one sampling.

I was wearing a peaked baseball cap in blue. I had attached a cloth badge to it which depicted an outline map of Iceland, together with the words, "ICELAND SOLO TREK 2014". As I climbed, a line of icy frost formed below the cap's peak, just ahead of my eyes. This was really not what I had expected. Ice on my cap? In July? Incongruous, I thought.

I settled into a steady rhythm, focusing on the road ahead, carrying my lightweight pack, containing a sandwich, a piece of chocolate and strawberry cake, two packets of cashew nuts, a bar of chocolate, two energy bars and a packet of chocolate raisins; more than enough to keep me going on this first day. I stopped for a break alongside a slim communications mast aside the road and munched my fill in the heavy mizzle that had now fallen continuously without respite now, for three hours. Even at this early stage, I had already had time to consider the size of the task ahead of me and the fact that it was going to be a very lonely challenge. Aside from a few passing cars, I had encountered precisely nobody. Walking in Iceland could prove to be a very hermitical existence indeed. A thought I now pondered with a degree of sombre inevitability.

On I went, until the road finally started to flatten out after a long nine miles slog uphill, however there was one thing that greatly worried me. Either side of the road, huge embankments of snow had built up, up to twenty feet thick, the result of many weeks' precipitation throughout the winter and spring. What lay beneath the snow was anyone's guess. I thought initially that it was the rocky mountainside, running down to the road verges, however, where some of the snow had melted, collapsed and given way, it revealed a mass of deep, grey water silent beneath, and quite a lot of it, gently stirring sluggishly with the chill wind. The snow had collected and frozen over what I believed to be a lake! This unnerved me considerably, because I knew that tomorrow's trek was on similar terrain to this, however I wouldn't be walking up the road, as I was now, but instead crossing high moorland. That too would be snow covered. How was I to know where the rivers and lakes lay, if I could not see them? I could easily be recklessly traversing the fragile white crust of a snow-covered lake; not a situation I particularly relished at all. Visibility would be an issue too. Thick fog like this would mean very restricted vision. Right now I could only see forty metres ahead, at best. High up on the moors it could be similar or worse. Iceland was throwing up some imponderables.

There is something disquietingly disorientating, almost surreal, when walking for hours without knowing exactly what lies in front of you. All I had seen on this first walking day, was the rain dripping off my jacket hood; snow piled up either side of me and a dark never-ending stretch of tarmac lined regularly with curved short yellow marker posts, which disappeared into a dense bank of cloud. This went on altogether for several hours. I had no precise idea where I was, however I knew that eventually the road would have to start to descend, and hopefully, it would emerge from this frustrating blanket of white.

And that is exactly what happened. I became vaguely aware of a slight brightening above me and dim, unfocused shapes started to appear in the distance. Within minutes, the sun was trying to break through and hallelujah! It made its very first appearance of the day. Fifty metres further on, and an extensive view materialised right before my eyes, as if I had been teleported there in Star Trekkian fashion. And what a view! The first and most obvious feature was the Lagarfljót River looking like a patch of spilt milk, in front of which lay a rather somnolent Egilsstadir, the town I had flown into the previous day. Of course, now it looked so different, and as I looked down on the buildings far below, the rain decided it had caused enough emotional unhappiness for one day and retired begrudgingly back into the clouds.

Immediately my flagging spirits lifted. I was identifying buildings in the town I recognised from the day before: Egilsstadir Church, a geometric design of strident shapes, clean and concrete, which stood statuesque reaching up into the sky; the airport terminal and its long, vacant runway where I had landed and of course, the numerous buildings around the centre: shops, offices, hotels and industrial units. Egilsstadir is a tidy, compact town of over 3000 inhabitants and the main communication and service centre for eastern Iceland. It lies on Route One, the main circular road that circumnavigates the whole country, so it is relatively easy to get everywhere else from here. Well it is in summer, anyway. In winter it is probably a totally different proposition, with serious quantities of snow dolloped on the roads and severe ice formations making travel rather difficult. As I descended to reach the town, I felt quite pleased with myself. My jacket had now stopped seeping water; my boots were now doing what boots should do, keeping my feet dry and all felt good with the world!

The temperature rose, to the extent I unzipped my jacket to cool down. Down, down I went walking in the same direction as R93, until I reached the outskirts of Egilsstadir. I was so pleased with myself. A simple enough walk with no route-finding needed. This marked the end of my first day of my trek. Apart from the weather, things had gone well. I arrived at R92 and headed for the campsite, located next to the athletics track. As I did so, I walked past a small inviting hotel, which temptingly seemed to say,

"Stay here! Stay here!" So that is exactly what I did. Since most of this trip I would be camping, I decided to live it up a little and keep dry!

Having checked into a regulation hotel room equipped with TV, en-suite and tea-making facilities, I headed out again to the airport. Björgvin was looking after my heavy rucksack and I needed to pick it up. En route, I stopped at an outdoor shop and decided to purchase a can of waterproofer, for the princely sum of 4500 kronur, about £20. I needed to ensure my jacket and boots would keep the elements at bay, after the problems I'd had initially, leaving Seydisfjordur.

It then took half an hour to reach the airport which lay on the northern side of Egilsstadir and Björgvin was waiting there to greet me. The airport was empty as no flights were scheduled for a while. It was now three o' clock, so I had arrived with an hour to spare. He apologised for me missing the bus the day before and I explained how I'd hitched a lift over the mountains in the pouring rain and nearly died. I said something derogatory about Spanish drivers, probably because I'm not the greatest fan of Fernando Alonso in Formula 1, and we both laughed. He agreed the mountain road could be very dangerous. My rucksack was standing there, propped up ready against the wall waiting patiently for me. It looked quite heavy, 18kg actually, and I knew that the serious walking and carrying was about to begin. With a deep breath, I swung it in a wide arc, narrowly avoiding smashing some air traffic computer equipment, the consequences of destroying it not worth thinking about! I shuffled my pack squarely onto my shoulders, and, indeed, it did feel very heavy. All walking would be quite different from now on. I felt like a pack animal that carries absurd loads up mountain passes and grimaced inwardly. Only 400 miles of this. I shook Björgvin's hand again, and, as I did so, my arm was dislocated from its elbow socket, ever so slightly, while my hand was crushed to a pulp, all in a friendly Icelandic way, of course. He looked me in the eye and said,

"Good luck." He meant it and I knew I definitely needed it.

As I walked back to the hotel, the sky started to look threatening once more, so I was pleased I had not camped out in the rain. Sure enough, the clouds squeezed out their contents onto everything below. I reflected on my first two days in Iceland, then somewhat surreally, retired to watch World Cup football on the television. This link with normality I greatly appreciated following a totally abnormal last forty eight hours.

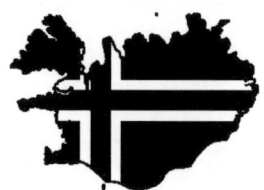

10. The Birds who mock

Bad birds seldom bring good weather- Icelandic Proverb

Egilsstadir – Teigasel - Skjöldólfsstadir 31.9 miles

The morning brought decision time, whether as planned, to head up into the hills, cross the snow-covered and misty heath to a lake called Sandvatn, followed by a wild camp high up on the moors, or to miss out this tricky moorland traverse and instead take a detour and aim for a lower level route, heading for the Jökulsá á Brú River along Route One, then turning left along a valley south-westwards along the R924. The first option was definitely the more unpredictable, perhaps, dangerous choice; the second, definitely safer, but longer.

I popped into the Tourist Information Centre for advice. Their response was quite categorical. It would be foolish to go onto the moors under the current adverse weather conditions. Never underestimate the terrain in Iceland seemed to be their message. What to do? I consulted my map and looked carefully at my proposed choices. The high level route was fraught with danger because of the sheer number of rivers criss-crossing the Bótarheidi heathland, past a remote farm at Flallssel. The lake itself, Sandvatn, was also a risk because if it was masked with snow, would I actually see it and unknowingly try to cross it? The low level route was about five miles longer, but straight forward enough, because it simply skirted the heath. I could not believe that on only the second day of my trek, I was already having to consider altering my route because of difficult weather.

There was never really a choice to make. It would have been complete madness to have ignored local advice, so with discretion playing the better part of valour, I revised my plans.

Before that however, I had taken time out to give my jacket and boots a good blast with waterproofer, to negate the leaks that had occurred the previous day. What this meant however was I inhaled a good dose of chemical fumes for a goodly five minutes and immediately felt light-headed and slightly out of it for a while, especially when a polar bear mysteriously appeared to loom large from the hotel foyer waving its powerful paws in playful fashion, so I gave him a manly cuddle and we had a boisterous tumble together, thankfully, with no ill effects. Then, a two headed reindeer appeared. It startled me initially by sneaking up from behind, but I soon got to know him and he could tell me an awful lot about Santa Claus and Christmas Eve.

I gradually came to, purging myself of hallucinogenic vapours, brushing polar bear hairs out of my jacket and set off purposefully along Route One. I passed the airport, waving to Björgvin, vaguely hoping he was watching me from his control tower perch. Probably not, as he had rather better and more important things to do with his time, dutifully directing local air traffic, it was to be hoped!

Before long I came upon a rickety bridge over the Lagarfljót, the river that ran alongside Egilsstadir and Route One. Timber was the principal material in this bridge, more than you would expect in a modern bridge really and I trusted the Icelanders to have calculated correctly the tensile strength of good ol' Scots Pine, as it carried me and my weighty pack over the impressive currents below. I then continued up a slight incline and reached the settlement of Fellabær, a satellite of Egilsstadir. Within moments, this was passed by and I was faced with a road northwards that became lonelier and more remote with every passing mile. The weather was again grey and damp and frequent showers accompanied me once more on my journey.

I soon became aware of a feathery presence above me, initially quite intriguing and interesting, but then as the novelty wore off, the intrusion became downright irritating, like a persistent fly that won't leave you alone, or a dripping tap, keeping you awake all night. This presence was in fact, not one, but a number of moorland birds, with long curved beaks, who exhibited quite an objectionable, abject attitude towards me. They kept challenging me vociferously and generally pushing their weight about in typical avian fashion.

At first, I just assumed that the birds were suggesting I had invaded their particular patch of road and moorland and so were quite justifiably annoyed and aggrieved at my trespass, however their behaviour became noticeably unusual for they appeared to be following me quite remorselessly and deliberately mile after mile, wheeling above me; occasionally swooping down for a closer look, then backing off, but still they remained; my uninvited companions across the heath. The moorland birds followed me all the way from Fellabær past Urridavatn along the Hringvegur – the ring road - a distance of seven miles or so. As I walked, any initial favourable impression of friendly local fauna I might have possessed was replaced by a general sense of foreboding and unease, that something about the birds was weirdly odd, slightly sinister and quite extraordinary. The birds suddenly began to shout all sorts at me, but in a language I could actually understand; some of it quite rude and abusive unfortunately, so I felt reluctantly compelled to shout back, but with a far more refined Anglo-Saxon brogue, after all, I was abroad as a guest, in someone else's country. The curlews were the worst. In Iceland they are called spóa and they particularly possessed a nasty, opprobrious side. The oyster catchers too were very unruly and plainly aggressive. They were joined by the occasional snipe, which did what its name suggests, and sniped away, very deliberately and unkindly, whilst remaining strategically in the background. A horde of redwings intermittently flew in to offer their own three pennyworth, name-calling at every opportunity and joining them were large, black tailed godwits, with their orange backs and, er, black tails. All of them harangued me, even mocked me, which I thought most unfair, after all, I was only a humble traveller, simply passing through.

Sometimes one of the more vocal birds would attempt to deposit on me something nasty, unpleasantly slimy and wet, however a singular wave of my walking pole soon discouraged such vulgar, anti-social behaviour. And all the while, they kept up their god-awful verbal racket, disrupting the consummate silence of the wild moors and surrounding mountains. I had to give them credit for their stamina. They would have outshouted and out-screeched the most vocal, fanatical football supporters on the terraces at Liverpool or Arsenal. On and on they went: chanting, belittling, launching diatribes of invective and vitriol quite uncalled for. My mother never prepared me for anything quite like this. I felt completely overwhelmed and humiliated. Flying above me, behind me, settling on the road in front of me, then running up to me and sneering, then at the very last moment, retreating in cowardly fashion, as I approached.

"Call yourself a trekker? You can't even walk across the snow! Sure you're cut out to walk across Iceland?" they mocked contemptuously, scoffing at my earlier decision to take the low level, snowless route. I was most put out at their brazen aggression, but at the same time, I did quietly appreciate their rather more conventional qualities: their sheer size, their beauty and especially their striking plumage.

I munched on a couple of energy bars – nuts basically stuck together with goo – and swigged from my water bottle, ignoring the blasted birds as best I could. An occasional sheep wandered into the road, to see what the fuss was about and to have a good look at me, but otherwise the road ahead was featureless, almost monotonous, just constantly winding across the heathland in long curves gently upwards. I tried to predict when my turn-off, R924, would appear, but it was still quite a few laborious miles away.

Thankfully it stopped raining and I was grateful for some respite from the perpetual drizzle. I had, frankly, had enough of this particular section of road and now I needed something to relieve the constancy and sameness of the surroundings, however as I crested a rise another half an hour or so later, I spotted a tell-tale yellow horizontal road sign indicating, to my great relief, and at long last, the junction I had been looking for. My four hour slog of nearly thirteen miles along Route One was drawing to a conclusion, thank God. Hopefully there would now be a change in the terrain, with something more interesting to see. I stopped to rest and take stock, while the birds continued unabated to give me grief.

"Bah" Look at you!" they shouted. "Worn out already? Pack too heavy? Feet getting blisters? Eh? Eh?" I watched them passively as they circled overhead, watching me, like a mobile form of CCTV. These birds had plenty to say for themselves and I had not expected criticism to come from such an unexpected source. This trek was now developing in a fanciful direction I could not possibly have imagined at the outset.

Alongside the junction was a very old, clapped out and dilapidated wreck of a skidoo, a vehicle with caterpillar tracks used for crossing snowy terrain. This was strange because there was absolutely no snow to be seen around here, so it must have been stranded here back in the depths of winter. Any lingering snow was hidden high on the moorland tops, way up in the clouds over my left shoulder. This skidoo had definitely seen better days and had obviously been abandoned by its hapless owner, who had given up waiting for the Icelandic AA to come out to fix it. It was weathered and rusty and missing a few components. The birds had, no doubt, foraged around for any useful bits and pieces, to add to their nests and now it resembled a piece of contemporary sculpture, normally exhibited in the more trendy Icelandic museums or parks in Reykjavik.

R924 led away to the left. Not a tarmacked road like Route One but a bumpy, stony affair with more than its fair share of potholes. It made a change to be walking on an unmade surface for it felt more organic, less manufactured and most pleasingly, it was inclined downhill. I really needed a downhill. I could see the mighty Jökulsá á Brú River to the right, known as the dirtiest river in the whole of Iceland, primarily because of the glacial debris carried along it, and what an impressive spectacle it was. Fast flowing, cutting a deep gorge through the scant topography. Bold sinuous meanders wove through black sandy mounds piled high at regular junctures along the water course, and its surface caught the light like a curved dagger blade gleaming menacingly in the sunlight. The river and I kept company all afternoon. Small farms would appear either side of the road. One was succinctly called, "Gil". That morning I had intended this to be my day's destination and the location of my first wild camp, however, right now, I felt pretty good; my legs were holding up to the rigours of the day and I felt I had a few more miles left in me, so I carried on, passing two more farms, one with a watchful dog, which seemed to be weighing up whether it was worth running down the farm track to savage me. It barked and growled noisily and aggressively to the extent I was seriously considering how to defend myself, if the worst came to the worst. My two aluminium walking poles were to be my first line of defence, possessing sharp points, good for gouging canine eyes or writhing around inside doggy nostrils. If that didn't work I could beat the living daylights out of the mangy beast instead, mind - the poles might distort and bend upon contact. Not good, for I needed them to last for the duration of my trek. My second, alternative means of defence was my polar bear knife, with a blade whetted to the calibre of Gillette and Wilkinson Sword. I pursed my lips at the thought of a glorious battle – homo sapiens versus Viking Mutt and I flexed my bicep muscles in anticipation of the skirmish ahead. I don't know about his hackles, but my hackles were rising, ready for our violent set-to. In the end, Mutt merely lost interest in me and couldn't be bothered anymore, so my polar bear knife stayed tightly sheathed in my pocket, a little while longer at any rate. My hackles calmed to their former condition, unrisen and soothed.

Finally I'd had enough of walking for the day. It was time to find a spot to stop the night. This was a significant moment for me, because I had never wild camped in my life. I had walked thousands of miles, but all my camps had been on recognised campsites with various facilities set on manicured lawns or rather more basically, in boggy farmers' fields. Now I was looking for my own private patch of ground. Nothing too plush, just a place away from the track, where I couldn't be seen, not that a vehicle had passed me for hours, but also next to a water source so I could wash and cook. After some reconnoitring, I climbed a promising- looking hillside for a couple of minutes just past a farm named Teigasel II. I don't know why it was called

Teigasel II but there was a Teigasel I further on. Perhaps the unseen occupants were related.

At the top of the slope was a depression which screened me from the road. Nearby ran a fast flowing stream that joined the Jökulsá á Brú lower down. A perfect spot to camp, although the ground was rather soft and lush underfoot. I set to work, quickly erecting my tent and tarpaulin in a matter of five minutes or so. I washed and cooled my aching feet in a nearby ice-cold stream and then cooked myself a rehydrated pasta meal that tasted surprisingly good, mind I was ravenous! All was well with me and the world. The sun made an appearance for a couple of hours while I drank several reviving cups of coffee. Curious sheep came to stare at me and I glared back.

"Rude to stare!" I bleated and they ambled off in a huff. Chores done, I was somewhat at a loss what to do, so I listened to some tunes on my iPod nano including the theme from the film Local Hero, - "Going Home", I think it was called. My own home seemed a very long way away indeed. Here I was, in a place as far removed from home comforts as I could imagine. Just me, my little green tent, my rucksack, my cooking stove and absolutely nothing else save the Icelandic landscape stretching before me. A slight breeze blew to sway the grasses around about and a nearby waterfall gurgled comfortingly as it wound its intricate way down the hillside. I sang "Going Home" aloud, with great gusto mainly to annoy the birds who had annoyed me constantly, but also to release the emotion of the past three days.

The sun dipped, but did not set, but then the air turned a lot chillier with a dash of Arctic spite. My feet that I had submerged in the stream earlier on, had not recovered their warmth, in fact my circulation appeared to have stopped, so I slipped into my sleeping bag with two icebergs for feet. It had been a long day and I was now ready for some well-earned rest.

x - x — x — x —x — x - x

What a difference a few hours makes! I became aware that my intentioned plans for a restful night would fall apart around 1am, when it started to rain. The relentless hammering of raindrops on the fly sheet woke me with a start. I was also exceedingly cold, from my chilled feet upwards. The small of my back particularly was absorbing the dampness and cold from the ground beneath me. My remedy was therefore to put on extra items of clothing – a pair of socks, my two mid layers and a waterproof top, followed by a fleecy hat pulled down low over my eyes. Now of course, I was all bulked up and my sleeping bag, which did not have a great deal of extra room for movement in the first place, was now stuffed to the seams. Consequently I was now tightly cocooned, as snug as a bug within the proverbial rug. We've all seen them, those pictures of young babies trussed up within an inch of their young lives like Indian papooses; or the victims of a voracious spider who has wrapped up its hapless prey in bundles of silk, ready for eating later at a more convenient time. Well if I was ready for eating, then it would have been a dish served cold, because I remained frozen to the core and parts of me started to shiver that had never ever shivered before. It was rather disconcerting, almost alarming to put it mildly. How can your backside shiver? Well mine did; a massive bottom wobble whereby my cheeks set about quaking and quivering with gusto, a bit like Beyoncé on heat.

Sleep, in this situation, was therefore impossible and instead, survival had become the order of the day. I didn't want to be one of those people found frozen to death in their tent months later, a bit like Scott of the Antarctic. I rummaged through my rucksack for extra clothing, all the while my backside palpitating uncontrollably. I even put on an extra pair of socks and another long sleeved base layer. That was pretty well everything I had in my rucksack to wear. I struggled back into my sleeping bag but continued to quiver and quake relentlessly. To make matters worse, the wind blew up and my tent flapped and thrashed about unrelentingly. Nature can be so cruel when it wants to.

My backside now decided to beat out a frenetic Charleston rhythm, the oscillations beneath me like an overworked vibrating phone. Cold had spread through every vein in my body. This night was indeed going to be very long. Thankfully, it was not dark, for at this time of year, night-times become dim, twilighty, but not pitch black, so at least I could watch my whole body and sleeping bag quiver and tremble the night away, which is precisely what I did.

Night times are very lonely events, depressing too. I have always considered that my natural effervescence dwindles as the day approaches nine in the evening, so that by midnight I can feel quite morose. If I am still awake after that, I definitely feel melancholic and downcast, and all my dark thoughts and petty concerns are exaggerated and amplified in keeping with the tenebrous depths of the hour. I have always been like that, churning gloomy nocturnal thoughts and ideas around in my head, keeping awake, however the brightness of the morning brings a new start, a re-invigoration of attitude and outlook, almost as if someone has changed my spark plugs as I fire back into action. All my anxieties are replaced with a sense of renewal and the dark night has gone for another day at least. I wondered, lying there, if others suffer in the night as I do, or whether it is just something unique to me. Lying there, in an Icelandic rainstorm, despite it not being completely dark, was a real challenge for me mentally. I was frozen solid, exceedingly uncomfortable and rather agitated in equal measure. Time was passing so slowly and I was worried that my sleeping bag was really letting me down. It was proving to be totally inadequate for the conditions and I was already thinking ahead to Sprengisandur, which would be far colder and wilder than this. How on earth would I cope with the cold in the highland wasteland without freezing to death? My mind was whirring and, as a consequence, along with the chill that wracked my body, sleep was impossible. It got to five o' clock and now the birds joined in, trying to keep me awake.

"Get up you idiot!" they shouted. "Don't come here invading our country and expect to get a good night's sleep! Brought the wrong sleeping bag, did we?"

That was it. I'd had enough. If I could not sleep, I might as well get up and journey on my way. I emerged from my sleeping bag, not an easy task with so many layers on. I was in a half-awake zombie-mode, in my catatonic trance. As I peered through my tent, I was surprised to see just how wet and damp everything was. Right next to my tent, three sheep stared at me inquisitively if not a mite startled by my intrusion. Staggering to my feet, I observed the Jökulsá á Brú, looking somewhat different to the previous evening, more atmospheric and a trifle threatening, flowing more deliberately and sluggishly beneath a misty mantle. Clouds draped the hillsides with their saturated cloaks and the grassy slopes were bound up with moisture by the bucket-load. What a contrast to the last evening. I could not believe it. I decamped without washing or eating, wiped my bleary eyes and dropped down the sodden hillside to the track, fifty metres below. I was desperate for sleep and for warmth. The sleep would come later, however the warmth could be achieved by hitting the road and getting my circulation pumping once again.

Once I had attained firmer and flatter ground, I felt a little better and set off rather gingerly at the unearthly hour of 5.45am. There was a layer of thick, low stratus cloud enveloping everything and the moors to my left, my original route on day two, looked decidedly intimidating and unfriendly. I was glad I had chosen to miss them out and detour round. The track followed alongside the Jökulsá á Brú, a dynamic companion if ever I saw one. It carved a deep fissure through the landscape and on its far bank I could see Route One, which I hoped to join a few miles further on. No traffic was moving at this early hour. I passed several sleepy, silent farms, and was accompanied for part of the way by small flocks of sheep that had emerged from the moors to access the firmer ground of the road, perhaps to give their feet a change.

Because my water was low, I needed to replenish my supplies and collect some from a river that crossed my path. The river was fast flowing and extremely cold, so I took great care to ensure I did not fall into it, picking my way down a slippery bank, next to a small bridge. As I refilled my water bottle and rested here for several moments, I was acutely aware of the extreme remoteness and isolation of this place, undoubtedly the most out-of-the-way location I had ever frequented. It made me feel slightly tense but, at the same time, quite exhilarated. As I looked round, I could see just one or two remote buildings, but otherwise, it was just basically nature in the raw, with tumbling distant waterfalls, clouded greenery and the splendidly intimidating, Jökulsá á Brú.

With a shrug of my shoulders, and a tightening of my rucksack chest strap, I got underway once more. I had decided to head for a bridge across the river, the only one in this part of the world, just past Hofteigur, a small farming settlement on the far bank. The bridge actually took far longer to reach than expected, so it was to my great relief when it finally came into view, over the crest of a right handed bend. Beyond it, one hundred metres away, was the junction with Route One, a symbol once more of a road to some form of civilisation. I was now rather hungry having completed nearly nine miles along the track and it was still only 9am. I needed some breakfast!

Starting a walk at an unearthly hour of the morning is quite strange, partly because you are not completely awake and therefore you are existing in a confused trance-like state. You are almost sleep walking. You feel slightly vulnerable because there is no one about, and here in this part of Iceland, there was precisely nobody to see; devoid of all people except me and one or two invisible farmers. I generally get on fairly well with my own company, relying on my deep intimate thoughts to get me by. If my spirits drop I tend to sing to cheer myself up, so this is exactly what I did on this Sunday morning, causing the accompanying birds to scream:

"Shut up, you tuneless idiot! Don't you know it's Sunday, a day of rest?"

I ignored them and simply sang louder.

It's funny how I tend to become rather introspective when on my own for an extended period of time. I don't know whether this is typical of others, but it is for me. I become quite contemplative and analytical, completely at odds with my persona when in company, when I tend to act the fool portraying a bubbly, effusive personality that actually is not me at all; it's the image I like people to have of me – this all-singing, all-dancing extrovert for whom nothing is too much trouble, who does not take life seriously and who laughs at everything, when really nothing could be further from the truth. I tend to dwell on issues and think very deeply about the troubles of the world, particularly with all the hatred and antagonism that exists between people. I often think about my general state of happiness and contentment – my relationship with my wife and son; my friends; and my mortality, yes my mortality. Once you pass fifty five, you definitely wonder how many grains of sand are left in the timer and the quality of life you have left before you. Your health generally. You wonder about all the aches and pains, the grumbles and creaks that increasingly afflict your humble body and you hope they are nothing serious, just passing complaints that will fade with time.

That Sunday morning, after a tuneless rendition of a couple of songs from my past, I reverted to inner contemplation: a time for reflection and deep thought, I simply trudged silently along the track. I had walked what? Forty miles so far, getting on for fifty, in two and a bit days. Not bad for an old codger like me, but this was just the overture, because I knew in my mind that Sprengisandur would define the success or failure of this trip. That bleak, lonely route across the highlands would be the real test, and it was slowly but surely drawing nearer. Something for me to focus on in the coming days and miles.

But right now, I felt mildly lugubrious, if that is not a contradiction in terms. You're either lugubrious or you're not; there's no mild about it. The reason, I surmised, was probably my lack of sleep and the persistent rumblings in my stomach. Also, the cursed weather was casting a damp cloud over my outlook in quite an assertive way, which did not auger well for the rest of my trip. As I walked, hobbling at this point, with my right foot giving me grief, I began to sing sections of the Abba song – "When All is Said and Done," sometimes humming, sometimes vocalising the words that sprang into my head. Quite why I was singing a song about a broken relationship and separation at this juncture I had no idea, or perhaps I *did* subconsciously, but it just reflected my pensive mood at the time. I thought of home and what my wife would be doing and whether my son was helping out as I had asked. I wondered if they were thinking about me or perhaps they were still in bed at the start of a new day. I hoped I was in their thoughts. This great solo walk of mine, apart from being a physical challenge, was actually becoming very much a mental one, even at this early stage. The battles within myself would prove to be equally provocative, for basically, there was nothing else to do. If there's nothing to see and distract you on a long stretch of road in the rain, you absorb yourself in an inner world, and my inner world could be quite a complex place.

When I reached the junction, I stopped and tended to my tender feet. No longer chilled like frozen fish fingers, my right foot was instead suffering a large blister on the sole next to my big toe. I was slightly dismayed at this, because throughout all my training and preparation for Iceland, I had never suffered from blisters, and now, on only day three, I had a blister the size of a 10p piece. Reparation work with three blister plasters, one on top of the other, seemed to lessen the pain and cushioned my foot slightly, so when I walked, I no longer hobbled quite so obviously. My credibility as a serious trekker was sustained. It didn't look good to be seen limping along, with a giant rucksack, as if one was about to fall over and expire. Mind the only people who could see me, were those peering from occasional vehicles that swept by me on the way to Egilsstadir, in one direction, and Akureyri in the other.

Feet sorted, I looked along Route One, which disappeared into the brightening gloom for a dismaying dagger straight three long miles. Occasional farm buildings set back fifty to one hundred metres, accompanied the thoroughfare, but otherwise it was just a long slog for an hour or so. Muttering an expletive under my breath, I set out, knees creaking somewhat and muscles stiffening, facing the oncoming traffic, basically one vehicle every ten minutes or so. There was nothing really to break up the monotony of this section, so as I walked, I considered the problems I had faced with the cold throughout the night. My sleeping bag was obviously not up to the job. I had been frozen! The chill from the ground had passed through my sleeping mat as if it wasn't there and my extra clothing had done nothing to alleviate this. I had no other clothes to wear. And this was just a bog-standard night at minor altitude. What was I going to do when I crossed the highlands? The temperatures there would be a good deal lower than here. I did not fancy being chilled for the eight days it would take me to cross them. I had a problem and I needed a solution.

I eventually reached my destination for that day, Skjöldólfsstadir, a guest house, a few miles further on along Route One, just after 1pm. It represented an oasis in the middle of a vast, untenanted land. It consisted of a couple of buildings next to which was a wigwam structure clad in wooden timbers, its entrance adorned with a reindeer's antlers. This apparently housed a hot tub. Next to it, in a large car park, a throng of German tourists milled around, but who disappeared as rapidly as they had appeared, on a noisy bus headed east. Skjöldólfsstadir, of unpronounceable name, like most Icelandic names, generally resembled a basic motel. It also accommodated next door: a petrol station, a rarity in these parts, along with a swimming pool and a restaurant. A campsite was situated in an adjacent field and it was here that I intended to camp, however, because I had not slept at all the previous night, I asked if a room was available, which it was, which pleased me greatly.

I was grateful to find a soft warm bed where I could crash out. Firstly however, I needed a decent meal – I had had no breakfast – and I had my sleeping bag problem to rectify. A bowl of lamb soup did the trick, accompanied by bread rolls and lashings of coffee. At least five refills I think. As I drank my soup, I observed that I was surrounded by numerous artefacts related to reindeer and the farming of these animals. Indeed there was an impressive reindeer head decorating the wall of the restaurant. Apparently, reindeer roam this area extensively, however I had seen precisely none. Perhaps the reindeer did not appreciate my garish appearance of bright blue jacket, with oversized rucksack to match.

I related my sleeping bag woes to a female member of staff and she kindly, and very generously, offered to ask her boyfriend, who lived in Egilsstadir, and worked in an outdoor camping shop there, to bring some sleeping bags over. This seemed to me to be exceptionally considerate and I thanked her profusely for her help and support. She said he would be over within the hour. I was impressed with the speed of all of this. Are Icelandic folk always this helpful? The answer, as I was to find out later, was, quite simply, yes.

The boyfriend and three sleeping bags arrived exactly an hour later. I knew immediately however, that they were not suitable. All really warm and snug, but far too bulky and heavy. My sleeping bag weighed 630g. These weighed four or five times that and would have made my pack too heavy. I thanked him for his efforts and consumed two more coffees. What to do? I could either carry on and grin and bear the cold temperatures. Not ideal. Or, I could return to Egilsstadir, the only retail outlet in this part of Iceland and find another outdoor shop and hope for better luck. This was really my only option, if I wanted to continue. I had not expected an equipment issue on this trip at all, and here I was, early on, with a problem jeopardising my whole mission!

With chagrin, I retired to my room. At least I could get some rest here, refuel and start out the next day. The plan for tomorrow was to leave my belongings at Skjöldólfsstadir, with the consent of the staff, hitch back to Egilsstadir, find and purchase a new sleeping bag, hitch back and then set out to walk up into the mountains starting early afternoon. Because it did not get dark at night, I was not constrained to walk at conventional times. If I wanted to walk at midnight, I could. Things were sorted. There was nothing else to do that day, but relax, dry my kit, and get some sleep.

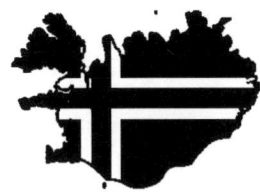

11. Foggy Assault

You will reach your destination even though you travel slowly – Icelandic Proverb

Skjöldólfsstadir – Saenautavatn – Modrudalur 27.8 miles

I slept soundly, no surprise there, considering the hassles of the day before. After a swift continental breakfast, I wandered outside to wave my golden thumb at passing traffic, as I attempted to hitch back to Egilsstadir. It was shortly before 9am. The sky was clear and this was probably the most pleasant weather I had encountered so far. I walked a little way along the road to what I considered to be a sensible hitching spot and waited for a car to come my way. And waited, and waited. The problem with this stretch of road is, it connects Akureyri to Egillsstadir, and that is all it does. People in Iceland tend not to make long journeys, and if they do so, they are more likely to fly. The only likely traffic to be passing this way were tourists anxious to explore this remote corner of the country, but they were still having their breakfasts.

In one hour, only ten vehicles had passed me by and none gave the slightest indication of wanting to slow down. My golden thumb was failing me and, to add to my troubles, various flies came to say hello, not just once, but several times. As I was wafting them away, increasingly annoyed at their unwanted hospitality, a car slowed and stopped. A kindly man who worked in Egilsstadir offered me a lift which I gratefully accepted, glad to get away from the unwarranted attention of the insects who were invading several of my personal spaces.

It took well over half an hour to reach Egilsstadir which I welcomed almost as a friend, and I soon discovered the location of the outdoor camping shops. The first was the very same shop where the sleeping bags I'd looked at the previous day, had come from, but they did not stock a suitable sleeping bag that met my requirements. I then walked to another shop a few minutes away, but the story was the same. The sleeping bags were too bulky and too heavy. A helpful assistant suggested I purchase instead some extra clothing layers to wear at night; clothes with good insulating properties. This, I thought, was a good idea. The tops he showed me were light, but warm. They could be rolled up small and stowed away in my rucksack easily. The only downside was the price, about 38500 Icelandic Kronur, round about a hefty £200. There was no debate. I needed them so I bought them. At least that lightened my wallet somewhat if nothing else, reducing my pack to about 17.5kg. The assistant wished me well with my trek and, through gritted teeth, I wished him well spending my precious £200.

With newly acquired tops in hand, I headed back to Route One, in order to hitch back to Skjöldólfsstadir. It was now just before 11am. Once again, the problem was finding someone to stop to pick me up. Several other hopeful hitchhikers were competing for the same traffic as me, so I decided to walk out of town, through Fellabær once more, towards the moors. It was now that the rain decided to fall. It likes to rain quite a lot in Egilsstadir particularly on foreign invaders like me unfortunately, which it did so with undue, almost spiteful relish. Two wet and frustrating miles later, thankfully, a car pulled over. It wasn't going to Skjöldólfsstadir, but it could take me just past the bridge over the Jökulsá á Brú, the turn off onto the R917 and a remoter area of north-east Iceland.

The return journey across the moors soon passed and in no time at all, I was waving goodbye to the German couple who had kindly given me a lift. They were headed to Vopnafjördur, by the coast and I watched as their vehicle disappeared gradually into the distance. A feeling of abandonment and isolation now took over however I had to put that to the back of my mind and simply get on with it. The rain had now stopped but this place was desolate in the extreme and there I stood, a serious number of miles from anywhere, with no food, no water, with just an empty moorland road for company. Oh and yes, the birds! The birds were back, offering their advice as I stood forlornly at the roadside.

"You'll never get a lift"! they shouted discouragingly. "You don't know what you're doing! Fancy coming to Iceland with a rubbish sleeping bag. Call yourself a trekker? You haven't a clue!"

I ignored them and gazed hopefully back along the road, looking for any sort of welcome vehicular movement. Nothing. Absolutely nothing. It now looked like I was in for a considerable wait. A time to take stock and ponder. A time to reflect and count the minutes as time shifted inexorably onwards, like dull clouds imperceptibly drifting across an overcast sky. I sighed a deep sigh. Thinking about it, quite a lot of my life had consisted of prolonged occasions of extreme torpor and ennui, particularly my early years as a child, when days seemed to last forever, especially when the weather was unremittingly bad and I had to stay in for what seemed like hours at a time, or later on, at my grammar school on a Friday afternoon, attending double Physics lessons when involved with crushingly boring topics like forces, or equally baffling concepts involving moments about a point. I never did get the point. The sheer monotony nearly killed me. I remember too when I used to watch the test card on the television. You know, the never-changing on-screen picture that television installers used to help tune in their televisions – this was before day-time scheduling - just the same unrelenting picture of a series of black, white and grey shapes and patterns, not forgetting that unbearably annoying, grinning girl with side parting, sitting in the middle of the blasted screen, playing noughts and crosses with no-one in particular, with just a stupid clown and irrelevant bloody balloons for company. I spent many a boring hour watching this, fermenting my bile, in a childhood obviously bereft of adequate stimulation and proper parenting, and, waiting here on Route One, provided me with exactly the same sense of frustration and unrelenting tedium. It also reminded me of the times when I dutifully attended Sunday church with my family and the blinking priest insisted on delivering a mind-crushingly inane homily that lasted the best part of twenty five minutes, delivered in a flat monotone that would have set cement. When you are only nine, it tests your patience sorely, and, to retain any semblance of sanity, I often considered trying to sneak out along the aisle to the side door and escape the acutely dreary overblown rhetoric. I never succeeded. My mother had an in-built radar designed for detecting the wayward behaviour of insubordinates at fifty metres, and I was hooked back before I had even travelled a mere five. Yes, there was no getting away from the fact that most of my childhood was pretty turgid, for all I seemed to do throughout my youth was to sit on a hot storage radiator, looking out the window at a never-changing scene of our residential street and develop piles.

An antagonistic bird suddenly squawked at me and I snapped back into the present, on Route One, going precisely nowhere. I wondered if I might have to walk all the way to Skjöldólfsstadir. Not a pleasant thought, especially since it was at least ten miles further on, maybe more. Allied to that, a gaggle of moorland birds, now joined their chum and resumed their chorus of vituperation, having nothing better to do, obviously. The only good thing to happen was the rain now stopped and a more settled bout of weather came my way.

Twenty minutes later, miraclulously, my luck changed, as my golden thumb swung into action and coerced a vehicle to stop. A Serbian gentleman picked me up and whisked me at frantic speed back to Skjöldólfsstadir. I gave a surreptitious V sign to the barracking birds as we departed, and in next to no time, I was back at the guest house eating another bowl of lamb soup. I was quite pleased with how I had managed my day; three lifts covering fifty miles or so and now I had overcome my sleeping bag problem, I hoped…

I packed up my belongings, consulted my map, and, at 13.30 precisely, I gathered myself and resumed my trek, heading off on an upward climb along Route One before turning off to Saenautavatn, way up in the mountains, thirteen miles further on. Saenautavatn lies alongside the R901, a high altitude track crossing the Jökuldalsheidi, a range of mountains, moors and hills southwest of Vopnafjördur. Saenautavatn is a sizeable lake and would offer me a good location for a wild camp. Despite my late start I thought that I would be able to reach it by about five or six o' clock. What I didn't consider however was that the weather, that had been fairly tolerable so far today, would take a definite turn for the worse.

I set off briskly, walking at a good pace, because I was anxious to leave Skjöldólfsstadir behind and get some miles under my belt. The next hour or so saw me climb over 1000 feet at a steady but productive rate, however, the higher I climbed, the more the weather closed in. Clouds emerged from the north and before I knew it, the rain was falling heavily and a dense mist had descended. Any views I had had, were now fading memories and the wind suddenly indicated its arrival with a vengeance, whipping up the sand at the side of the road around me. Consulting my map, I discovered I had inadvertently put it in its map case the wrong way round and, as I attempted to remove it, so I could see the relevant section, it inconveniently blew on a sudden inopportune gust of wind across the soaking ground. After a bit of swearing, I retrieved a rather sad-looking, bedraggled piece of paper, resembling some idiot's failed attempt at origami, and tried to place it back in its plastic cover. All that happened was one piece of paper had now become at least four soggy pieces. Frustration now set in and my blood pressure started to rise. The birds thankfully, had run for cover and did not attempt to give their three pennies' worth. Just as well, the mood I was in.

Map restored once more, in a grim sorry state, I continued on, upwards, getting wetter and wetter. I resigned myself to another passage of travel where I could see next to nothing, with raindrops dripping constantly off my jacket hood, giving a dispiriting watering can effect a mere few centimetres in front of my eyebrows. The temperature had dropped considerably with the height gain and I considered putting on another layer to keep out the chill. Visibility diminished rapidly to almost nothing when I came upon a road junction, hopefully leading off into the mountains. Good! That was what I had been hoping for, but was this the junction I required? I was not sure. The place mentioned on the road sign was not indicated on my map. Strangely, the river, in the gorge on my left at this point, seemed to be on the wrong side of the road. I checked and decided that I was either lost, or the river had moved. This was not a particularly good state of affairs to be in. Getting lost out here was not to be recommended at all. I was reluctant to take this mountain road if it was not in fact the correct one, especially with almost zero visibility. I checked again, and was positive the map must be wrong*. The river should be on the right but it was on the left, or was it the other way round? Whatever, I was completely disorientated. It is amazing how quickly your circumstances can change when you are walking. One moment you are in full control, comfortable with your situation, your equipment, your outlook generally and within a minute or so, you can feel unnerved, confused and decidedly edgy, all brought about because you doubt exactly where you are. All I know is, my mind suddenly became very focused and alert, as I switched into survival mode. Time to make some important decisions.

Occasionally a car would emerge from the mist like a ghostly carriage. I had seen two vehicles pass me in the last half hour, so I decided it would be prudent to take action and seek assistance. Now, if *you* were driving through the fog on full beam and a faint apparition emerged waving walking poles maniacally in front of you, would you stop? No, and they didn't either. I shook my fist vehemently after them. Must be French, I thought. Why didn't they stop? Thoroughly disconsolate and becoming increasingly worried, I carried on walking away from the road junction. I ummed and ahhed whether to go back and take it, but what if it was the wrong way? This was not the time or place to get lost in this god-awful weather. Another lonely car appeared out of the mist, tiptoeing its way through the murky haze. Drastic action was required! As it drew nearer, with its headlights vainly searching for the road ahead, creeping slowly through the mire, I managed to get it to stop by basically throwing myself onto its bonnet, with my face squashed against the windscreen in some grotesque, paralysed,

*I found out after my trip that Route One had been re-routed in this area and my map did not reflect the recent changes.

gargoyle pose, hands outspread like the angel Gabriel. I crossed my fingers that it would not crush me to death but somehow it managed to anchor on rather abruptly and came to a shuddering halt; its headlights picking out the swirling spectral fog in two mysterious yellowish, lustrous beams splaying forwards like toppled ice-cream cones. Peeling myself away from the windscreen, upon which was imprinted quite disturbingly, a misty, rather frightening outline of my deformed shape, I clambered down and staggered around to the passenger door.

"Thanks for stopping," I whimpered, as a window was wound down. "Do you know where the junction for the R901 is? Have you gone past it?" The startled couple inside the car looked at this saturated, somewhat deranged figure, who had frightened them to death and who had made them violently perform an emergency stop, rather against their wishes, and answered hesitantly that they had not gone past any road junction for quite some way. This baffled me because my bedraggled map clearly indicated R901 heading off into the mountains.

"You must have," I implored, and thrust the remnants of my soggy map in their direction, as if to say look for yourself. Hesitantly, they then attempted to fit the map pieces together, but the nature of the task was nigh on impossible. Every time they moved the map, another sodden fragment came apart in their hands, like tissue paper. I reached through the window to help them. The male driver had the map pieces propped up on his lap against the steering wheel. His partner, a substantial, but not unattractive, female sat alongside him. As I reached over to adjust the map, my hand inadvertently brushed the woman's comely breast and she flinched, just a little, well more than a little really. It was like she had suffered a substantial electric shock. How does one describe it – almost as if she had been struck down with instantaneous rigor mortis through my rather inappropriate physical connection? I could now imagine her thoughts at that precise moment:

"We've been hijacked by a lunatic who has emerged from the mist, a sex maniac and now he's going to ravish me in a most unpleasant way. After all, he's soaking wet, for God's sake! And English!"

I withdrew my hand pretending I hadn't noticed my overly personal contact with her rather pleasant and perfectly formed rotundity, and said again,

"There must be a road junction round here somewhere."

"Where exactly are you trying to get to?" the man asked, oblivious to his partner's sudden brush of intimacy. I then reached in again, to show him on the map, and blow me, my hand touched the woman yet again, this time more substantially. She froze in her seat, but still said nothing about my breastly encounters. Had she enjoyed it, I considered, momentarily?

"I'm headed for the mountains to Saenautavatn." I might well have said Timbuktu, because they hadn't a clue where Saenautavatn was. In fact, they hadn't a clue where they were whatsoever. I was amazed they'd set out at all! I had a better knowledge of Iceland and I didn't even live in this bloody place!

By now, my patience had worn thin. All I wanted to know was, where the effing junction was? The woman, relaxed slightly and composure somewhat regained, said,

"The mountains? You're going to the mountains?"

"Yes," I replied. "I'm going to Saenautavatn." She obviously considered me to be an inept fool. And an opportunistic sex maniac to boot.

"Promise me," she implored, with quite a surprising reconciliatory tone, all things considered, "that you won't go into the mountains. It's very dangerous in weather like this. Promise me!" She sounded like my mother when I had asked to play on the railway line. "Promise me!"

"I promise," I lied.

"Promise me you'll stick to the main road," she shouted almost deliriously now. I had considered this option a while back, but dismissed it because I wanted to explore some of Iceland's more uncivilised terrain, not just the tarmacked ring road.

"Ok, I'll stick to the road. I'll be all right," I assured her, and then I reached across her, taking care not to engage her attractive form a third time, (even though I may have wanted to), and retrieved what was left of my map. I thanked them for their help but the woman was hastily winding up the window to put some form of physical barrier between her and me. I waved them goodbye, although she probably interpreted my friendly smile as a lascivious letch. They hastily went on their way, almost recklessly so, without a backward glance, probably to report me to the authorities.

So there I was, on Route One, ruined map, hopelessly lost, visibility nil and now, a wanted felon. I walked on for another hundred metres, through the impenetrable gloom, and then, within a split second, a miracle occurred. The wind dropped, the rain ceased and the clouds started to lift. And as they rose, they revealed the most stunning landscape imaginable. I simply could not believe it. I fell to my knees and thanked God.

Ahead and to the right and left was a tremendous range of mountains, the Jökuldalsheidi, that stood proudly and impressively. I was in awe. Moments previously, I could see nothing and now, in a brief moment, I could see everything and everywhere. I was dumbstruck and, to compound my delight, there, not a hundred metres further on, was my delicious R901 junction, headed off at right angles to my left, with two yellow road signs clearly saying Modrudalur 32 and Saenautasel 13.

I was in raptures of joy. The landscape was hypnotically barren - grey sand topped with moss, with mountains like serrated knife blades. I laughed aloud and long. How we are governed, dictated to, by the elements! I could clearly see the way to go now, along a rough but distinct track, snaking its way amongst mounds of the high ground, enticing me in, just as Theseus was, into the Labyrinth, to face the Minotaur.

The Jökuldalsheidi rise over 2300 feet and basically this whole area is covered in huge quantities of ash deposited after the devastating eruption of Mt Askja way back in 1875, far to the south. In every direction there was evidence of this monumental geomorphic fly-tipping, with massive quantities of pumice thrown out inconsiderately, but in considerable quantities, by the volcano. The beauty of this area lay in its starkness and in its sameness. Mile after mile, the track wound through a landscape that changed in shape, but remained constant in style and substance. Lunar is an adjective that would describe superbly what I was seeing, and this was definitely a superb lunar place to be, helped I might add, by the upturn in the weather and the clarity of the atmosphere. I felt rejuvenated, reborn. This was why I had come to Iceland - to absorb and to be a part of, this immediate geology, this land-making, this divine origination, and I was thrilled, immensely so.

I marched onwards, the track rising and falling gently, so progress was made relatively quickly. My first reference point was a road junction that led down to Saenautasel, an old turf building that was a farmhouse way back in time, but had been abandoned after the eruption: farming and general living, now being almost impossible. Today, Saenautasel is a summer refuge where travellers can retreat from the worst of the weather. I contemplated stopping here, but because it lay 2.5 miles off my general route, I decided instead to keep going forwards 2.5 miles nearer tomorrow's intended destination of Modrudalur.

The sun started to lower in the sky. Saenautavatn, a large lake, and my original intended stop for a wild camp came and went, then Grjótgardsvatn, a smaller lake beyond the first, and it was here I decided to look for a suitable place to stop. The air was still, the evening quiet, except for the occasional sheep and the odd feisty bird. I pitched camp, slightly hurriedly, because I was afraid that if the weather changed, I would end up cooking in a rain storm, and up here, with no shelter at all, things could get very inclement and unpalatable indeed. But the rain and wind held off, and instead, I enjoyed a wonderfully remote camp, feasting on a rehydrated chicken curry and a slab of chocolate, way out in the wild, at an altitude of nearly 1900 feet. I sat on my triangular stool next to my little green tent, my belongings scattered around me in their variously coloured bags. My walking poles standing erect in the dusty sand, as sentinels protecting my temporary kingdom. Everywhere I looked was mine for the short term. No one could deny me this. A stark, detached outpost with nobody around for miles. A wonderful feeling! I had discovered myself in this tiny portion of Iceland and it felt good. As I sat there, reflecting and philosophising, I sipped my coffee that tasted sublime; the air smelt fresh and I savoured every last sweet second as the sun dropped inexorably in the Arctic sky.

There was some rain in the night. I felt warm enough however with my new insulating layers, but what really interrupted my sleep was around 3am when I heard the sound of what seemed to be an aircraft flying low over my tent. I awoke with a start, then realised that it wasn't an aircraft performing an emergency landing, but two geese – I think it was two – which had come to reconnoitre my tent, in the middle of their patch. They almost crashed through it, but luckily landed nearby and then the pair of them decided to squabble between themselves as to why anyone should want to camp up here in the middle of nowhere, or rather, precisely in the middle of their domain, when there were perfectly good man-made facilities back at Saenautasel and even Modrudalur, several miles further on.

I listened to them for a while, each one putting across their gabbling point of view, then I slowly drifted off again, to dream of irate Icelandic women falsely accusing me of various perversions and fetishes, whilst slicing my precious map into a million pieces, then swallowing them in one fell swoop, as if to say; "Serves you right!" As for the cold, this night had been far more agreeable and comfortable than when camping alongside the Jökulsá á Brú, the previous night. Thank goodness!

I arose, slightly stiff, to discover the geese had waddled off. It was not raining, which made a pleasant change. I now had a chance to try out my bog-in-a-bag toilet, far away from anyone. Now I am not really known to be a reticent character and yet here I was, miles from anybody else, dropping my trousers and draping a discreet towel across my lap, probably to hide my sanitary movements from the wildlife, especially the recalcitrant birds who would no doubt shout,

"Look at him! Look what he's doing, despoiling our land! How disgusting! Go and do that in your own back yard, not in ours, you disgusting piece of work!"

I ignored them and continued with my open-air No 2 – an airy experience, not unpleasant in fact, just primeval and necessary, and as I sat there, I was rewarded with the most fantastically, far-removed view of this volcanic desert, stretching away in front of me. I could have sat there all day, just taking it all in, however I had places to go to; there would be more vistas like this. My problem came afterwards. Once I had performed my sanitary ablutions, I needed to hide the effluent from innocent passers-by, not that anyone would be passing by this way any time soon. I looked around for a suitable spot to excavate a hidey-hole but there was nowhere really suitable to dig to hide my shiny black plastic bag of unpleasantries, the ground being slightly difficult to excavate, so instead I collected a pile of rocks and built a modest symmetrical cairn, about a third of a metre in height, to commemorate and conceal my first wild camp Icelandic ablution. I was rather hoping it would decompose rapidly and not be preserved in the midst of time as a primeval 21st Century fossil or artefact, to be discovered years later by an unfortunate geology undergraduate looking for unique volcanic outflows. My volcanic emission would only have measured a miserly 0.4 on the Richter Scale of earth movements.

It was with some reluctance I left the campsite and headed out along a dusty track westwards. The extreme barrenness of the scenery was something so alien to me, I might as well have been on another planet, however this notion was suddenly disrupted by a 4x4 vehicle that came thundering past me, kicking up a dust trail that lingered long after it had passed. Its enthusiastic occupants waved at me and I waved back, almost in a mutual appreciation of each other venturing in such an outlandish place. I resumed my inter-planetary thoughts. These mountains could so easily be from another world I surmised. I fully expected a Neil Armstrong figure to appear over a crest, muttering his "One small step for man" platitudes in a monotonous drawl as befits an unemotional astronaut. And then another vehicle passed me – this time a larger coach, and then another. I was slightly taken aback by this. Tourists? Out here? But these were tourists embarking on an Arctic cross country safari and it was probably costing them plenty of kronur to experience this unworldly place, whereas me? I was paying precisely nothing! I smiled an economic smile and sallied onwards.

The track dipped and then started to huff up a steep climb. I watched the two distant coaches toiling away uphill and then gradually disappear over the crest, leaving me in my own personal world once again. It was strange not having the distractions of modern life to interfere in my thoughts and meditations. It was just me and nature and we had emotionally connected.

The hill took a bit of climbing, and I was pleased with the assistance given to me by my walking poles. Without them, walking is purely a lower body operation, but with them, you involve your arms, shoulders, your upper torso, in pushing downwards, in a disjointed but efficient, skiing action. What it meant however, was I could ascend slopes expending much less energy and move more quickly, than without them. I liked my walking poles. We had bonded and they would prove to be such an important piece of kit later in my trek.

A little while later I encountered a vast plain ahead of me, called Geitasandur meaning "Goat sands". It was fractured only by the track I was walking along, a blemish on a grey canvas. Icelandic roads, basically stony uneven affairs, have yellow marker posts, sunk every fifty metres so when it snows, drivers can orientate themselves. Across this plain I counted seventy three posts all in a perfectly straight line, making it, in my estimation, to be over two miles wide.

As I walked, there was no protection from the wind whatsoever and along here it really tormented me, whipping grit up into my sandblasted face. As a result I pulled my hood cord tighter and battled onwards, leaning into the wind. It felt like someone had seized my shoulders and was forcing me back against my will. Perhaps this is what it felt like to be a front row forward in a rugby scrum, anyway it was curiously invigorating! Apparently this area is notorious for its frequent sand storms and I could now understand why. I had never seen so much sand, dust and rock in all my life. Local microclimates of air turbulence would readily rouse the ash and debris into the air, making life very unpleasant indeed for exposed trekkers like me.

Eventually post number seventy three was reached and passed and the track turned and meandered upwards once again. This time it climbed around a mountain called Miklafell and it was here that my sense of isolation was disturbed by an unexpected spirited coach party of Dutch tourists, who had parked up to view the extensive panorama below. As I approached, they all turned and stared at me to the extent I began to wonder whether something horrible was up. It probably mimicked the sort of stare Himalayan Sherpas gave when they encountered an abominable snowman and right now, I felt distinctly abominable.

"Where have you come from?" they asked enquiringly.

"Well, today I have walked about nine miles from the east," I said sounding like one of the Magi, bearing gifts for the infant Jesus. I was hoping that would give them the answer they were wanting.

"What are you doing here?" came the next probing question. Abel Tasman, the famous Dutch explorer, probably asked similar questions of local natives when he first discovered Fiji and other remote Pacific Islands, centuries earlier. This however was not Pacific, but Arctic, well almost.

"I'm attempting to walk across Iceland from Seydisfjordur to Reykjavik and this is day five of my walk. So far I've covered about 115 km," I estimated. (This was quite a good estimate in retrospect.)

"What! You've walked all the way from Seydisfjordur to here?" they gasped, almost in deep shock, grabbing hold of each other for support. They were plainly not walkers. "In five days! You've walked all that way in five days!" they shouted almost accusingly but, seeing their incredulous demeanours break into fulsome smiles, I assumed correctly that they were pleasantly approving of me. They were very impressed with my accomplishment, so much so I too, began to feel quite proud of myself, almost too proud. I decided I was going to enjoy my five minutes of fame and I briefly considered selling autographs at a very reasonable 100 Kronur a time. I broke away from the animated throng and climbed a small rock, affected a wistful stare and a classic explorer's pose as I looked into the far distance and pretended to consult my torn map, weathered in a vicious storm of yesteryear. I puffed out my chest, but they took this to be a sign of hunger, and immediately thrust some juicy wine gums into my gloved hand. Without thinking I greedily stuffed them, all three of them, into my mouth at once and began to chew with the relish and abandon of a returning around-the-world traveller back from his pioneering adventures to faraway places. The throng murmured in unison; my rapacious feeding frenzy leading them to believe I was on the verge of starvation, because at least five of them dashed back as one, on board their coach, returning moments later, with wide smiles and benevolent looks and began to stuff some boiled sweets into all my pockets and every last available orifice, being rather too personal and over-familiar for my liking. Paramo jackets have pockets everywhere, as discovered by my Hollandaise friends. Laden with sweets, I soon resembled the fat Michelin Man who used to sit atop his garish yellow tyre delivery vehicle in times gone by. I could hardly refuse such confectional generosity, but the fervent Dutch were not finished with me just yet and now they all wanted to take my photograph or be photographed with me. Had they mistaken me for someone else? Was Edmund Hillary or some famous Arctic notoriety of distinction due to pass this way? Should I ask for commission? Eventually they were photographed out, mainly because their lithium batteries had expired, in the frenetic clicking of shutters with accompanying flash. They retreated, bowing and shuffling backwards, paying due reverence to their newfound deity. I felt like evangelising and pronouncing solemnly: "Go in peace, in the name of Christ.

Amen." The only reason I didn't however, was because my mouth was still stuffed with all manner of sweet delights and my mother severely taught me never to speak with my mouth full, or to take the name of the Lord, our God in vain, lest I be smite down with a heavenly thunderbolt. Instead, I mumbled my gratitude whilst consuming at least a further two kilograms of much needed sugar and glucose. The madding throng now reluctantly climbed back aboard their coach, gazing wistfully at me for one last time, to the extent I felt I was being visually raped. Their coach then departed with everyone aboard waving frantically out of the side and back windows. The driver even tooted his horn enthusiastically. If this is what a party of ageing Dutch tourists were like, what on earth were their national football supporters like? I'd never seen such passion and zeal! It was quite suffocating to be honest. The only explanation I have, in retrospect is, that they had all partaken of the evil weed that is "Cannabis Sativa". I hoped they would return to earth by tea-time.

As quickly as they vanished, lustily and patriotically singing their National Anthem, "Het Wilhelmus", a solitary car appeared over the brow of the hill and parked close to me. I wondered momentarily if the Pope had arrived to canonise me as the new patron saint of Holland, ousting the incumbent Saint Plechelm into the depths of history. Instead, two athletic looking occupants got out and started taking photos, not of me, but of the impressive Icelandic vista all around us. I detected English accents and said, quite correctly,

"Ah English. First I've come across since I set off." There then ensued an excited discussion between myself and the pleasant couple, named Annette and Graham from Keswick, who lived a mere hour's drive from my home village. We congratulated ourselves on being here and then talked wistfully about our homeland, the United Kingdom. It always amazes me how staunchly patriotic one becomes, when one ventures into conversation overseas. Latent nationalistic tendencies that have lain dormant, suddenly arouse immense fervour in, and intense devotion to, one's mother country, yet as soon as the conversation ceases, the passion wanes as fast as it arises. Strange, as if one feels legally obliged to extol enthusiastically one's country's virtues when overseas, at least for a few minutes, at any rate. After this compulsory patriotic sabre-rattling, we then shared our experiences whilst being here in Iceland. Graham and Annette were reaching the end of their stay and were on their way to catch the ferry in Seydisfjordur. They asked about my plans and I told them I was headed to Reykjahlid then down Sprengisandur, across to Gullfoss before heading on for Reykjavik. We talked about the wilderness that is the highlands and the problems it poses, particularly for the solo trekker. Annette said,

"You have to respect this landscape. It's similar at times to the Scottish Highlands, but more extreme." I agreed, thinking of the Torridons on the west coast. "The weather too, it's so changeable it can catch you out."

Outside Modrudalur near Miklafell

I'd of course already experienced sudden climatic change the day before in the fog and I recalled very briefly the woman I'd unfortunately fondled. Shaking my head, to mentally divest myself of such a sudden lascivious thought, I said I was fully aware of the difficulties that Sprengisandur imposed. We talked about food requirements, energy levels, navigational skills and river crossings.

At the end of it I was in no doubt that Sprengisandur did indeed present a difficult challenge, especially after all the rain we had had since I'd been in Iceland. We then took photos of each other, Dutch style, and swapped email addresses. We shook hands like typical wimpy English folk, all limp wrists and clammy fingers, but as I waved them off, I had the feeling I might one day possibly see them again. I really hoped so, they were my kind of people...

Alone once more, I set off for Modrudalur a few miles further on, all downhill. The track swept round in a wide arc before straightening, and there, at the end of a long straight road, was the unmistakable outline of Modrudalur Church, set in amongst several other random buildings. I was quite excited, because Modrudalur was a place I especially wanted to visit, being the highest farm settlement in Iceland at over 1500 feet. It was also very remote, lying to the south of Route One by several miles. It used to be a service area on Route One, before the ring road was diverted further north, making this place somewhat redundant. As I drew closer, I could see farm buildings of some sort to the right and some turf structures to the left. As I looked way over to the left of the road, I observed the magnificent mountain named Herdubreid, meaning "broad-shouldered" with a sloped table top. This had to be one of the most attractive and impressive stand-alone mountains in Iceland and it quite simply filled me with awe.

Modrudalur took longer to reach than I expected, along the arrow straight dusty road and I was greatly relieved to finally reach a rather attractive collection of buildings, set in precisely the middle of nowhere.

I headed for the café in one of the offset turf buildings and bought myself a much needed lamb soup, that I later considered to be the tastiest in the whole country, pleasantly meaty, full bodied and well-seasoned. I even went back for a second helping. My feet and legs were tired and aching, even though today's distance had been a moderate fourteen miles. My pack had seemed heavy today; perhaps it was the cumulative effect of walking for five consecutive days. Anyway, I decided to take advantage of the basic accommodation here, get myself a shower and wash through some of my more whiffy clothes. I then had a look around the site. The church was similar in style to many Icelandic churches with a square bell tower at the front and a simple nave. The windows had straight pointed arches above them and the whole building was painted in a cream colour, whilst the roof was red. It was the sort of building you could have built out of Lego without requiring any special bricks to do so. The church was very charming so I took numerous photographs of it from every possible direction, then went to explore the other adjacent buildings. There were two sets of turf buildings. One set appeared to be a group of houses in the traditional Icelandic style of old, layered sods for the walls, all topped off with a turfed roof. The other set housed the café, and some petrol pumps which I found rather incongruous – the old and the modern, juxtaposed within a building constructed essentially from grass and soil. Apart from the hostel where I was staying, the other buildings were all associated with the farm here, and that was just about it. From time to time, coaches would drive up and disgorge parties of eager tourists who took photos of the church, as I had. After twenty minutes, they then clambered back aboard their impatient coach that disappeared along R901 in a cloud of grey dust. The whole place then became remarkably silent and a serene tranquillity settled once more, like a soft eiderdown.

Modrudalur felt to be a wonderfully spiritual place and I sat in a meditative mood on the steps of the hostel, calmly absorbing the distinctive aura that permeated every last square inch of this godly location. What an ethereal place to experience! I became quietly emotional as I looked westwards across the incredibly desolate plain, perhaps reflecting on my own physical isolation and mental disposition. I was beginning to notice how fragile I felt psychologically, especially in the quieter moments of my walk. While I was busy, or distracted by the rigours of the day, I was fine, but whenever I stopped, I felt quite vulnerable and detached, almost forsaken. With a mighty sigh, I stood up and took three deep breaths. Time to be doing something, I thought.

The rest of the day was spent pottering about, drying my clothes on a clothes line situated beneath a small pitched roof. The wind was building up and it did not take long for my various items to blow dry. After my tea, again eaten in the café, I retired for the night and contemplated the next two days of my trek. I was concerned because these days were both long twenty mile plus days, so there was some serious walking ahead. I had never walked more than seventeen miles throughout my training and my longest day so far, day two, was only eighteen miles. Would my legs cope with the distance? Only time would tell.

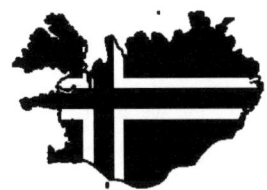

12. Fly me to the Moon

Hunger, work, and sweat are the best herbs – Icelandic Proverb

Modrudalur – Grimsstadir – Reykjahlid   48.3 miles

I awoke refreshed and alert. My legs felt fine and any latent stiffness from the day before had dissipated. I was so pleased to see it was a bright, sunny morning, much warmer than it had been in previous days.

I breakfasted in the café quite early because I knew I had a long slog ahead. Firstly I had to walk five miles to reach Route One, then a long haul northwards for at least twelve miles, before leaving Route One and following a track to a place called Grimsstadir, which was close to exactly nowhere. The waitress who served me said,

"The weather will be good today, but because of that, look out for the flies."
I noted what she had said and rummaged in my pack for my fly mesh and
placed it readily in my jacket pocket. I gorged myself on apple juice, two
bowls of granola, numerous slices of ham and cheese, sweet-tasting bread
and marmalade washed down with two coffees. A full day's work, I
deduced, required a full breakfast. I quickly stocked up my pack with
chocolate and energy bars and, with a last wistful look back towards
Modrudalur, set off to the north.

The flies were indeed up and about, intent on causing mayhem and after a
few deft swipes with my topspin backhand, I decided to wear my fly mesh,
basically a flimsy piece of nylon gauze. It had square corners, so placing it
over my head meant I now looked decidedly uncool, a complete prat
actually, however if it kept the damned flies at bay, so what? It also felt
rather constricting and clammy. I wondered how long I could stand wearing
it.

Ignoring the discomfort as best I could, I headed along a flat dusty track
with the magnificent mountain Herdubreid way off to the west, surely in
my top five mountain scenes, beyond which lay the highlands of the interior
– my goal in nearly a week's time. It was actually a lovely morning for a
stroll and a small range of mountains presented themselves on my left
including the peaks of Sandfell, Geldingafell and Vegahnjúkur. They were
blessed with sharp serrated ridges and conical forms that dropped steeply to
the roadside. On another day it would have been wonderful to climb up to
their summits to take in the view, but right now I had some serious mileage
to cover.

I kept up a lively pace and was pleasantly surprised when I reached Route
One as promptly as I did, after merely an hour and a bit. I was expecting to
have been travelling on this last section of R901 for a while longer, but

perhaps I was just benefiting from the consequences of an energising breakfast.

Upon reaching the junction, I encountered a few more vehicles than I had been used to of late, roaring off in the direction of Egilsstadir to the right, and Myvatn to the left. It is amazing how quickly the modern world suddenly re-emerges after a remote sojourn in the wilderness. I was actually quite sad to leave R901, because it had been an absolute thrill and a real privilege to walk this route, a step back in time to the creation of our planet and a path that I would definitely like to wander along in the future.

As soon as I turned left onto Route One, the road climbed steeply, carving a path through the mountains. I paused for a minute or so to gather myself and then I was off, pushing my walking poles determinedly into the road surface. Because it was so warm, the pole tips sank into the melting tarmac leaving a trail of neat holes behind me, a dot-to-dot picture as proof I had passed this way. As I climbed higher, I was becoming very aware of the sultry heat. Such a contrast to the previous days. Time to take on water. Already I was sweating like a pig in a sauna and emitting an odour that drove the flies into a wild frenzy. My fly mesh, though uncomfortable in the heat, was doing its job, but at the very moment I attempted a swig from my water bottle, a fly snuck in through a tiny exposed gap benesth my mesh and made a bee-line - or is it fly-line - straight down the back of my throat. I gagged instantly and repeatedly coughed trying to dislodge this unexpected morsel of protein, however, with a few quick swishes of saliva, I successfully moved it back onto my tongue and spat it out. Unfortunately I had momentarily forgotten I was wearing my mesh, so all that happened was a rather dead, soggy fly, immersed in my unctuous spittle, was now splattered across my gauze in a rather distasteful display, of what may possibly have been conceived to be a microcosm of modern art.

I stopped, rinsed my fly mesh in a nearby stream, took the opportunity to take on water, making a mental note not to spit inside my head covering ever again.

As I walked onwards, the route was proving less spectacular than R901, at times almost boring, and I soon realised this day was simply about clocking up the miles to Grimsstadir, getting from A to B and not much else. The heat was now severely oppressive and I unzipped all the various openings on my jacket, creating my own air conditioning system. I did not want to remove my jacket completely in case the flies started curiously exploring the numerous crevices and orifices about my body.

To take my mind off the relentless trudge, I tried to think about anything except walking. I thought about the World Cup where England had had their usual success - an ignominious first round exit. I thought about home and my family, which was not a good idea, because I then started feeling morose and lonely. Either side of the road the scenery remained fairly constant - a river winding its way to the north on the left, and a range of lavary hills to the right, made of a stuff called tufa. This panorama continued for nearly two hours and the scorching heat was inducing intense cravings in me for drinks distributed by that industrial giant, Coca-Cola. At that moment I would have paid an awful lot of money for a refreshingly cool glass of the fizzy stuff. I wondered why Iceland did not have roadside cafés, like back home, thoughtfully located on all busy trunk roads across the countryside, then I quickly realised why there were none, because daily passing traffic out here can often be counted in meagre and paltry amounts, just odd numbers of vehicles a day. I kept drinking from my water supply but was well aware I had to make it last. Rivers at this point were inconveniently set back from the road, detours over challenging terrain. I plundered on, as Route One gently wrestled with itself in mild contortions, changing direction occasionally but not often enough for my liking actually.

God, how I wanted, no desired, almost in a sexual way, an iced glass of coke! Sweat dripped down my face and down the small of my back. I was leaking profusely, pouring like a colander.

At that precise moment, ahead of me in a lay-by, stood a camper van. Not a mirage, but a genuine aluminised reality. A man emerged and crossed the road to take a photograph of something mountainous to my right. I watched and closed in on him, furtively like an opportunistic stalker. I coughed and made him jump, so much so, he inadvertently took a photograph and his Nikon digital SLR, nearly jumped out of his hands.

"Do you have any drink?" I asked, slightly desperately.

"You English?" he replied, regaining his composure.

"Yes, near Manchester," I responded. I never said Burnley. People have no idea where Burnley is. Even people in Accrington and Clitheroe don't know where Burnley is. It's one of those nondescript Lancashire towns, lost in the industrial heritage of the north-west, full of decaying terraced houses, the birthplace of Chumbawamba, and a football team that cost no more than a couple of bags of chips and a tatty pie. "Do you have any drink, it's very hot," I implored, trying to hide the desperate urgency in my voice.

"Yes, of course, in my van. You are welcome… ." He did not have time to finish his sentence because I had transported myself, Star Trek style, into his stylish camper van, where his wife looked at me with a somewhat startled and surprised expression. Her husband appeared behind me, two seconds later.

"Hello," I said. "I'm Mark. God, it's jolly hot today, isn't it?" trying to think of something sensible to say. She nodded uncertainly in agreement and then her husband explained why I had hijacked his vehicle.

"He's come for a cool drink. He's from Manchester," as if that explained everything.

And with that he poured me a delectable glass of fizzy strawberry, that was utterly divine. I drank for several seconds and proffered my glass once more, hopefully for a refill, that was thankfully forthcoming. Again, words cannot describe how good that liquid nectar was, as it dribbled down my throat, sating my thirst. Strawberry ecstasy! Time stood still. I relished every last drop.

Whilst still in blissful rapture, I then thanked them for their kindness and generosity. I established that they were from Holland, but had nothing to do with the narcotised Dutch tourists who had plied me with their happy sweets the day before. Apparently they were over here in Iceland with their own group of Dutch chums. Altogether, an armada of Dutch camper vans had travelled across the North Atlantic and invaded Iceland two weeks earlier. They had travelled around Iceland in the manner of Willem Barentsz and Cornelis Nay, noted Dutch Arctic explorers, and having left their mark, were now on their way back to Seydisfjordur to catch the ferry the following morning.

For that reason they were using up all their supplies of food and drink and that was why I was welcomed inside, to share in their strawberry pop. I thanked them gratefully and told them all about my trek so far. They were impressed that someone my age should attempt such a journey. Half of me felt flattered and half of me felt like saying,

"Easy on, old chap! I'm not ready to pop my clogs just yet!" My reference to clogs I deemed to be appropriate for the Dutch company I was keeping. Anyway, I didn't really say anything, I just glugged some more pop down, satisfying my liquid cravings.

They wished me well and I wished them well. Strange that when I really needed a drink, there was someone there, at exactly the right time to help me, but, as I was to discover throughout the rest of my trek, this would happen a lot more than once…

I shook his hand. Certainly not up to the standard of an Icelandic handshake, but still pretty good. The Dutch had been good to me the past twenty four hours and I made a mental note to support the Dutch national football team next time they were playing.

Back on the road, a lone bird appeared, of unidentifiable species, because the sun was shining in my eyes. It hovered over my left shoulder, keeping pace with me.

"Enjoy that did you? Didn't bring enough drink for a warm day, eh? Good planning that! You'll learn." And with that he soared high above, until he disappeared over a ridge, leaving me alone once more. The flies were now back to their annoying tricks, but I was well protected. Fortress Archer was currently impregnable, if rather fetid, not that the Dutch camper van couple had complained about my noxious pong; perhaps they were too polite. The road kept climbing, but not steeply and the miles were being ticked off relentlessly. I detected a flattening out, as the road plateaued, then a slight drop and finally, at last, the road started to descend properly, gravity now my ally. My whole body was now beginning to resent the physical exertions of the day, as twinges and gripes were felt in knee and ankle joints. My back voiced its own concerns along with my shoulders that protested in sympathy too. Time to show some grit, so I ignored their plaintive pleas and headed forever onward. It was simply a matter, I concluded, of putting in the hours and I would arrive at my objective. No harder than that. I was now afforded an extensive view that stretched endlessly westwards in the general direction of Myvatn, my destination for the following day. I was, in fact, looking at a desolate vista incorporating the Odadahraun, a massive lava desert, the result of many volcanic outpourings over 12000 years, the most recent being from Krafla in 1984. In places the lava had been colonised with a covering of green vegetation but otherwise everything, as far as I could see, was a dusty grey colour, with Route One slicing through it. Lush was not a word ever considered in these parts.

I chanced upon a viewing point, having covered sixteen sweaty, protracted miles. Wearily I cast down my rucksack, which was weighing heavily on my tired body. Thankfully, the temperature had dropped from the excesses of midday. Chewing on an energy bar, my fourth of the day, I scrutinised my map. I was required to leave Route One shortly and head northwards towards Grimsstadir. The diversion lay half a mile ahead. I then hopefully scanned the horizon for two tell-tale white columns, which would indicate I was nearing my destination for the day. These were the vertical supports of the bridge over the Jokulsá á Fjöllum, a glacial river sourced in the Vatnajökull Glacier to the south, and the second longest river in Iceland.

My eyes squinted against the sunlight and followed the road as it dropped down, and there, to my intense joy, protruding upwards like flag poles, were the two white lolly stick appendages I sought, the bridge of the Jokulsá á Fjöllum! My heart pounded. I knew that I was back in familiar territory, because twenty two years earlier I had driven a hire car over this very bridge, on the way to Dettifoss, one of Iceland's greatest and most powerful waterfalls.

With renewed spirit, but with sore and overworked aching limbs, I set out once more and shortly afterwards I abandoned the tarmac, to discover a stony, dusty track half right, headed for Grimsstadir, a tiny hamlet which lay a few miles further ahead. I had expected this particular leg of my journey to take about an hour, however Grimsstadir was to prove annoyingly elusive. My feet now decided they had had enough and my stride length shortened considerably. I suddenly heard an unexpected commotion above me. Blow me down! The birds were back.

"Ah ha! Look at you now! You're buggered! Your knees are shot and you can hardly walk! Call yourself a trekker? More like a wanker!"

This I thought, rather cruel. I'd completed over twenty miles in the intense heat and my legs and feet had every right to complain. A curlew took it upon itself to stand on the track ahead of me, defying me to approach. I felt like Robin Hood when he first confronted Little John with quarterstaffs, crossing the bridge over the river in the legend of old, but unlike Robin, despite my unhealthy condition, I overcame the curlew challenge, wafting my poles at it in semaphore fashion and continued with an intense grimace on my face as the hapless bird flew skyward. My legs were almost screaming now. My muscles had given up and simply wanted to rest. Urging myself onwards, with the disdainful bird now high above me, I carried on, almost pleading for Grimsstadir to show itself.

It took another whole hour before this remote oasis appeared. I could barely muster a self-congratulatory whimper as I staggered in, crossing a small rickety wooden bridge. I was bushed, zonked out, completely in bits and upon reaching a collection of rather basic-looking buildings, I headed for one displaying an Icelandic flag. I had thoughtfully booked a room here. In my planning I assumed I would need a bed after such a long day, and now, how sensible that forward planning had been proved. Once I had ascertained I was in the right place and established there was food to buy here, I flopped down into a plastic chair, totally fatigued and drained. I wearily ordered everything on the scant menu: some tomato soup, a grilled sandwich and two coffees. These were devoured somewhat impolitely rather like a scavenging vulture decimating a fresh carcass, and when I had finished, I sat there with bits of food around my mouth with a bone-weary and spent look, hair plastered to my face and eyes staring madly. I then tried to stand up, however my legs now mutinied and were seized with a severe form of rigor mortis. Flexible movement was now virtually impossible. My legs were shot, my back was shot and my shoulders were shot. My age was finally catching up with me. I found a comfortable chair outside and hobbled into it as best I could. I could feel my leg muscles throbbing away. Time, I thought, to just sit back, do absolutely nothing and recover. Time to appreciate that in six days I had now walked ninety nine miles with a substantial pack, not bad for an old geezer.

Dinner, two hours later, was lamb chops with vegetables. My body was now in a very slightly happier state, but still rather fragile and creaking, but the physical rebellion that had taken place in my body earlier on, had now been greatly subdued. I felt bit like a UN peace-keeping force, summoned to maintain law and order in a broken body to keep the warring factions apart. My warring factions, primarily in my lower half – my hips, calves, knees, ankles and the soles of my feet were now quiet: muted and repressed, almost as if tired of fighting against me. I now sat in a rather compact room filled with a mish-mash of tables and chairs at which were seated a number of trekkers and tourists, either residing at this establishment, or else camping nearby. While I was eating, I struck up a conversation with two Spaniards, Julio and José. We noticed a TV in the corner of the room and we asked the proprietor if it was possible to watch the World Cup, which it was. A very agreeable evening then ensued watching Holland play Argentina. I remembered to support Holland, in acknowledgement of my friendly coach supporters earlier on, but unfortunately their national team lost on penalties. As I watched the match, I conversed easily with Julio, who spoke reasonable English, and problematically with José, who spoke absolutely none, but understood some basic Anglo-Saxon. We talked about our time in Iceland. They were cycling the ring road and were finding it hard going. I told them

I was headed across the country solo and they were duly impressed. It transpired that they were headed to Myvatn, as was I, the following day, so I jokingly said I would race them there. Julio laughed and understood. José said nothing because he clearly had not. Finally, at about 11 o' clock we all retired and I gingerly shuffled off to bed, not really looking forward to tomorrow's exertions – the longest day of the whole trek. My knees moaned softly, wincing at the thought and my ankles lamented vociferously. It was going to be quite an ordeal!

Apart from suffering major leg cramps during the night, that elicited paroxysms of contracted pain and stifled gasps of agony, that basically meant me stuffing my face into my pillow, so as not to wake the rest of the residents into thinking I was being murdered, or worse, the night was generally uneventful. The hot weather of the previous day had gone, leaving a drab and blustery morning in this far-removed outpost in northern Iceland. Grimsstadir would prove to be the farthest north I would explore on this trip; everywhere else I intended to visit being of a more southerly latitude.

I once again stocked up on food at breakfast. Today was an estimated twenty four miler, and I had only ever travelled this far once in my life before, as a spritely thirty year old who ran half marathons and a single marathon for fun during the running boom of the nineteen eighties. This trek today was going to be a significant test for me and one I hoped I could rise to.

I ensured I ate plenty of bread and cheese and other foods high in carbohydrates. I did enjoy my bread, in fact I felt I was developing an obsessive craving for it, almost like a pregnant woman craves mustard and chocolate. Sometimes, when I was walking, my mind became full of thoughts involving granary loaves, wheat germ, wholemeal and seeded batch, crusty rolls and ciabatta sandwiches. Lord knows why, because at home I just ate basic white sliced bread and only a couple of slices a day at that. Right now I craved all things made with flour and yeast. My mind fermented wildly at the thought. Next, I filled my water bottle and added to it several heaped spoonfuls of sugar, not for sweetness, but for pure energy. Today I was crossing the lava desert, however any idea that I could access water on the way could be dismissed. The lava simply cannot retain surface lying water, for it immediately soaks through, deep underground. Any water for my hydration requirements would therefore have to be carried and transporting water meant significant weight. My pack was currently about 17.5kg, plus two litres of water, taking me up to 19.5kg, right on the limit of what I could physically cope with over an extended distance. What I did not want to do was to provoke my back into another round of back spasms that had afflicted me back in April. That would be end of my mission, there and then. With somewhat of a fateful and determined grimace, I lifted my load onto my back and set off, into a stiff, blustery breeze.

Almost immediately, my two Spanish cyclist friends overtook me, as we headed for the bridge over the Jokulsá á Fjöllum. As they passed I shouted I would catch them up shortly, in a jovial sort of way. Little did I realise that I actually would!

It was three miles to the river and on the way there, Route One curved in a wide looping arc to the left. I watched the Spaniards follow the road, battling with the strong wind that was blowing into their faces. Their bikes were heavily laden and it appeared as if they were cycling through treacle. I saw that I had no need to follow the road they were on, but instead could follow a more direct route cutting a corner across the lava field, so that is exactly what I did. The bikers disappeared way out left and I focused on traipsing through mounds of volcanic debris in as straight a line as I could manage. I emerged somewhat dusty, just before the bridge, one of only two crossing points on this river, the other being at the coast. The Jokulsá á Fjöllum is truly a beast, flowing speedily, carrying masses of detritus down from the glacier to the sea. How they managed to build a bridge across here is anyone's guess, but it was a terrific feat of engineering – a suspension bridge supported between two substantial gleaming white structures at either end.

I ambled across the river – the last source of water before Myvatn - taking time to take photographs before heading westwards. A slight incline and the road flattened out, meandering gently as far as the eye could see. On the right were a group of mountains - the Reykjahlidarheidi. I knew Mount Krafla was in that vicinity and as I walked, I tried to guess which summit it was. Krafla had been a very active volcano in recent times and was again due to erupt soon. Hopefully not while I was sauntering by, but it would have made a good photograph.

It is strange the mood one assumes when walking relentlessly all day, hour after hour, where the scenery appears to change only slightly. There is little around to feed and maintain your enthusiasm. Volcanic dust and lava formations can, with time, cause your exuberance to wear thin and the scenery can become, well, almost dull. How then does one fill the void in the time between setting off and reaching one's destination twenty odd miles up the road? Weirdly, I sought solace in counting. Not just any old counting – no that would be far too unimaginative and mundane. No, my counting involved a certain rhythm, a certain metre based on four. I found instinctively that whenever I walked four paces, the natural pattern in saying the number I was counting, fitted perfectly with my steps, so that it felt easy, balanced, co-ordinated and in tune. And I must have counted thousands of numbers that day, to the regular and constant beat of four paces, to the extent I became lost in my own personal world of metamathematics, sensing the beat, whispering the number under my breath, aligning my breathing with my arms that reached forward, holding my walking poles, completing yet another morsel of dusty distance across this interminable terrain. Sometimes the numbers ran into the hundreds, as I became lost in my own cogitative dream world, where I slipped quietly by, tallying, computing the world quadrasonically through the sub-Arctic landscape. As I counted, I did not think. I purely existed in a sublime state of equilibrium that enabled me to have a heightened awareness of my breathing: slow, measured; respirations of purpose and controlled release. I was increasingly aware of patterns in the ground beneath me – confused jigsaw pieces of old eruptions discarded in cinereous or taupe grey shapes that either tessellated precisely or lay randomly, waiting for me to disturb them with a deft scrunch of my boot. In this balance of movement and breathing, this synergy of mind whilst progressing over the coulee, I felt totally at ease with myself and my body. I became absorbed in a world of detachment and withdrawal, where inner hidden processes were now maintaining my body, minute by minute, hour by hour; a vegetative state with brisket, where I was aware but not aware; a contemplative trance but not a trance. All I know is it allowed me to walk miles that day, accomplishing distance against an unchanging, unending backdrop. Occasionally I would jerk from my meditative muse and marvel at some more appealing or dramatic rugged feature with old lava disgorged into all manner of weird and wonderful configurations. It was veiled with a thin layer of vegetation, that slightly spoiled its barren character, but otherwise the alien nature of the landscape was quite hypnotising. The scenery changed very little and after three hours, my body started, once more to seriously niggle me. The wind was difficult to walk against and my whole body was still complaining from yesterday's exertions. My back ached somewhat so I took a strategic time-out to give it some rest. I thought about the Spanish bikers and realised they still had not overtaken me even though

I had covered nine windswept miles! What had happened? Had they punctured?

I sat propped up on a sandy lava bank and stared back the way I had come, when I perceived two distant figures pedalling rhythmically, but painfully slowly, towards me. It was coincidentally, Julio and José. When they reached me they stopped and leaned on their bikes, with weary grimaces.

"Hard work?" I suggested. They both nodded.

"The wind, it just stops you," explained Julio. I had tried to lift Julio's bike earlier in the day back at Grimsstadir, but couldn't. It seemed to be loaded with concrete or its equivalent. Steam rollers have weighed less.

"I think it's easier to walk rather than cycle," I suggested. "With a bike, the wind just catches you and holds you up." They again nodded in agreement. "Either that, or I'm walking really quickly," I said with a cheeky laugh. "Bloody Spanish, never been any good at cycling!" I was ignoring the remarkable historic exploits of the acclaimed Spaniard, Miguel Indurain, possibly the greatest road cyclist ever. We all grinned, including José who probably guessed what I was saying. "I'll see you at the finish," I said optimistically and waved them off. They climbed back on their bikes and once more set off into the stiff breeze blowing relentlessly across the lava. This was not a day for the faint hearted.

I watched them gradually disappear along the road and swigged some of my sugar water. I wasn't even half way. This day was all about pacing myself. Too fast and *my* wheels might come off at eighteen miles. This was not the sort of place to run out of gas. It was now about midday and I could see me still going at six. I staggered under the weight of my rucksack as I reluctantly swung it back onto my shoulders and set off in pursuit of the Spanish once more, a little like Francis Drake and his English fleet chasing the Armada in 1588.

My mind switched back to Sprengisandur, the route I was due to follow in four days' time. I had felt distinctly uneasy about this particular leg of the trip for some time, because it was so long, cold and remote. I was worried about the weather Iceland was currently having, much wetter and colder than it should have been, however this was the year of El Nino and unpredictable weather patterns. I was worried about running out of food too. Basically I had allowed four days to walk down Sprengisandur to reach Nyidalur, the halfway point, where a food parcel I had sent on ahead, awaited me. From here that food parcel would have to last another four days until I reached Hrauneyjar, and civilisation once more. The problem was the distance I was expecting to walk for both sets of four days. I had calculated it was sixty nine miles for the first half, then a restock of food, followed by another sixty six miles. This meant I would be walking an estimated sixteen or seventeen miles on average each day, across difficult terrain in inclement weather. Could I keep up that sort of mileage in much cooler conditions than at present, crossing swollen rivers that may be dangerous? All sorts of issues were now crossing my mind. Unfortunately my estimates of distances to cover each day up till now had proved to be under-estimates, by two or three miles. What if I was to run out of food, in Sprengisandur, or couldn't do the distance,? I had had this conversation with Annette and Graham back on R901. We all knew that Sprengisandur was a really hard walk, and during inclement weather it could be really marginal. What was I to do? I was unsure. All I knew was, I had to take advice on reaching Reykjahlid and come to the correct decision as to whether I could walk safely down Sprengisandur or not. It was so important to make the right call.

Around 3pm, I noticed that the range of hills, on the right of Route One, I had been headed towards for some hours now, were imperceptibly getting larger and therefore, nearer. Hoo bloody ray! This was a relief, because, if nothing else, a change in view on that side of the road was to be welcomed no matter how impressive or otherwise. On the left hand side I was looking out for Námafjall, an area of geothermal activity with fumaroles and solfataras, or mud springs. The whole hillside would be conspicuous with its distinct red, yellow and orange geology and the whole area would also reek of sulphur. I had visited Námafjall twice before and it really was a place to be reckoned with. In bad weather, it suggested to me what Hell must have been like: a dark, sombre, overbearing place, almost wicked and frightening. At least on a day like today, I would be seeing it in a more favourable light.

And then it appeared: faint at first, then more identifiable; very distinctive in colour, contrasting strongly with the grey and the green landscape either side. Various shades of orange, ferrous, ochre, peach, saffron, sienna, bisque, amber and maroon were evident; a veritable technicoloured dreamcoat painted onto the hillside; a swathe of shades and tones of which Van Gogh would have been proud.

On seeing these hills from afar, I changed gear from fourth to fifth. I was quite excited and I coaxed my tired joints and limbs to keep going. I knew there was now an end in sight, to this lava desert. As I drew nearer towards Námafjall, I could see groups of people wandering on its lower slopes, inspecting and enjoying the rawness and sheer energy of the geology displayed here. Steam issuing from various fumaroles added to the atmosphere. I was captivated. On my right side I passed a road leading to the Krafla caldera, a distinctly evil feeling place. In times gone by, Icelanders believed Hell to lie beneath volcanoes. I could well understand, in threatening weather, why they would so easily believe that. Even now, on a windy but relatively mild day, weather-wise, the air buffeted me with intimidating energy.

I wanted to stop here and spend some time savouring the crudity and the intense spirit of this place, however what dissuaded me was the sight of a massive and steep ascent as Route One curved uphill unremittingly, up and over Námafjall before sweeping downwards to Reykjahlid and Myvatn beyond. My heart sank. I knew I had already covered over twenty miles and this ascent was almost one hill too far.

My whole body now decided it had done enough hard work for the day and started to groan and whimper, saying, "Enough!" The argument against this was however, enough wasn't enough, and I quite simply had to knuckle down and get on with it. Rest and recuperation lay on the other side of the hill, and I was unfortunately still on the wrong side. Various cars passed me by and their occupants stared at this hobbling, overburdened wreck limping his way onwards in irregular, faltering steps. With gritted teeth, I dragged my suffering body the final miles up and over the mountain. The final miles elicited a strange, exhausted state where I was just aware of my tired feet, my aching muscles, the yellow marker posts and precious little else. My breathing was regular and rhythmic, but my motivation was almost spent. Upon reaching the crest of the hill, the road meandered in a wide curve until I could at last see a shimmering expanse of water ahead of me. Myvatn! And just in front of it was Reykjahlid, my destination at last.

Stuttering along with tentative paces, I hesitantly limped into town. The last two miles had taken me an hour and three quarters. Tourist Information informed me there were three campsites, so I headed for the nearest one conveniently right by the lakeside - Bjarg Campsite. As I walked wearily down onto the grassy field, my base layer and trousers drenched in sweat, I noted two bicycles propped up on their stands beyond an array of tents near the outdoor sink facility, so I wandered over and there, to my delight, were Julio and José, pitching their tents and making camp.

"Not you again!" I joked, in a weak, fatigued voice as I approached. My mouth could hardly function, such was my exhaustion. They turned round and smiled a warm smile of recognition.

"Hello!" they said. "You made it!"

"Only just. By God, that was a long way," I sounded like I was still under the anaesthetic at the dentist, slurring my words appreciably. "And that hill at the end nearly finished me off. How long have you been here?"

"We arrived an hour ago. The wind was terrible. It made it so hard. It was very difficult." I was amazed. I had been beaten by the Spanish cyclists to Reykjahlid, but only by an hour! My GPS indicated we had travelled 26.4 miles, a marathon distance on a marathon day carrying a full load. I had survived on two litres of sugar water, but my feet and knees were now shot. Forty eight miles in two days is rather excessive for a body like mine and it was crying out, pleading mercifully for a rest.

I sat down and looked across to the far side of the lake where Vindbelgjarfjall, at 1719 feet, an extinct volcano, sat proudly on Myvatn's western shore. Myvatn, or Midge Lake, was a beautiful feature that accommodated various volcanic features in its vicinity such as pseudocraters within the lake itself, explosion craters such as Hverfell three kilometres distant and weird lava formations as found at Dimmuborgir, towards its southern margin. A veritable collection of relatively modern geology. I felt truly privileged as I sat here, almost at the end of my tether, in such thrilling surroundings, despite the many tiny flies that tried to distract me otherwise.

It was time to erect my tent, eat some tea and basically do nothing. Tomorrow was a rest day, thoughtfully built into my itinerary, and a day in which I was going to have to decide how my trek progressed from here. To wander down Sprengisandur or not? I needed to make an important decision.

13. Day of Rest

A man's fate should be hidden to preserve his peace of mind - Viking Proverb

I lay in my tent until 8am, quite late for me on this trip. The bright yellow inner tent, just centimetres from my face, gently flapped and swayed in the mild breeze blowing from the shores of Myvatn. Sleeping in a solo trekker's one man tent has its problems, not least the lack of space to do anything really except lie there. Some say it's like lying in a coffin, but I could not be dead certain about that, as I have never lain in one – not yet anyway...

I calculated I had covered 125 miles in seven days to get to Reykjahlid, a reasonable effort so far, at an average of nearly eighteen miles per day. One worry I had had before setting out, was how my body would hold up when trekking day after day, with no rest. Well the answer, so far, was just about, although the extended walks of the last two days had left me in something of a fragile and tender state. The first hour each day was the worst, as muscles creaked and groaned back into action overcoming soreness and inflamed tissues. I tended to hobble about like an old doddery fool before breakfast, but as I got going, the stiffness and aches waned, as I returned to what I considered to be, my former lithe and athletic self.

This was my rest day, as it was too for the Spanish cyclists. I had decided to head for the Nature Baths which I had passed on the way to Reykjahlid. These were geothermically heated bathing pools and I considered a prolonged dip in their warm, soothing waters was a necessary treat to allow my ailing lower portion to relax and recuperate. My whole body actually required a bit of tender loving care, because the physical demands made on it so far were taking their toll. I felt as if I was a failed MOT car with bits hanging on precariously like an old, rusted exhaust pipe and dented wing mirrors. I must have looked one heck of a wreck. The Spanish meanwhile, seemed remarkably perky and were up bright and breezy. They were headed for the Krafla volcanic area nearby, for they wanted to explore the new lava field created in Krafla's most recent eruption and the infamous Viti crater.

First of all however, I was headed for the Visitors' Centre, opposite the campsite. I stiffly limped my way there, shaking the lactic acid from my legs. The soles of my feet were rather tender and sensitive, and as I walked, I must have looked like someone hopping uncomfortably across hot coals. I had heard from Julio there had been a problem with landslides down Sprengisandur. Was this highland route under threat? I went inside and talked with an friendly assistant there called Steinunn, who informed me that there had indeed been a landslide towards the southern end of the F26 that had blocked the road, but things had now quietened down, the route had been cleared and was now open once more.

I asked about the viability of me walking solo through Sprengisandur. Steinunn consulted a colleague and said that the inclement and unseasonable weather was making things tricky along the F26, that being the road that cut through the interior of Iceland. I asked what she meant by that. She replied that you always had to respect the weather and terrain in Iceland. When the weather changes, the terrain has a habit of catching you out. So what was I to do? She looked at me with her teal green eyes and I looked back at her. It was almost as if she was weighing me up. Would this frail limping man, who appeared to barely have control of his legs, have a fighting chance of walking down Sprengisandur?

"It'll be difficult," Steinunn eventually said.

"What would you do?" I asked her. She seemed to be avoiding the question and waffled generally. She spoke of people who struggled to cope with the elements down there. Sprengisandur was not a place to take lightly

"But what would you do?" I repeated. She looked across to her colleague and then back at me. Our gaze held steady for all of ten seconds. She did not say anything, but in those ten seconds, her eyes told me everything I wanted to know. Their deep colour suggested it would be rather rash of me to attempt to walk solo down Sprengisandur at that juncture. The weather of the past two weeks had aggravated the rivers and the temperatures were much colder than usual. One did not mess with Sprengisandur and a solo trek could prove quite extreme and injudicious right now.

I averted my gaze and looked skywards. I shut my eyes tight and agonised briefly over my decision, then I looked back at her. We didn't have to say anything. We both instinctively knew. Sprengisandur was a no-go. At that moment I felt very strange: hollow, quite nauseous and perturbed. I needed to sit down.

I had been planning to walk across Iceland for the past eighteen months. I had been so precise, so meticulous in my preparations, so particular to ensure everything was organised to the nth degree. I had sorted through the logistics of equipment, route finding, food and fitness. The one aspect I had no control over however, was the climate, and right now, the climate was doing me no favours whatsoever.

Now the realisation struck me that my trek in its original form was over, and it hit me like a punch to the stomach. To trek through Sprengisandur would be pushing my luck too far. I could handle the terrain, a heavy pack, the long distances and the bad weather, but not all at once over a long period of time. The bad weather would impact on my progress as well as making river crossings dicey. My food might not sustain me and my sleeping bag and extra clothing might not even keep me warm enough at night. A no-brainer really. I could not take the risk. Instead I would revert to Plan B.

Steinunn informed me that Plan B involved catching a high suspensioned bus from Reykjahlid, down Sprengisandur along the F26 to Hrauneyjar. It was from Hrauneyjar that I could carry on my trek in its modified form. It was now Friday and the next bus to Hrauneyjar was three days away quite early in the morning, on Monday. There was really no other way.

With heavy heart, I decided to purchase a ticket. Steinunn understood my predicament and looked at me sympathetically and said I had made the right decision. She smiled at me as she handed me my ticket and then, rather emotionally, I went outside.

I now felt totally empty and bereft. Up to now, my sole purpose had been to walk across Iceland. That was it. That was my long term goal. For the past week, I had endured mile upon mile of relentless slog with the sole intention of reaching a predetermined location each night, as part of my long-term mission to conquer Iceland. But now, the mission had changed, a dilute form of that intended. I felt quite depressed and just at that moment, to match my negative state of mind, the wind started to gust and heavy squally rain fell; the very type of weather that was causing me so many problems.

I sought refuge in a coffee bar away from the wind and the rain that was blighting my mood and texted home to say I was now changing my plans. As I texted, I quietly sobbed and tears welled up in my eyes. This past week had been so hard for me, mentally, physically, emotionally and now I had to face the reality I was simply not up to it. The weather and the conditions down Sprengisandur had defeated me.

Texts came back immediately sympathising with me and my plight, but telling me my safety was paramount and I was sensible to change my plans. I just felt so empty. I drank my coffee and headed out. The weather continued to mock me and I headed back to my tent where I lay for an hour or so. My legs were still sore and my knees ached, but it was my inner spirit that had taken a severe blow.

It is amazing the recuperative powers of the mind and, while resting, I reappraised my decision, but each time I came to the conclusion I had made the right choice. Being out in bad weather in the wilderness is something not to be considered lightly. I was not sure I would have coped with it. I was not even sure I would have survived it. My instincts were normally right and my instincts had been telling me not to go. If anyone knew my limitations it was certainly me.

After lunch, I felt a little better and decided to walk to the thermal pool. It was located three kilometres back up Route One and, in improving weather, I sluggishly hobbled my way there.

Námafjall is a very impressive, a most exciting and truly an intimidating place. In bad weather it can appear evil and menacing. I remember when I first visited here twenty years ago, on a very dark and sombre day. Storm clouds piled high into the sky and it really felt quite sinister and alarming, and it is no exaggeration to say it was like entering the gates of Hell. No wonder, people back in history were so superstitious and so greatly affected and terrified by sudden unpredictable whims of climate or geology. Twenty years ago, I could almost taste the raw energy coursing through this place. Right now, in kinder weather, it just felt dramatic. Mounds of lava were stacked high in volcanic scrapheaps, a strident terracotta-red and jet-black in colour, alongside steaming vents that sent white plumes of thick smoke billowing ceaselessly into the air. I turned right towards the thermal pool, captivated by the whole whirl of destruction and devastation here and I wondered what this place used to look like before the seismic catastrophe befell.

The thermal pool itself was sublime. I gave little initial gasps of indrawn breath as I tiptoed tentatively in my swimming shorts into the cool Icelandic air. These were followed by sighs of joy and relaxation as I submerged myself in the steaming blue-green, mineral rich waters of this natural spa and tended my aching limbs. It felt good and for the next ninety minutes I just gently exposed my muscles to the deep warmth of nature, perfect de-stressing after the pivotal decision-making of the day.

Body reinvigorated, I made my way back to camp. The sun decided to shine across Lake Myvatn and a subdued version of myself ate a hearty tea. I had picked up my latest food parcel from a hotel here and restocked my rucksack. Between mouthfuls I sighed deeply. My solo trek was evolving into something new. My emotions were troubled. My mind was distracted. This solo walking malarkey was a lot harder than I could possibly have envisaged. After tea, I sat and watched the sun lower over the distant horizon. Tiny midges danced on the breeze and campers busied themselves with their tents and their equipment. I sought solace in my own thoughts. I was desperately tired and I needed a full night's sleep.

14. Cue for Thufur

Reykjahlid – Graenavatn – Kálfborgarávatn - Kidagil 28.0 miles

Young and alone on a long road, once I lost my way: Rich I felt when I found another; Man rejoices in man – The Hávamál

Because this was my second rest day, I arose late as I had done the previous day. I was considering walking to Hverfell, a volcanic explosion crater a few kilometres south of Reykjahlid and then walking around its dramatic perimeter, as I had done many years before. This quite appealed to me because craters are always exciting places to walk round. You always think there is a remote chance that the blooming thing might suddenly decide to erupt, not too much to cause your sad demise, but just enough to see a bit of the molten stuff, feel the intense heat and smell the sulphur, a sort of seismic fix. Seeing red hot lava erupting from the earth's core was high on my bucket list, so perhaps today would be the day.

I ate a rather inadequate breakfast of granola and watched the Spanish cyclists, Julio and José, pack their tents away. They were now leaving Reykjahlid and were heading for Akureyri along Route One, so this would finally be the parting of our ways. I had enjoyed their company hugely and I would miss our amusing disjointed and confused conversations, that made me smile so much. They checked the loading on their bikes, each of which was heavy as a Sherman tank, and with a friendly handshake within the middle range of Icelandic intensity, they were gone. And suddenly I felt quite alone.

I watched other campers packing their kit away, dismantling tents, with the metallic clicking of folding tent poles and the determined rolling up of sleeping mats like squashed Swiss rolls. I am always amazed how sleeping bags fit into stuff sacks a fraction of their size, but they always do, confounding somewhat the scientific principle of the Conservation of Mass. Over the course of the next half hour, I watched numerous travellers pack up and depart, and go their separate ways, so that the campsite now appeared quite empty and devoid of life, leaving just me and my green one-man tent, lost and all alone. The sense of abandonment was immense and I felt really troubled and upset.

"Sod it!" I said suddenly. "I'm not staying here! I'm going to walk down Sprengisandur."

I totally surprised myself. All my careful reasoning about the dangers that lay in the highlands were now cast to one side in a flash. I felt a huge surge of adrenalin flow through me as I stood up and reflected briefly on this unexpected turnaround. This was a spur-of-the-moment decision based upon the irrational logic of being isolated and left behind. My mind was now racing. All I could think of was to resume my solo trek across the whole of Iceland. Nothing else mattered and all valid reasons for catching the bus were discarded and ignored. This could only happen however, if I could cancel my bus ticket purchased the day before. I half ran, half walked to the Visitors' Centre, where Steinunn was sitting behind the desk as I'd hoped.

"I've had a change of mind," I shouted, breathlessly. "I'm going for it. I'm going to walk to Kidagil and then down Sprengisandur." She looked at me peculiarly. "I know, I know, " I apologised. "I know I said I was going to catch the bus, but I want to give it a go. I think I've enough food. I just hope the weather is kind to me."

Steinunn continued to look at me strangely as if she only partly understood. Talk about an almighty u-turn! Whether she agreed with my decision or not, I had no idea, however she managed to cancel my ticket without any problem.

One concern I still had was that my rucksack would be too heavy and it would slow me down. If I did not get to Nyidalur in four days, my food would run out and I would be in trouble. I would go hungry and keeping warm would then become a real issue. Failing to reach Nyidalur in the allotted time was unthinkable and for that reason, I had to go through my belongings casting aside everything but the absolute essentials.

Steinunn said she would be happy to post on a parcel of the items that I deemed to be surplus to requirements, to the hotel in Reykjavik, where ultimately I would end up at the end of my trek. I was desperate to reduce my pack weight, because the lighter the pack, the less food I would need to eat to carry it and the faster I could walk. I dashed back to the campsite. In a frenzy of activity, I de-camped and threw several unused items away. Other items, such as my head torch and my fire strike, (I had storm matches too), I packed into a box and handed to Steinunn who promised me she's post them on. I trusted her to do so.

"I've got to give this a go," I repeated, not entirely convincingly and she smiled at me with her big green eyes. Were they telling me to forget my foolish ambition or were they telling me to follow my dream? Instead I thought they were saying that whatever I decided, I should stay safe. Steinunn wished me well. We shook hands, quite firmly, and then I was gone. I was elated at my sudden decision to go back on the road. My trek was resuming once more, and moreover, I was actually heading south for the very first time since I started, which was quite an important psychological boost.

What had caused me to change my mind? Well I did not really want to spend another two days in Reykjahlid, despite it being a great place to stay. I was here to walk, to be a trekker not a tourist and I was still very much in exploratory mode. This sudden rush of impulsion was something very new to me. I was always known for making very considered decisions, weighing up the options carefully, looking at all the pros and cons. This decision was just downright rash, based on a burst of capriciousness, an erratic whim, a knee-jerk reaction to being forsaken by my Spanish friends.

But at that moment, the feeling of euphoria, as I set off south, dominated all rational thought of self-preservation. It was almost as if I was bound up in a type of hysteria and it was snowballing relentlessly to the edge of a high cliff. As I walked, the rain came on with a moderate drizzle, not enough to dampen my new-found spirits, but enough to make me consider the fact I had not eaten much breakfast at all. I was on the lookout for a café that I knew lay down the road on this eastern shore of Myvatn. It felt so good to be moving again! I shouted aloud with jubilation. My joyous, emotional cries bouncing off the lava cast asunder round about. My purpose for being here was restored. As I walked, an oyster catcher flew above me and called,

"Can't make your bleeding mind up can you? One moment you've given up, next moment you're off again! Bloody useless, you!"

I grimaced to myself, and halted my stride, almost as if the belligerent bird had brought me to my senses. I stood stock still in the middle of the road, contemplating the enormity of my decision I had just made setting out for Sprengisandur once more and suddenly, I wavered again, my mind in total turmoil. I really hoped I'd made the right decision to carry on. What's the saying ? –

"I used to think I was indecisive but now I'm not so sure."

A passing car hooted at me to get out of the way. I laughed a nervous hollow laugh and slowly, with a sense of uncertainty, followed the road past the huge crater that is Hverfell, which had thoughtfully decided not to erupt that day, to reach a roadside café. Here I sampled some sardine-like fish on toast and a large slice of cake, backed up with coffee. My mind was scrambled. One half of me wanted to continue, the other half was saying,

"Hold fire! Sprengisandur is dangerous, you duck egg! "   I was at the centre of a cerebral tug-of-war: Should I? Shouldn't I? I honestly did not know.

Within ten minutes I was back on the road. The "Carry on" camp had won out, for the time being anyway. I set out past some contorted and weird-looking lava formations at Dimmuborgir, frozen in ugly, distorted shapes from way back in tectonic history.

At the bottom end of the lake, I came across a really good view of some natural features called pseudo craters which broke through the surface of the still water on Lake Myvatn. These craters were made when hot lava emerged in the water of the lake. Gases within the lava exploded through it and formed these low-lying craters before me. They appeared perfectly formed, quite exquisite and unique, and enhanced an already mystical and spectacular scene.

I continued round the southern end of the lake and stumbled across some isolated farm buildings beyond which was a road junction left, towards another smaller lake called Graenavatn, meaning "green lake." This was my turn-off. I hesitated slightly because this next section was unmarked on any map. I was simply cutting my own pioneering track for the next sixteen miles across stark, anonymous terrain towards the F26 - the road down Sprengisandur.

In order to reach my objective, I had to locate a remote bridge over the Kráká river, then forge a trail to the north of a lake called Sandvatn – sand lake. There are many lakes sharing this name across Iceland, perhaps indicating how widespread the abundance of black volcanic sand is. I hoped to wild camp by the side of this lake and I was really relying on all my navigational skills to get me there safely. Finding the bridge was crucial because there were no other suitable crossing points. To miss it would mean a detour of a goodly thirty miles.

I set off down a level dusty track and fairly quickly reached Graenavatn. This was a quiet backwater, away from the traffic and bustle of Myvatn, a mile or so behind me. It was surrounded by a few houses and nothing much else. The track faded away and then I dithered which way to go. As I was consulting my map, a solitary 4x4 truck appeared unexpectedly ahead of me. I asked the driver if he knew where the bridge across the Kráká was. He fortunately did indeed know and suggested I head for a red roof-coloured farm building I could vaguely make out about a mile distant. The bridge, he said, lay next to this.

Encouraged by this advice, I selected a route roughly in a straight line to the farm and, sure enough, after half an hour, I encountered the Kráká River, flowing sedately through the countryside in a moderately shallow gorge. After a short while scanning its course, I detected a metal and wooden structure jutting above a slight crest. Bingo! I'd found my bridge! I let out a whoop of joy, causing the sheep grazing here to look at me in peeved irritation for disturbing their pastoral peace.

The bridge was a rickety, flimsy structure in need of a general overhaul, however I ignored the decay and avoided the gaps between the planks and trod warily across it. Now where? Well my map said head west, so I set a course between two really isolated farm houses, joined by an apology of a road, full of potholes and dusty sand. Both farm houses exhibited some rather outsized aerials and satellite dishes, probing skyward. Communication in Iceland is vital, and every house, no matter how primitive and dilapidated looking, has the latest in high tech equipment, so they can connect easily with everyone else. It did indeed look somewhat incongruous, in such a remote and rustic setting, to see such modern technology.

I passed by both houses and was now on the lookout for Sandvatn Lake. I knew it to be around here somewhere. It measured over a mile in length, so it was quite a significant puddle, but where was it? The ground westward was now leading me uphill, so I was hoping to finally view it from a high vantage, but once I had attained the high ground, it was still nowhere to be seen. Time to keep walking.

Twenty long minutes later I found it, shimmering and silver-like, as the sun broke through the clouds and reflected sharply on its surface. The intention was to pass by on its northern shore and pick up a marked track beyond, a simple enough task, I thought. The distance involved was about three quarters of a mile and before me lay a green expanse of slightly undulating bumpy ground. Fifteen minutes worth, I reckoned.

Never underestimate the terrain! The fifteen minutes worth proved an absolute nightmare to negotiate. It would best be described as a large aggregation of tussocky mounds, springy and firm to step on, but conversely spongy and soft. You simply had no idea whether your next step would rebound or sink in; a sort of unpredictable lottery involving walking. The tussocks were up to a metre and a half across, consisting of what appeared to be root balls and soil. Between each tussock was a narrow crevice, ranging from a shallow few centimetres up to two metres deep, so if you put your foot into a deep one, you had a good chance of injuring yourself, even breaking your leg. It would be best described as a grassy form of limestone pavement with clints and grykes, but instead of rock, you were standing on a peculiar type of vegetation, unique, I was later to discover, to these Arctic climes, and its name was thufur, formed, my subsequent research told me, by: "differential heaving of ground ice, within its sedimentary core." Whatever it was, and however it was formed, it was to get right up my flared nostrils.

I tried a first traverse, but walked into an impassable dead end, so I had to backtrack and start again. A second attempt also proved futile. Picking a route through was indescribably difficult; a mere five minutes on this stuff roused within me a great ire, in which I vented my spleen quite severely, accompanied by a tirade of quite foul and offensive language, that would even have shocked my mother, and she was from London's less refined East End. It was quite hopeless to cross, especially with a heavy rucksack that endowed me with a high centre of balance. Several times I fell over with appropriate vocal exasperation of the four-lettered variety and gingerly regained my feet. I stood studying the terrain, but it all looked ridiculously tricky. *My bloody track at the far crappy side was still frustratingly three quarters of a bastard mile away and I had been going for nearly twenty sodding minutes!* A happy bunny I was not.

In the end, still cursing aloud, I headed right back to where I had first encountered the wretched thufur. I now considered that the best way forward was to reach the lakeside and follow a route along its narrow shore. At least this would not be tussocky. Getting to the shoreline took me another ten frustrating minutes, and when I reached the beach, it consisted of a metre wide, at best, strip of black sand. Sometimes the beach disappeared to nothing, in which case more tussocks needed stumbling over. Sweating and swearing, I set out, disturbing nesting geese and ducks on several occasions. To be blunt I was quite hacked off by the whole thing by now. It had looked so easy an hour ago, but instead it was taking me a dratted age to overcome.

After over an hour of toil and stress, during which further profanities and references to God were uttered, I finally reached the track, thankful I had solid ground beneath my feet once more.

"What the bloody hell was that all about?" I shouted angrily looking back at the green clumpy minefield behind me, which showed me two defiant fingers as I continued westwards once more. I had never come across anything like it before and never wished to ever again. Give me a good old peat bog any day.

"Struggled did we?" came the call from above. "Never walked across thufur before? Hard, isn't it? We, of course, can fly over it. Tread warily, or you'll come a cropper!" Following that piece of advice, the oyster catcher flew over to the middle of the lake and settled on the surface, watching me from a distance. At least he did not swear at me this time. Mind, he was right, I would have to tread warily, for thufur and solo trekkers do not get on.

I was however now in a bit of a quandary. The intention had been to camp beside the lake before setting out the next day for Kidagil. The thufur did not lend itself to being the finest camping ground in the world, in fact I cannot think of a surface less suited to camping than thufur. Instead, I decided to plod on and see what opportunities for a wild camp presented themselves in the next hour or so.

The track was straightforward to follow and I was now looking for a larger and longer lake, with a larger and longer name: - Kálfborgarávatn. It should have been visible to the west, however the only thing that confronted me was a steep rise, with the track turning southwards, the wrong way. Heading on a westerly bearing, I left the track and started climbing. It was hard going as I laboured up the hill with my base layer drenched in sweat and sticking to my back with all my fraught exertions.

After ten minutes of awkward stumbling and scrambling, the crest was attained and there, to my left, looking pristine, was Kálfborgarávatn. I smiled a weary smile of success. Now, where to camp? The lake was over two miles long. I momentarily considered just forgetting about a wild camp and instead just heading straight for Kidagil, where there was a chance of getting a proper bed, but I soon put that idea on the back burner because I was overly tired from the challenges of the day, and sometimes it is prudent to be content with the distance you have achieved, in this case a notable 21 miles. Kidagil could wait until tomorrow, even though it was only five miles away, as the crow flies. That way I would have the prospect of a more pleasant short day, after all the efforts of the past twelve hours.

I decided not to camp by the lake because, as I had crested the rise, I became aware that the air round here was thick with flies, and big ones at that. I put on my head mesh firstly to stop myself going mad, but also to prevent me swallowing them as I breathed. I had never come across so many flies in all my life, many more than on the road to Grimsstadir. They were everywhere. If they were this bad around here, down by the lakeside, they would be even worse.

I found a flat spot with a convenient embankment by a small pond. The embankment would serve as a seat and it also offered a marvellous view across the lake to a lofty hill called Brunnfell beyond. I was scanning the ground, trying to see where my route would take me tomorrow, for I would have the option to either pass by the north end of the lake, or else I could take a longer detour around the southern end. The advantage of the southern route was that the river flowing from the lake here would be much easier to cross than the river at the northern end, according to my google earth research, carried out weeks earlier.

Tent pitched, I then proceeded to cook myself a rehydrated meal. When it was ready, there followed the farcical situation of trying to eat a meal with my head mesh on. It was a matter of lifting the mesh for a split second, then shovelling a mouthful of food in, then dropping the mesh, before any of a million flies tried to enter my mouth. It was as bad as that. I did however get quite adept at feeding myself and drinking my coffee in this way. It was all to do with timing and making sure I blew out at just the right second, to remove any flies before opening my mouth to eat. Luckily the flies appeared to be of the non-biting variety, they were just a flaming nuisance. The birds round here probably could not believe their luck. They could simply walk around, beaks a-gape and the flies would come to them.

After my meal, I watched the sun go down. Akureyri was situated some twenty five miles north-west of me. I wondered whether the Spanish cyclists had reached there safely. No doubt they would not be suffering quite as badly from the swarms of flies as I was. I wished them well and scanned the horizon, reflecting on today but also appreciating the tranquillity of the panorama before me. The sense of detachment from the rest of the world seemed utterly profound. I considered how many people had actually camped in this very spot before and reckoned, probably nobody! This was a wild place. Just me, the flies, the birds and the lake. As I sipped my coffee, now going cold, I absorbed the spiritual essence of this moment. When God created Iceland, he did so on one of his good days. I then grinned and wondered what sort of day he had had when he created places like Slough and Luton, back home. It was now about eight o'clock and I retired early for the night, thankful to lie down, hoping that I would have some pleasant dreams that did not involve the dreaded thufur!

Remarkably I did sleep well, thufur-free, low-flying geese-free too. Nothing disturbed me and the rain stayed away as well. The flies were still there in their thousands to welcome me as I opened up my tent flap the next morning. Did they never sleep? Today was to be an easy day, mileage-wise. If I went north of the lake it was five miles, if I went south of the lake another extra 2.5 miles. Whichever route I chose, definitely an easy day. Strange how one can get it so, so wrong, as I was soon to find out.

Over a meagre breakfast I was starting to worry about my food. I was loaded with packets of chocolate raisins and cashew nuts along with some chocolate and energy bars, but basically, during the day, that was it. The problem was, I did not always feel I was getting a return on my food, energy-wise. Sometimes I felt a listlessness barely an hour after a meal break; perhaps this was because these foods only gave me spikes of energy, instead of slow release energy to sustain me for longer. I was also getting a little bored eating the same food every day, and crucially, meal breaks did not always motivate me; they were almost a chore. Strange. I had not expected me to react to my food in quite this way.

I decamped with no problems having built another cairn to the goddess Defaecatius and set off towards the lake. Immediately I came across the infernal thufur I had encountered the day before at Sandvatn, so to avoid it, I followed a stony clearing and walked along it, fifty metres away from and parallel to the lake. I had decided after all, to take the easier southern longer route around Kálfborgarávatn, because I did not want to struggle crossing the difficult river following the northern option. Eventually, I had to leave the stony track and head down to the water. I followed a narrow beach round its shore, and came upon a slim, shallow river draining from it and with a couple of convenient sandy islands, was able to step across with relative ease, without getting my feet wet. At this juncture, I stopped to chew on an energy bar. I had been travelling half an hour but already I actually felt quite lethargic and so hoped a burst of food would do me good.

Setting off again, an area of cursed thufur about quarter of a mile across presented itself. The tussocks themselves were not too bad, however the flooded wide ditches between them meant I was having to choose my route very carefully. One false step and I could be submerged up to my waist, or even worse, I might not be able to get out again. Ten minutes of thufur, and I felt distinctly uneasy. It was getting harder to find a way through and for the first time on my trek, I felt rather unsafe and at risk. Underfoot it was getting marshier and the tussocks were doing their very best to throw me into the water surrounding them.

"This is not a good place to be," I said aloud, as a sort of warning to myself. "You need to get off this stuff."

I looked around but the only way off was to reach a rise in the ground beyond the thufur. I picked a bare spot on some higher ground, fifty metres away and headed for it. Those fifty metres were an absolute nightmare, because retaining my footing was almost impossible. There was no flat surface to stand on, and everything was distinctly spongy, causing me to repeatedly trip and stumble. My feet were getting wet and several times I nearly fell in. The relief I felt upon scrambling out of this wretched stuff was almost palpable as I sat, getting my breath back on a raised bank. This was supposed to be an easy day, I thought to myself. I could still see the blinking spot where I had camped across the lake. I had been walking an hour or so and had barely covered a mile.

Now I was above the thufur, the options left to me were: either skirt round it then drop down to cross another patch of the blasted stuff or head over the hill at the side of me. The hill was called Kálfborgaráfell, a steep sided affair summiting at nearly 1800 feet. I chose to scramble over the hillside, not wishing to become entrapped in a boggy thufur field, however the hill's steepness caught me by surprise. Because of my lethargy, I had to keep stopping at regular intervals, and as I did so, some indistinguishable birds came to observe me.

"Aha, look at you now!" they squawked. "Feeling lethargic are we? You were warned about the thufur! Why didn't you go the northern route? Not so many problems that way. "

Right now, I truly wished I had gone north. The thufur had been too hard, but I think anyone would have found it hard, not just me. And this hill I was climbing was exhausting work with my heavy pack and my lack of energy. I just felt so listless. I couldn't even be bothered to shout back at the birds, as they dived low over my head and then gradually lost interest.

A slow slog up Kálfborgaráfell brought me eventually to the top. On the other side, it was no surprise to see a steep descent, followed by another climb over Brunnfell, the hill I had so admired the previous evening. Once over this second mountain, I calculated I should almost be on top of Kidagil. The descent of Kálfborgaráfell however was painfully slow and awkward so

I took extra care not to twist an ankle. I then cautiously crossed a narrow valley before heading upwards again. This next ascent was very steep, my pack now weighing very heavily on my shoulders, so I had to resort to scrambling, using my hands to pull myself up. Again, I needed a time-out to get my breath. It was not a warm day, but my base layer was soaked in sweat once more as I toiled ever higher. I decided to count one hundred paces then rest, but one hundred proved to be too many, so instead I counted merely to thirty, gulping in air with every foot of height gained. It was so hard, I felt like giving up. I could not believe that such a short walk would be so difficult. I dragged my wretched energy-less body up the slope until finally it plateaued out. I could see across the valley, but where was Kidagil? I looked around desperately. In the space of an hour or so, I had gone from feeling fresh and alert to being totally spent, almost exhibiting a sense of panic, in a deep trough of despair where I felt utterly dispirited. What was happening to me? Fifty metres further on, the land dropped away and I saw, for the first time, a bridge crossing a river called the Skjálfandafljót, the only river crossing for miles. This was my bridge near Kidagil! I had found it. I was so relieved to see it, I shouted out with joy, but my shout was more of a feeble, plaintive cry really. I did not care, I was precisely where I should be, almost at the end of this particular leg of the trek having just crossed a rather remote and inhospitable part of Iceland. To my right I could see several buildings, one displaying a flag, set back from the road. Way to my right was a farmhouse, that I knew to be at a place called Sandvik. Everything was slotting into place, just like my google earth image I had fixed in my mind. I looked back to the flag, fluttering frantically in the wind, far below.

"Kidagil," I exclaimed, and for the first time that day, I almost had a spring in my step, well, a half-stumble really. The route down to the bridge was quite tricky, such was its steep gradient and its rugged approach. I picked a way down, but it took me a full half hour just to reach the road on the near side of the bridge. The bridge was of similar design to the one over the Jokulsá á Fjöllum, that I had crossed a few days earlier – a sturdy, compact suspension bridge, with wooden planks, through which you could see the swirling river below and on the far side, I spotted a road sign saying "Sprengisandur F26". My heart missed a beat. The trek southwards was about to get very serious indeed.

The trouble was, the self-doubts I had back in Reykjahlid, barely two days ago, concerning the adverse wet weather and my ability to cope with it; the swollen rivers and my issues with insufficient food, had re-surfaced. Today had not been a good day for me. The going had been tough, so tough I had walked barely seven miles in half a day. How on earth could I manage eight gruelling days down Sprengisandur walking seventeen miles over and over again, if I was struggling to complete half that, on a day like this? After all, the weather here was reasonable and dry. Down in Sprengisandur, it could be the total opposite.

I turned right and headed a short distance on R842 to Kidagil, a remote guest house with a wide open car parking space in front of it. It was a single storey building with shallow pitched green roofs and white walls. To one side was a camping ground, on which stood two camper vans and that was it. I climbed the steps into the foyer and went inside.

At once a man approached me and I instantly knew who it was. This was Magnus, to whom I had posted not one, but three food parcels, for me to collect here.

"Hello Mark," he said, offering his hand. He knew immediately who I was too, because he had been expecting me. He shook my hand firmly, but I had been expecting that and so, in self-defence, I also shook his hand quite firmly. We smiled a mutually respectful smile. "How's it been?" he asked.

"Bloody hard work, to be honest," I replied. "I've come over from Kálfborgarávatn today and it's been a nightmare, boggy and difficult to walk on. I had to walk over Kálfborgaráfell and Brunnfell to avoid the bloody stuff."

"I expected you to come here further north round Sandvik," he said. "It's easier there. "

"I would have done if I had chosen the northern route round Kálfborgarávatn, but it's always easy in retrospect," I muttered. We were talking in the restaurant and I leant against the bar. "I'm shattered," I said. "Do you have a room here for tonight?" He nodded and I removed my pack and sank, brain frazzled, into a chair.

A young female waitress in the canteen asked if I would like to have something to eat and drink. That seemed a great idea so I chose asparagus soup and bread and a large mug of coffee. I asked the waitress almost immediately about conditions down Sprengisandur. She told me it was very remote and not to be taken lightly, which I already knew. What had the weather been like down Sprengisandur, I wanted to know? She informed me the weather had been terrible for the last few weeks. Magnus came back and basically reiterated the same thing. Sprengisandur was being exceptionally difficult this July. The rivers were overflowing and it was cooler than expected for this time of year. I knew all this already of course. He looked at me, assessing the condition in which I had arrived – tired, out on my feet, hungry, low on morale. I could see what he was thinking by the look in his eyes. In my own eyes, I could see it too. The euphoria of the previous morning when I exploded back into action had completely evaporated. Pragmatism, borne out of my exhaustion and hunger, was now overcoming all fanciful and absurd notions I had of trekking through Sprengisandur on a diet of cashews and chocolate raisins in the pouring rain.

No, Sprengisandur was once more off the agenda. I knew it. Magnus knew it. The bloody birds knew it. But this time, there was to be no change of mind. If I attempted it, it might be the last thing I ever did. I sat back in my chair, and played disconsolately with my spoon. Soup never tasted so wretched.

I think Magnus appreciated how difficult the decision to not walk down Sprengisandur had been for me. However he too knew the road southwards and the hazards it presented. I, as a solo traveller, would have to be right on top of my game in every respect to succeed. At this time, my game was simply not good enough to cope with the trials and tribulations that would arise. Magnus offered to take me a few miles down Sprengisandur, the next day to catch the rugged overland bus that passed this way three times a week and I gratefully accepted his offer.

I now felt like I did at Reykjahlid, when I originally thought my trek in its original form was over; hollow and empty, stressed, devoid of any pleasant feelings. Adding to my malaise, I was also exhausted. I needed to recharge my batteries before I did anything else, recalculate the food I needed and reinvigorate my fading morale.

For the rest of the day I relaxed, washed my clothes, dried my tent out and wandered around the guest house and its grounds. There wasn't too much to explore actually and I wandered back to the roadside, looking down the start of the valley down Sprengisandur, the beginning of a highland lava desert over one hundred and twenty miles across. It felt so remote looking down the void between the hills. North Iceland was such an out-of-the-way place, so detached from Iceland itself, let alone the rest of the world. Here, life went very slowly. The only vaguely active thing around here was the weather and the river that flowed with such immense kinetic power nearby.

I sorted through my three food parcels. All were stashed with nut and raisins, dehydrated meals and chocolate bars. One included a safety rope for crossing rivers. I had also thoughtfully included spare batteries and toilet rolls. The only thing was, most of this stuff was now surplus to requirements if I was not walking down Sprengisandur, so I donated it to Magnus and the staff at Kidagil.

I had now been on the road for ten days and walked over 152 miles. In that time I had experienced two completely rain free days, but the rest had been rather changeable, with rain showers ever present, some of them prolonged and heavy. It had been a shame, because I felt I was not seeing this country at its best, instead it had often been shrouded in cloud and mist. When the sun shone, it was glorious and my spirits rejoiced. When it was dismal, I sank into a lonely depression, usually at the end of the day, when the walking was done and I had eaten my fill. In hindsight, walking with a companion would have been so much easier. We could have carried more food and we could have been a source of inspiration for each other, basically keeping each other going. In other words my own company was not proving to be sufficient to console me. It was not looking good for the rest of my trip.

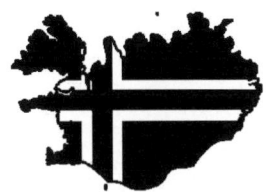

15. South through Sprengisandur

The unwise man is awake all night; worries over and over again. When morning rises he is restless still, his burden as before – The Hávamál

I awoke and breakfasted early. Magnus said he would take me at 9.30 to Aldeyjarfoss, several miles down Sprengisandur on the F26, from where I could pick up the bus. We actually set off at 9.15 and it felt very weird to be travelling in a car, almost illegal!

I was surprised how quickly the track became rough and demanding, an undulating rocky surface with all manner of potholes. Dramatic scenery lay either side of the road, in the form of imposingly steep green slopes upon which were traced vivid, white streaks like boldly painted brush strokes, as waterfalls cascaded over towering ledges. Sheep wandered through the area oblivious to the splendour of their surroundings. Magnus' slightly battered car rattled and thundered along, in fact at times I worried for it remaining intact, such were the vibrations resounding through the chassis. Magnus took it all in his stride. He had driven this route many times before.

After twenty minutes, the car stopped precisely in the middle of nowhere.

"We are here," said Magnus. "The bus will be along soon." I could not believe it. A bus? Stop here? This was the most far-flung bus stop I had ever been to in my life. In fact, there was no bus stop. No familiar sign saying, "REQUEST STOP" with a friendly circular London Transport logo. No detailed timetable telling you the schedule of bus arrivals and departures. All there was, next to this desolate track was a fabulous waterfall, Aldeyjarfoss, that roared and tumbled on a fine haze of water droplets thrown up by the spray that drifted on the breeze in wondrously sheer gossamer curtains. It was stupendous! Basalt columns hung like organ pipes as a silent igneous backdrop to the crashing, swirling cascade ahead of it, around it and below it. It was breathtakingly stunning. Aldeyjarfoss lies on the path of the Skjálfandafljót River, flowing from the Vatnajökull Glacier northwards. At this point, here at Aldeyjarfoss, the Skjálfandafljót drops an impressive ten metres before continuing uninterrupted to Skjálfandi Bay. Magnus appeared not to notice such devastating beauty, but I did. I was in raptures.

Magnus was impatient to be gone, somewhat surprisingly. How could he not linger here? Too much of a good thing maybe... I shook his hand firmly with all my might and thanked him profusely for helping me out. He wished me well and fixed me with a unblinking stare that connected. Be careful, it suggested. Be very careful. My returning stare suggested I would, you could count on that. Within seconds, he had gone, his car tyres complaining bitterly on the irregular, rugged ground and then silence, save the crashing water and the sigh of the wind. I was alone once more.

I walked a few steps towards the waterfall at this ridiculous bus stop. I looked back from where we had travelled and in the far distance I could clearly see the rounded peaks of Kálfborgaráfell and Brunnfell, my route of yesterday, that had caused me so many problems. They were high, steep sided tumuli – no wonder I had struggled. Avoiding the thufur had meant I had partaken of an absurdly exhausting alternative. I smiled a faint smile of resignation at my haplessness. As I did so, I suddenly heard an engine determinedly revving and a long white vehicle marked "Reykjavik Excursions" appeared round a sharp bend, weaving almost uncontrollably, as it was thrown about at the discretion of the landscape. I had not expected its appearance so soon, and, concerned that it might not stop and so leave me at the mercy of this outlandish wilderness, I stepped almost in front of it and waved my arms about like a possessed lunatic. People on board stared out at me with frantic alarm. Who was this imbecile trying to force the bus off the road? Was this one of the notorious Sprengisandur bandits they had heard about in Icelandic folklore, come to kill them all cruelly and rob them of their precious belongings? They quickly realised my intentions were instead that of an uncomplicated traveller concerned quite simply in getting from A to B, with A being this precise spot and B being a guest house at a place called Hrauneyjar, so they all calmed down somewhat and rather sheepishly retrieved all their money and expensive possessions they had stashed, in extreme panic, down the backs of their seats and into every available nook and cranny. The bus pulled up sharply and manoeuvred to face the way it had arrived. People streamed out armed with cameras and other high-tech gizmos and were drawn immediately to the waterfall below, picking their way over the rocks for a better view.

I spoke to the driver and bought a ticket to Hrauneyjar. He wasn't sure of the price and in the end I think he quite simply made a price up, which we both agreed was fair and reasonable. I breathed a sigh of relief that I had now established a way to further my journey down Sprengisandur.

After half an hour, everybody, photographed-out, climbed back on board the bus and I chose a vacant seat towards the rear half, next to a Danish student. Moments later, we were underway, following the F26 southwards. The ride would take eight hours at an average speed of 15 miles per hour. Eight hours? If I had walked it, it would have taken me eight long days of physical torment, prolonged exposure to the elements and maybe a bit of a soaking in one or two of the many glacial rivers that crossed this route. Eight gruelling days involving nights of remote wild camping and snack food, with added flies for extra protein. But now, in a mere eight hours, I would be transported in a bumpy jolting journey, over wild rivers, along desolate mountain tracks and along wide lava filled valleys to more southern Icelandic climes.

As we travelled, I made a subjective assessment of this highland route. For centuries this route was regarded as off limits to all but the insane or stubbornly determined. Its very name "sprengja" means to ride a horse to death, for any brave horse-back travellers passing this way would have had to proceed at such a severe pace for there was no horse fodder or grazing ground to sustain their charges en route and human shelters there were none. Riders would have to travel at frenetic speed to safely gain the havens of settlements around Akureyri to the north and Thingvellir to the south-west. Basically the Sprengisandur route was off limits. It was not until the nineteenth century that intrepid travellers attempted to open up this route once more, although, to this day, in winter and early spring it is almost impossible to negotiate because of extreme weather and difficult ground conditions for all but the most prepared and equipped adventurers. In summer however, when Sprengisandur has been reopened, conditions underfoot reveal F26 is definitely walkable and certainly a lot easier to proceed along than the dreaded thufur I had been snarled up in just a day earlier. It is certainly remote but the problem is, there is little shelter to protect you from the elements save some valleys and leeward facing hillsides. Not really the place to be caught in a gale, sandstorm or blizzard. Your tent would quite easily be lifted and transported skyward. Another thing struck me as the bus travelled round tricky hairpins and awkward bends, was the fact that although there was plenty of water to be seen, quite a lot of it flowed a course well away from the road. When we did reach a river that crossed the track, all appeared fordable with care. This was because it was so unseasonably cold, glacial meltwater was at a premium, still frozen high up in the glaciers. I wondered what it would have been like in warmer weather, when these rivers become impassable torrents, swollen with water released initially many miles away.

I followed the road on my walking map. There were one or two climbs but nothing as steep as Brunnfell. The biggest difficulty traversing Sprengisandur was covering the vast distance without any let up in the wind and the weather; a truly bleak wilderness, a cold desert in its truest sense. I imagined myself walking across this exposed landscape hour after hour, with little variation; just endless volcanic scenery and limitless black sand and grit, mile after mile. Quite an ordeal.

After several hours, I sensed we were nearly at Nyidalur, my next intended food parcel pick-up point on Day Four of my crossing of the highlands. I was intrigued to see the state of the rivers around here, because I knew that they could be notoriously difficult to cross. As it was, the cold temperatures had kept the water locked in, so fording Nyidalur's rivers by bus at this time, was fairly straight forward. Behind the rivers stood a group of isolated buildings and upon one was fixed an Icelandic flag being whipped around atop a tall mast. This was Nyidalur Mountain Hut, the location of my food parcel. The driver announced we were stopping here for forty five minutes.

I was anxious to get off, and as I did so, a cold blast of air severely greeted me. I had not expected it to feel quite so bracing and immediately pulled my hood tight around my head. The air temperature here was heavily influenced by Nyidalur's proximity to Tungnafellsjökull, a gleaming white glacier nearly five thousand feet high, a mere few kilometres east of us. It was like standing next to a deep freeze with the door ajar. Allied to the cold, there was a stiff breeze blowing. This was not the place to be hanging about. I sought refuge in the mountain hut, where the resident warden was to be found. I asked if my food parcel I had sent here, had arrived. She indicated a pile of parcels all of various sizes and wrappings, indicating that quite a lot of people used this place as a refuelling stop in this wilderness. I eventually found my parcel towards the bottom and smiled a satisfactory smile when I recognised my distinctive handwriting on a label. I was quite impressed with the Icelandic delivery system in reaching this remote location. Using my polar bear knife, which had been relatively redundant up till now, I sliced open the brown paper and tape, to reveal a box containing a few packets of chocolate raisins, some 80g portions of granola, powdered milk, three dehydrated dinners, two bars of chocolate, coffee, sugar, four energy bars, spare batteries, a fresh pair of underpants and that was about it.

"Jesus!" I thought. "How on earth was that meant to sustain me up here, in these temperatures, for four days?" I had seriously underestimated the amount of food I would have needed to keep me energised and warm in this exposed terrain, especially walking the long distances into a headwind with no respite. Thank God I had erred on the side of caution and caught the bus. I don't think I would even have got this far on my own. As far as I could see, the only way to travel down Sprengisandur, with such unseasonable weather and survive, would be to do it with a companion, where you could carry more food and supplies and share the burden. On my own, this leg of my trek was simply too much, too extreme for me.

I explained to the warden that I had changed my plans and would not require all the contents of my food parcel. I did take out however a bar of chocolate and the spare underpants! Time to become slightly more sociable, for a little while anyway! The rest was placed on a shelf in the hut where passing travellers, especially those with a craving for chocolate raisins and energy bars, could help themselves.

Back outside, I took various photographs of the glacier and the hut, ate some chocolate and generally just savoured the atmosphere. This was a wild place, a place where you respected nature and all it could throw at you. If I had walked here, I would definitely have stayed in the hut, because I'm not sure I could have survived a night wild camping in such cold temperatures. The wind definitely had a sharp bite to it, which would have tested the insulative properties of my sleeping bag and my extra clothing to the limits. I shivered at the mere thought of it.

Nyidalur seemed to be something of a watershed, in the geographic sense, for when we set off shortly afterwards and headed south, the rivers now flowed southwards. We also started to lose height as we headed relentlessly for Hrauneyjar. Fording points indicated that the rivers were more swollen at this southern end, and required more careful negotiation. Perhaps the rainfall had been more intense in the south, if so, what a remarkably saturated summer they had had. I had heard on the grapevine that back in England, they were enjoying a prolonged heatwave with temperatures in the thirties. Although I would not have appreciated such hot weather here, making it too hot to walk, I would have preferred many drier and clearer days. As if on cue, at that moment, the skies opened and rain poured down. I sighed a sigh of disapproval at this, as we headed for Versalir, an outpost towards the bottom end of Sprengisandur I had visited many years ago. The miles were now being covered more quickly as, almost imperceptibly, the track was becoming easier to travel along; longer straights, less boulders to avoid, fewer rivers to ford and eventually a civilised tarmac road once more.

A large lake called Thórisvatn appeared alongside the road, the second largest lake in Iceland. Evidence of industrialisation now appeared in the form of power lines and pylons, breaking the monotony of the natural landscape. They led to Sigalda, a hydro-electric power station opened in 1977. This was built in remarkably quick time to meet the energy demands of a rapidly evolving energy-guzzling nation. Out here it looked impressive with massive concrete structures fused to the landscape. It reminded me of the robust clunky architecture of Hitler's architect, Albert Speer, though I may be doing the architect who designed Sigalda, a gross injustice here.

After eight hours, the bus pulled into a car park outside Hotel Highland Guest House at Hrauneyjar, my destination. Flags fluttered outside a motel-styled building complete with a line of petrol pumps. And that was it. A remote building built at the southern end of Sprengisandur. I climbed off the bus, beneath darkening skies and retrieved my rucksack stashed away in the boot. It was still quite breezy and I was not really sure what I was going to do, now I was here. I went inside the hotel building to find out. Behind a reception desk sat a young and attractive girl and I instinctively knew who it was. I had communicated extensively with Hotel Highland over the previous few months to ascertain if it was all right for me to send a food parcel here. My emailing chum was called Stella and I intuitively knew it was Stella behind the counter. I introduced myself and said,

"It's Stella, isn't it? I'm Mark and I sent you a food parcel from England, which hopefully has arrived for me." Stella initially looked surprised and her teal blue-green eyes opened wide. Then, with a sudden realisation and recollection of our emails, she smiled a welcoming smile.

"Hello Mark. Good to see you. Welcome to Hrauneyjar."

Apparently there was no campsite near here, which I found surprising, because it had been my intention to camp at Hrauneyjar. What to do? I could wildcamp but I sensed that this area was not appropriate for wild camping. I was not sure. I asked Stella how much rooms cost for the night. The prices weren't cheap, however I negotiated a deal where I acquired a very basic room for about 65 euros. The room itself was small, containing two single beds, a couple of shelves, a hanging rail for clothes and that was about it. A bathroom was situated along the corridor and toilets beyond that. Functional and minimalistic summed the place up, however it was warm and clean and that would do me quite nicely. It also contained a restaurant serving a good selection of fast food and soup. After a long drive, I was ready for something to eat, preferably not involving nuts, raisins, noodles or chocolate.

I consulted Stella and her companion Karen for advice as to the way forward the following day. I wanted to access a campsite which would allow me to head north-west towards Gullfoss. Apparently however, there were no convenient campsites. They suggested following the F26, then R32 to Stong. Just before that, across the Thórsá River lay Hólaskógur, where a travellers' lodge was situated conveniently near Háifoss waterfall. This seemed a good idea because it put me right at the start of the power lines route to Gullfoss, my very next objective.

Because I was now eight days ahead of schedule, I had time on my hands. I had considered making a detour to Mount Hekla, Iceland's most active volcano, currently overdue a considerable eruption. Tomorrow's trek would go straight past it, however a senior member of staff where I was staying warned me off, saying that Hekla was still covered with a sizeable amount of snow and the weather forecast was not good. In other words, keep off our volcano!

I spent the evening recording copious notes on my Psion word processor. I found the activity of recalling my thoughts and actions on a daily basis remarkably therapeutic as well as giving me something to do in the long evenings. As I ate my meal, I typed, sometimes for an hour at a time. Nobody here seemed to want to talk to anybody else. It reminded me somewhat of London, where a single person can feel very alone whilst surrounded by millions of people. I thought back to the beginning of the day, way up in the north, at Kidagil. Sprengisandur represented a vast, almost impregnable barrier between the north and the south. To think, that once September arrives, the weather closes in and within weeks, the highland pass is closed by extreme winds, extensive snowfall and ice once more. Nights darken and lengthen and Sprengisandur remains shut until the following May or June. Here, at Hrauneyjar, snow would be piled high, masking everything. July and August were simply fair weather interruptions to the normal state of affairs. This would normally be a very dark, bleak and uncompromising place, often snowbound and cut off from civilisation. I was just glad it was mid-July and not the middle of winter.

16. Lost Memories

When passing a door-post watch as you walk on, inspect as you enter. It is uncertain where enemies lurk or crouch in a dark corner – The Hávamál

Hrauneyjar – Hólaskógur 15.8 mls

A new day, and once again it was raining, which was quite depressing really. It was as if someone had left the tap running and gone away on holiday for a fortnight. I just wished they would return to turn it off. Iceland was overdue a proper summer.

I ate a continental breakfast to recharge my batteries, before getting ready to tackle the murky weather. I retired to my room and repacked my rucksack. All my possessions were organised in different coloured waterproof bags.

Yellow for technical items like batteries, chargers etc; red for cooking items; orange for my water filtration system; light blue for washing and toiletries and dark blue for clothes. Food was kept in a grey blue bag and I made sure I had enough food to last me for three days until I reached Gullfoss.

My pack weighed between 17 to 20 kg depending how much food I was carrying. Generally I disliked carrying my pack after picking up a new food parcel, because the extra weight made a substantial difference, particularly on my long-suffering shoulders. It also meant I had to consume more food to carry the extra weight, but that was just part of the deal when trekking a long way; your body continually faces a challenging situation. I checked my map, my hat, my gloves, my walking poles and then reached for my camera. Where was my camera? I could not find it anywhere. A quick search on and under the bed revealed nothing. No matter, I must have hidden it away in my rucksack, inside my clothes bag, maybe. A rummage however, revealed nothing. Strange, I thought. I checked again, then again, but still no sign of it, an Olympus Compact bought specially for this trip. I hunted around the room, lifting pillows and covers to no avail and then looked for a third time in every pocket, bag and compartment of my rucksack. I checked my jacket. Nothing. This situation reminded me of all the multifarious times I had hunted down my car keys at home, which somehow always seemed to be trying to escape. Many an abusive hour had been spent looking for my keys and now that scenario was being played out in the hunt for my camera.

I was now starting to feel slightly uneasy, because there was nowhere else in the room to look. I wandered down to the restaurant to see if I had left it there, but there was no sign of it. My furrowed brow now reflected the anxiety that was building inside me. I looked in the reception area, the toilets and the showers. The trouble was, there were not many places I had visited while I had been here at the guest house and I had already looked in all of them. Another search through all my stuff, this time emptied out onto my bed again revealed nothing. I rechecked the restaurant and the toilets, but increasingly I was facing up to the inevitable, my camera, with all of my precious photos from Seydisfjordur to here, had gone. I returned to the reception area but still there was no sign of it.

The last time I remembered having it was when I first entered the hostel when I saw a sign requesting guests to remove or cover their boots before entering the building. My camera was fixed to my chest strap, so I loosened this, placed the camera behind me, removed my rucksack and tended to my boots. That was the last time I could remember genuinely seeing it. I hunted round the foyer where I placed it. Surely I picked it up again, but frankly, I could not remember for certain. In the end, it appeared to me that I had left it on the window sill behind me and someone had seen the opportunity to take possession of a nearly new Olympus camera, containing up to two hundred photos of a middle aged man trekking across Iceland. My heart sank.

I informed reception what had happened and they were actually quite upset for me. Several members of staff went through my belongings including the manager. They hunted through my room and checked the restaurant and toilets as I had done, but my camera had simply vanished. If it had been taken by a fellow traveller, I considered that quite mean, because surely we all belonged to the same club? Stella, the young receptionist said she would have cried if she had been in my shoes.

"I am crying," I replied, "but on the inside." Stella looked at me, her eyes downcast, genuinely upset for me, for she knew exactly how I felt. I was completely devastated. I was not so bothered about the camera, but the memory card containing all my personal moments on this trip: Seydisfjordur, Egilsstadir, R901 - the mountain road, Reykjahlid, Kidagil,

Nyidalur. All gone. My special cache of treasured recollections. Gone forever.

I sagged into a chair, deflated in spirit, almost in a state of shock. Stella did not know what to say but smiled sympathetically at me. I just sat quietly, reflective, almost resigned.

After ten minutes I stirred myself and asked that Stella take my personal details on the off chance someone returned it, which she did. I then hauled my rucksack onto my back, said my farewells, shook hands with Stella and the hotel manager, not noticing his iron grip this time, and set off along the road. I felt completely empty and flat; not at all enthused about the prospect of walking to Hólaskógur some fifteen miles away.

The whole walk now seemed pointless and for the first hour or so, I saw nothing as I walked. I was in a dense fog of disillusion, feeling as sorry for myself as it is possible to be. Mount Hekla, the most active volcano in Iceland, rose majestically to my left, but it might as well not have bothered, for I was not really interested. It could have erupted there and then: I would not have noticed. I stopped a couple of times for refreshment, not looking, just standing and staring into space. It almost felt as if someone close to me had died and I had started to grieve and mourn. Ridiculous really, it was only a camera, but those photos were so special to me, so meaningful, so personal, based on a lifetime's aspirations, and now they had vanished. I sighed a deep sigh, said, "Bother!" a few times and walked on. To make matters worse, the persistent rain got heavier and the sky darker, to match my mood; a sombre, miserable time.

The road stubbornly refused to bend and this particular stretch was quite boring, the most interesting features being the pylons running across the landscape transmitting power in the general direction of Selfoss, a medium sized town, to the south. It was now simply a matter of ticking off the miles and reaching the bridge over the River Thórsá. Once across the river, I could head for Hólaskógur.

Once more, to help pass the time and the miles, I reverted to my well-tried practice of counting as I walked. Four paces for each number. A steady, deliberate rhythm in which I harmonised my breathing, my stride length, the swing of my arms and my thought processes. Everything else was shunted into the background as I entered a secure, distant, dream-like meditative state, yet I was still awake. I could hear myself saying the numbers just beneath my breath, each number an accomplishment in itself, said in a breathy, slightly melodic chant; a eulogy to myself: "Less distance to cover - a step nearer my goal. Less distance to cover - a step nearer my goal." On and on I went, maintaining this canticle incessantly. As I trudged inextricably onwards in my forlorn, rather pensive depression, sounds around me seemed amplified somehow – the comforting crunch of the gravel and ash, the singing of the wind, the rustle of my clothing and the birds accompanying me on my way. A calmness now gradually transcended my emotional condition so that the stresses of my early morning dismay at losing my camera, were subjugated to an archive of my memory, on hold so to speak.

Eventually, after a four hour road trek, I reached the bridge, a robust steel and wooden structure 185 metres in length. It crossed a powerfully flowing river at this point, the Thórsá, the longest river in Iceland at 144 miles. The Thórsá is fed by the glaciers of Vatnajökull and Hofsjökull, as well as draining the sands of Sprengisandur to the north and, looking at its swirling, animated potency, it was clearly not a river to be trifled with. Whilst crossing the bridge, I was astonished to see vast quantities of glacial debris being hurried along in its current, giving it a distinctive blue-grey tinge, similar to the colouring on a dolphin. Not a river to fall into either, and I really hoped the rivers I would encounter the following day, were much calmer and friendlier than this. A stiff wind blew across the bridge which had recklessly low and dangerously flimsy crash barrier sides. Not a bridge to cross in a gale I surmised.

Once across, I consulted my map to work out where to find Hólaskógur, but I reckoned I could already see it with my own eyes, a chocolate brown wooden structure about a mile away to the left. To my right, just over the bridge was an imposing building of the Sultartangi Hydro-electric Power Station situated at the end of the Sultartangi Reservoir, created back in the 1980s. It reminded me of the futuristic headquarters of International Rescue on Tracy Island in the children's TV programme, Thunderbirds, that I watched as a child, but perhaps I was letting my imagination run away with me. Anyway, Thunderbird One did not suddenly take off in clouds of white talcum powder and disappear over the summit of Hekla.

My task was to reach Hólaskógur and, after a couple of false starts, I found a deep sandy track used by Icelandic horses, that led there, judging by the many deep hoof prints, and I reached the hut a weary forty minutes later. Everything looked quiet, but on opening the door, I came across a lady, Jóna, the warden, lurking quietly inside, almost as if she had been expecting me. Thankfully she could accommodate me for that night, so now it was just a matter of resting up and washing through my clothes, some of which had started to acquire an odour akin to that found in a pile of rotting cabbages.

That's the trouble with long distance trekkers; they become quite quickly socially unacceptable, repugnant even. The pints of perspiration generated over several days soon degenerates into a suppurating, putrefying stench that could stop a charging polar bear at fifty metres. You know when it has gone beyond the pale when innocent passers-by suddenly freeze midstride, assume an expression of absolute horror and blanch with revulsion as your whiffy noxious charms gently float their way. They then retch uncontrollably in great distress, requiring immediate first aid and a comforting arm.

My base layers were bad enough, emitting a fruity fragrance of the skunky variety, but it was my socks that were now causing a great deal of concern, not just for those in the immediate vicinity but for all the people in the whole of southern Iceland. Me? I tended to be oblivious. What went on in my boots tended to be ignored or unnoticed. I knew I occasionally had a problem with my feet because I suffered at times from fungal decay brought on by athlete's foot; my feet giving out a full bodied mushroomy smell that tended to induce sudden depression and contemplation of suicide in those around whose sensitive noses detected it.

So right now, my socks needed some form of revival and renewal, if not immediate condemnation. The difficulty being, I did not have the right type of biological soap powder to neutralise the pong, I simply had a half bar of Dove Beauty Soap and no amount of Sodium Lauroyl Isethionate or Strearic Acid contained therein, could possibly overcome the festering, pungent reek. Thinking about it, I should have known there was something wrong back at Hrauneyjar, when a young girl suddenly gasped, held her throat, grimaced violently, heaved and then burst into tears as I nonchalantly walked by in my bootless feet. I was heading towards the restaurant, with invisible rancid vapours rising skyward from my sweaty footprints, that left a faint but distinct trail across the linoleum similar, I considered, to misty handprints pressed onto a cold window in winter. You get the idea. Her parents looked daggers at me; I had no idea why, but in retrospect, it was probably they who stole my camera, for deeply offending their olfactory organs.

Hólaskógur was a two storey building that could accommodate over sixty people in comfort. It had two extensive kitchens, one on each floor and was warm and spotlessly clean. I knew I would like it here. I occupied a bed on the first floor, and because there were very few people staying here at the time, I had the whole floor to myself. I spread my belongings out around my bed, and reflected once again on the fact that I no longer had my camera. I felt like my cat had died and I so wanted to turn the clock back twenty four hours to make everything all right again. Various what-ifs came into my mind. What if I had ignored the sign requesting me to remove my boots back at Hrauneyjar? What if I had decided to walk down Sprengisandur after all, instead of getting the bus? I was sick of what-ifs. All I knew was someone was walking round with my photographs and that hurt me intensely.

The warden, Jóna, allowed me to wash my whiffy clothes and I put them, still rather, er – fetidly fragrant, outside to dry on a clothes line. The wind was gusting violently however there was plenty of rain in the air, and sure enough, all that happened was my clothes got wetter, so I quickly retrieved them and placed them inside the hut, fermenting gently, in front of the radiators upstairs. Before long, a haze of low cloud hung across the room and the air tasted of an aroma not unlike sickly, soured milk. Dismayed, I shut the door tight, sealed the gap at the bottom of the door with a discarded towel and hoped no one else noticed the malodorous mephitis barely contained within.

A lazy early evening saw the arrival of a Swiss couple from Basel. They were touring Iceland and we soon got chatting. He was a teacher of unmotivated challenging teenagers and she was an administrator. We discussed all sorts of topics and whiled away a very pleasant evening.

It is always interesting to get other people's perspective on politics, culture, religion, family values and so on. We also discussed humour and I tried to get them to understand that British humour was often based on disparaging remarks and self-deprecation where the objective was to take the mickey out of yourself and others; something the Swiss couple did not initially understand. I said that British people liked to insult each other as a form of jocularity, as a way of engaging with each other. Still they did not understand. Surely an insult was offensive? I said an insult could be a form of banter and offered to give them a perfect example.

I knew a British school party would shortly be arriving at the guest house, because Jóna had told me, shortly after I arrived. I said to the Swiss couple that when the British party appeared, within five minutes we would have hurled abuse at each other several times over, but would be best of friends as well. The Swiss couple looked very dubious at this. Sure enough, shortly afterwards, the British group turned up, carrying various heavy rucksacks and boxes. They were chatting amongst themselves. I detected a thick Scottish accent.

"Oh no, not the bloody Scottish!" I exclaimed loudly, on purpose in their direction. "That's all we need out here! I've travelled hundreds of miles to get away from people like you!" The Scotsman looked across at me and grinned.

"Bloody English!" he responded. "I thought it was too good to last! I thought I'd come here for a quiet night," he retorted. "We should have finished you lot off at Bannockburn!"

"You're one to talk. Bloody Scots don't know the meaning of the word quiet! Mind you went mighty quiet at Culloden!" I responded. I then heard a Welsh voice. "Christ almighty!" I said. "Bloody Taffs too!"

"Ah shut up," said the Welshman, and grinned at me. Then I heard a Yorkshire accent.

"Oh God," I shrieked, "Not a bloody Yorkshireman as well!" The man from Yorkshire asked, "Where you from them?"

"I'm from Burnley," I answered.

"Jesus Christ," he said. "Tha' knows nowt about cricket over there. Mind, tha' knows nowt about owt! I coom to Iceland and bump into soomone from effing Lancashire! Aye. Tha' knows nowt about owt!" We all laughed like drains and shook each other by the hand, Icelandic style. The Scottish handshake was particularly firm and combative. They then went to unpack and make their evening meal. I turned back to the Swiss pair.

"See?" I explained. "Not a friendly word said, yet we all get on. It's just banter and a very British thing."

The Swiss couple smiled, half-understanding but not really comprehending. Then he said, "I think I get it. It wouldn't work in Switzerland, but I do get it." We looked at each other and I knew I had made a connection with him. His wife just looked bemused.

After tea, I sat quietly making notes on my Psion Computer as usual. People were interested in this device because basically it was technology from the 1990s. I was using it because it ran off a couple of AA batteries and did not need recharging, unlike most modern electronic contraptions, which can barely last eight hours without being plugged into the mains. Having recorded my personal thoughts on my Psion, I sat and reflected once more on the whereabouts of my camera and exhaled a deep breath of lamentation. This grieving lark was simply adding to my woes. I was also already thinking about tomorrow, the power lines walk; crossing rivers and deep ones at that. I had already been warned twice about the dangers of the next day's walk. Back at Hrauneyjar, the man who informed me in no uncertain terms that I should not climb Hekla on my own, had also stated that the power lines walk was a difficult challenge.

"The rivers are deep," he said, "waist deep and fast flowing."

I knew that that meant trouble, because all my Icelandic guide books had stated that flowing water, above knee height, can quite easily knock you off your feet. Jóna had also mentioned the rivers and was slightly concerned for my safety. I could detect the anxiety in her voice and the fraught look in her eyes.

"When you cross the rivers," she had said, "make sure you follow the line of the tracks made by 4x4 vehicles. Look on the opposite bank to see where these tracks emerge. Do not, under any circumstances, leave the line of the tracks." I assured here I would take the utmost care. "Have you got river shoes?" she asked. I assured her I had. I told her I knew the theory behind crossing rivers, I had just not had any practice at it." She looked at me, her knowing blue eyes, warning me silently.

"Don't worry," I assured her. "I will be very careful."

"The river bed is uneven," she continued. "Sometimes there are potholes where the river is very deep. You must really look to see where to put your feet." I made a mental note of everything she told me. I felt rather uneasy about the whole thing. I knew the rivers on this section were going to be my biggest challenge from the outset. I knew that this day was going to be very difficult when I scrutinised the route, months earlier The only problem was, that challenge was now just a few hours' sleep away.

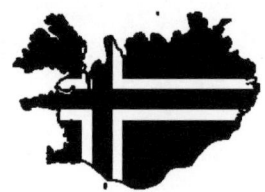

17. Current Affairs

The man who stands at a strange threshold should be cautious before he cross it, glance this way and that: who knows beforehand what foes may sit awaiting him in the hall? - The Hávamál

Hólaskógur – Helgaskáli 17.8 mls

I slept relatively well, but awoke with a start as I instantly knew what day it was. My sub-conscious was ahead of me; it knew what was coming. I jumped up and peered through the steamed up windows. Outside, a blanket of fog enveloped everything and rain, as usual, was in the air. My stomach felt queasy as I began to think about the challenges and demands of the day. The rivers! Ah yes, the rivers!

I sat back down on my mattress on top of my sleeping bag. All night my socks had been drying in front of hot storage heaters. They were dry now and stiff like putrid-smelling crisp breads and the air hung thick with a sallow haze; a pungent odour permeating everything. Quite depressing really and it added to my fragile cheerless state.

I ate my breakfast very deliberately, making sure I gained every last ounce of energy from my strawberry granola. I also ate plenty of milk chocolate and consumed two cups of coffee. That was it; my main meal to start the day. The intention was to follow the footpath behind Hólaskógur and visit Háifoss, Iceland's second highest waterfall. Then I would join the power line track to Gullfoss. Basically this meant following a sinuous mountain track that ran alongside some pylons that was occasionally used by power maintenance vehicles. I wouldn't reach Gullfoss today, it was simply too far, but instead I would head towards a mountain hut called Helgaskáli, some eighteen miles away. I was hoping to either stop there or camp nearby. Gullfoss would have to wait until tomorrow.

After breakfast, I gathered my belongings and went to thank Jóna for her hospitality. She again earnestly told me to take care and to be observant when crossing the rivers. I assured her I would. We shook hands and she looked at me with her steel blue eyes in a manner I felt was rather kind and protective, which was nice. I opened the door and was gone, to face the ordeals of the day.

I turned uphill towards Háifoss. I did not feel very happy at all, in fact I felt quite down-in-the-dumps and very lonely. This was the day I had been dreading for months – the power lines day – the day with the significant rivers – the day I had scrutinised for hours on my computer back home, studying every last nuance of the rivers that lay across my path on google earth. And I was very worried indeed. I knew all the names of course – Stóra- Laxá, Svartá, Fossá, Leirá, Tangá – rivers that I hoped would not prove to be too swollen or taxing for me to cope with.

It is hard to explain but without overstating the case, I felt that this could indeed be my very last day on this earth. I had thought this many months previously, when I agonised over my choice of route across Iceland. But it was indisputable, this service track was the only sensible route linking this part of the world with Gullfoss. All other routes added up to three or four days extra hiking; but this route was also bloody dangerous. I had never said anything to anybody back home, about the dangers so as not to worry them unduly, but my decision to walk this way was, for me, marginal at best.

I came to the awful conclusion that I may well have eaten my last breakfast. It was as bad as that. I actually felt like someone on death row and I was walking to my execution. All my senses were heightened. I could hear the birds mocking me, as usual. I could feel the cold wind around me once more and the squally rain whipped into my face. I gripped my walking poles very deliberately, placing each one quite precisely, quite purposefully, in front of me. My stride length was greatly reduced from normal, almost as if I was trying not to reach the place to where I was going. Well, it was true. I did not really want to reach the rivers for I was very afraid of the rivers, particularly these rivers; I had been for months, but now they were right at the top of my agenda and my eleventh hour was approaching.

Why would I want to put myself in such grave danger? After all, I had eschewed the perils of Sprengisandur on the grounds it was simply too testing and foolhardy for me as a solo traveller. I suppose it comes down to the plain fact that this whole trip, this whole challenge was really about discovering myself; finding out what sort of person I was. All my life I had never done anything particularly hazardous; health and safety was partly responsible for that, but conventions of modern life ensure that everything we do is very cosy and comfortable. Any risks are usually stage-managed, for instance sky-diving, with an instructor strapped tightly to you making the real decisions about when to pull the cord to release the parachute, or white water rafting, where you are supported by experienced rowers, who can steer you round the worst of the whirlpools and eddies. Everything is sanitised to protect you from real-life traumas.

The power line route, and in particular the swollen rivers, gave me the chance to confront real danger, alone, unaccompanied, with no one to bark out the orders, but simply me making instant judgements – life-saving options of right or wrong. I was going to confront my fears, to see if I could overcome them. This was to be my Shackleton moment, the point of no return. There was no guarantee however, that I had the resolve to see it through. Today would tell me, one way or the other. Right now, I was nauseous with fear.

The path continued steadily uphill. The route was obvious and the pylons were coming ever nearer. I felt consumed with anxiety – even ill - but I carried on remorselessly. This was something I had to do; totally illogical but compelling. The rain got worse and I cursed the fact it was yet another unpleasant day.

"I've enough to worry about, without the rain making it difficult!" I shouted to myself.

A curlew appeared above me and said, "Well you'll have to take extra care then, won't you?"

After half an hour, I stopped and turned around. There behind me, in black, were two shadowy figures, about 200 metres away. I wondered where they were going. I gathered my breath and resumed my reluctant trudge up the path, with my footsteps growing shorter and shorter. I really did not want to be here. This was the first time ever I had sensed such genuine, unadulterated fear on a walk. All right, I had encountered some dodgy moments over the years, falling into bogs, getting lost on the moors, being attacked by farm dogs, but nothing on this scale. Dread and an intense sense of foreboding coursed through my body and I shivered and twitched desperately in an attempt to rid myself of it, but to no avail. I stopped once more and looked back. The figures were still there. No closer, no further away, just there, sort of watching me, morbid spectators of curiosity, like the crowd at a bull-fight. I wondered momentarily if they had any significance in this situation; overseers on my plight, but just as quickly as this thought had arisen, I dismissed it as psychological tosh.

I continued upwards. I knew the waterfall was not far and soon I came across a junction of paths. The path left, led down to the waterfall, the path ahead, led to the rivers. In a way, I was glad I was turning left, delaying the inevitable. The figures were still behind me. They stopped when I stopped. They moved when I moved. This was weird. They now started to make me feel very uneasy and a frisson of anxiety consumed me as I shuddered violently - exaggerated spasms of fear almost causing me to halt my progress completely. Indeed, I nearly threw up, such was the turmoil within me.

The path to the waterfall took just a few minutes, even when travelling slowly. I could hear it quite clearly, the rush of the water dropping violently onto the rocks below. Unfortunately the weather had totally closed in and I was immersed in a shroud of cloud. I could see barely five paces in front of me; the shadowy figures now gone from sight. I wondered if they were still following in my footsteps, or whether they had gone straight ahead to the rivers instead. I could not tell. Sounds became muffled now, as I picked my way gingerly down a slope towards the cascading water.

"Typical," I thought. "I'm not going to see a thing! The weather's just crap!"

Feeling quite angry at this point at the unfairness of it all, I reached a platform, perhaps a viewing point but could see next to nothing, just thick cloud. The rain dripped off my hood and across my face, as my very own tears of despair. I had long wanted to see this waterfall, probably not in these stressful circumstances, but right now, the weather had defeated me. Not the first time on this trip, I surmised. I felt totally wretched and dispirited. What the hell was the point of it all? I stood vacantly staring at the cloud, behind which I could hear crashing and tumbling water. I did not really care about anything anymore. I was just existing in my own selfish, feeling sorry-for-myself moment. A deep sigh of angst and disquiet filled my soul, and I turned to leave.

At that very moment, as if by magic or divine intervention, the clouds separated, first a little, then a lot, to suddenly reveal Háifoss in all its glory. It was immense! Dynamic and raw and powerful! A surge of amazement ran through me as I silently witnessed this true wonder of nature. Water fell in curtains of white-steel shards, fracturing and disintegrating over a stubborn rocky shelf, before smashing mightily into the depths below, slapping disdainfully the tumbled, fractured boulders at its base, before undergoing a remarkable transformation and continuing in total contrast as a ribbon of silver and black, rather demurely and sedately down the valley. It was awe-some. Here I stood, paying homage to a truly remarkable spectacle, and for a minutely short while, this amazing vista distracted me from my apprehension; the view belonged solely to me.

Suddenly I was aware of a movement behind me and there, picking their way down the path, was a young waterproofed couple, clad in dark, heavy capes and hoods. My shadowy guardians had arrived and, as they did so, the cloud lifted further to reveal more of the valley downstream. All possible varieties of Dulux colours were displayed in the vegetation that cloaked the hillsides – moss green, olive green, myrtle green, Buckingham green. Fabulous! The young couple stood next to me and we silently shared and appreciated the awesome panorama. I broke the silence by saying,

"Have you ever seen anything like that?" They replied in the negative. "Thank goodness the cloud lifted or we'd have missed it."

They agreed and we thanked our lucky stars. All the while the water plummeted relentlessly with the gravity, disappearing at great speed below. We took photographs of each other, mine being taken on my mobile phone now, but it was better than having no photos at all, evidence of our being here. I said farewell to them after establishing that that they were not going my way but were instead following the river downwards back to Stong. I was slightly disheartened at this news because I was secretly hoping they were going my way and we could have helped each other out. Never mind, I thought. Never mind.

As fast as my spirits had been uplifted upon seeing the inspirational Háifoss, they now sank just as quickly, as once more, I resumed my walk along the fateful river path. I again became immersed in black thoughts, negative thoughts. I reached the junction and turned left. The moment of truth was fast approaching.

There is something somewhat suffocating about an impending sense of inevitable doom and this is exactly how I felt as I drew nearer the Fossá river. A feeling of being physically crushed and squeezed, a claustrophobic vice from which there is no escape. I rounded a turn, and to my absolute horror, there is front of me, in this imposing and malevolent place, was a fast-flowing mass of churning water, hostile in the extreme. Any vestige of optimism that I had previously clutched on to, now disappeared in an instant.

"Oh, my God!" I screamed in sheer terror. "How the hell am I meant to cross that!" It was not meant to be a question but a statement of unequivocal fact. The river seethed and boiled. To me it appeared to be a maelstrom of savagery. I would not have lasted more than two seconds if I had attempted to set foot in it.

I paced the bank, with fearful thoughts spinning and swirling through my head.

"I can't do it, it's too much," I despaired. "I'll have to go back."

Going back would have involved a diversion of some fifty miles through Árnes and Flúdir, adding three whole days to my schedule, but at least I would be alive. I then thought that everyone would think I had bottled it, when faced with such adversity. In their eyes, I would have proven myself to be inadequate, a failure. All my life, in my professional career, I had considered myself to be the "nearly man": I nearly got a headship of a school in which I had been teaching; I nearly won first prize for being the inspirational teacher of the year in north-east Lancashire. The story of my life really. No, I just had to go on; it was time to stop being the nearly man. But then common sense, allied with my acute survival acumen, fired in and once more I repeated aloud,

"I can't do it!"

For several minutes I struggled with this dilemma, and all the time, the rain poured down. What an abject scene. I was standing there, quaking, almost mentally broken, aside this raging torrent, agonising what to do. I looked once more at my map, covered with a sprinkling of water droplets, when I suddenly noticed two faint dotted lines leading north-east, away from this awful place. I looked once again and it dawned on me that this was not the actual crossing point after all! This was simply the place where the track met the river. The river crossing was actually a few hundred metres along the bank! Christ! Talk about nearly man! Nearly dead man! I had nearly entered the water at a ludicrous, suicidal crossing point. Jeez, that had been close, I thought to myself! I nearly wept with relief, and instead swiftly set out to discover the detail behind the real crossing point, around the corner.

It took me all of three minutes to reach there; my heart in my mouth as I rounded a turn in the track and there it was. The Fossá, and this time, the genuine fording place to cross the river lay ahead of me. Whilst it was not in the same league as the awful place I had left behind, it was still quite overwhelming and intimidating. The river was about thirty metres wide and the route went straight across, as evidenced by the vehicle tracks emerging on the opposite bank. I vacillated for several minutes weighing up the pros and cons.

"Sod it!" I screamed at myself. "Just do it!" Immediately I took off my rucksack, removed my gaiters and loosened my bootlaces. I rummaged for my river shoes, placed conveniently atop the various items in my pack. I also looked for two plastic bags. I thought that any physical barrier that would protect my feet from the freezing water was better than nothing, and placed these over my socks. They were a bit too big in all honesty, but I wore them nevertheless. I could just squeeze my feet inside my river shoes. I then replaced my gaiters, tied my boots to my rucksack and heaved it onto my back, ensuring the straps were loosely fastened. In the event of me falling over, I would throw my rucksack off rather than have it pinning me to the river bed. Actually, if I fell over, there was not the slightest chance of me regaining my feet anyway, such was the strength of the current. No, if I fell over, I would perish, just like that. One slip of my foot would mark the end very swiftly. I quickly banished that morbid image from my mind and focused on the task ahead.

The river sloped away gradually from the bank in front of me, but after that, its depth was anyone's guess, though I imagined it would range from knee deep to waist deep. I sincerely hoped it went no deeper. With a deep breath,

I stepped forward. To delay anymore would make my mental torture worse, so without a further thought, I placed my right foot into the water. It felt cold but not too cold. My left foot followed, supported by my walking pole, which I pressed deep into the river bed against a hidden rock. Now, my right walking pole. The water became deeper and stronger, pressing against me; a fluid battering ram rushing around me. I was aware of the sound of the river developing into a thunderous roar and I shouted above it:

"I can see the bottom, I can see the bottom!" I maintained this chant throughout, partly to drown out the noise of the river, but also to impose my personality on the situation. The water now reached up to my waist as I stepped in a particularly deep pothole. I could not actually see the bottom at all. My breath was sucked from me. It was cold but my waterproof trousers and jacket were up to the task, protecting me from the coldness of the torrent. I edged forwards step by step making sure that my feet were planted firmly, before moving off again. The placement of my walking poles was so exact, an exercise in precision that would have been appreciated by a darts player going for 180. I could not rest. Such was the latent capacity of the current, to stand still would have expended more energy than I could afford, so I just kept on moving. The water surged around me, as I wallowed waist-deep, battling to stay upright. Not the time to fall over, I thought. For some obscure reason, I suddenly thought that this was no way to treat my very expensive Paramo jacket. It was not designed to be immersed in a river such as this, or any river for that matter. This thought was abandoned as my foot slipped slightly and I pitched forwards with my face inches from the rushing flow. I tensed and my heart missed several beats, but I instantly thrust my walking pole into the river bed to support and protect me from calamity. My walking pole stayed rigid and unmoving, as I regained my balance and composure. On I went once more through the turbulent force that was trying to up-end me and treat me like a piece of flotsam. To drift in this current would be instant death.

"I can see the bottom, I can see the bottom!" I continued my determined mantra, forcing myself in resolute industry across the river, step by step until I gradually sensed the water was diminishing in depth and I could see the bottom more transparently. In a few more faltering paces, I was climbing the track on the opposite bank. I had conquered the Fossá. My relief was immense, as anxiety peeled away. In fact I have never felt such a powerful onrush of emotion in my life, screaming with joy, with passion and raw elation; a scream that rent the air like a hot knife cleaving butter. Such a divine moment, and one that would remain with me forever. The adrenalin rush was prodigious and my emotional state intense, I could almost taste it, almost metallic. I was joyous, triumphant, exultant. I had done it! I had bloody done it!

I stood on the bank looking back, quaking with emotion at the tumbling torrent I had overcome, when, to interrupt my all-conquering mood, a rather quaint, slightly battered, high-sided 4x4 vehicle appeared behind me with a guttural roar on the opposite bank. Its driver climbed out and looked at me.

"Helloo," he shouted. "Do you want a lift across?"

"No!" I shouted back. "I've just crossed that. I don't need a lift, thank you very much!"

"What!" he yelled. "You've just crossed that?" pointing at the river.

"Yes, and it's bloody deep!" I screamed with euphoria in my voice.

"Fucking hell," he shouted, observing the seething river. "You've done well. Wait there." He climbed back into his cab and set off the way I had just crossed. His 4x4 twisted and rolled, bucked and swayed, in fact, for a second, I though a couple of times it would turn over. He was a skilled driver however and he soon gained the bank next to me, wound down his window and grinned. "Fucking hell," he repeated, "that was interesting!" with an element of understatement.

"It was," I concurred. "A bit cold too!"

He asked what I was doing there and I informed him I was trying to reach Gullfoss via Tungufell following the power lines. He nodded.

"I came that way yesterday," he said.

"What are the other rivers like?" I asked anxiously.

"There are five big ones, but this is the worst," he said. I shouted a cry of relief.

"Yessss!" That was exactly what I wanted to hear, although it did not quite match what I had been told previously by Jóna, back at the hut, who had informed me that the Laxá, the third river, was the worst, not the Fossá. I was yet to discover who was right. The driver asked where I was going and I told him I was walking across Iceland, hopefully reaching Reykjavik eventually.

"How old are you?" he asked me.

"Fifty nine," I replied.

"You have done well for fifty nine," he stated. I felt quite proud of myself. "Good luck," he said and waved. Then he reversed his vehicle, turned round and proceeded to drive back across the river, where he stopped, reversed his vehicle once more then faced me again. Over the course of the next ten minutes he proceeded to drive back and forth across the river, with me as an intrigued and rather wet onlooker. He set up a camera on the bank, and kept returning to it, making slight alterations and adjustments. It was then I realised what he was up to. He was one of these adrenalin junkies who likes to film themselves in extreme situations. This was his white water moment. I laughed hysterically, in fact I felt hysterical about everything. I had survived!

It took me a good twenty minutes to dry my feet and my legs and put on another pair of socks, followed by my boots. The rain was relentless, so my feet were actually not particularly dry. I chewed on an energy bar, waved a final farewell to the 4x4 driver, who was still there messing about with his camera, then set off along the track. One down, four to go, I mused. I was hoping I managed all the rivers with equal aplomb.

Power lines walk

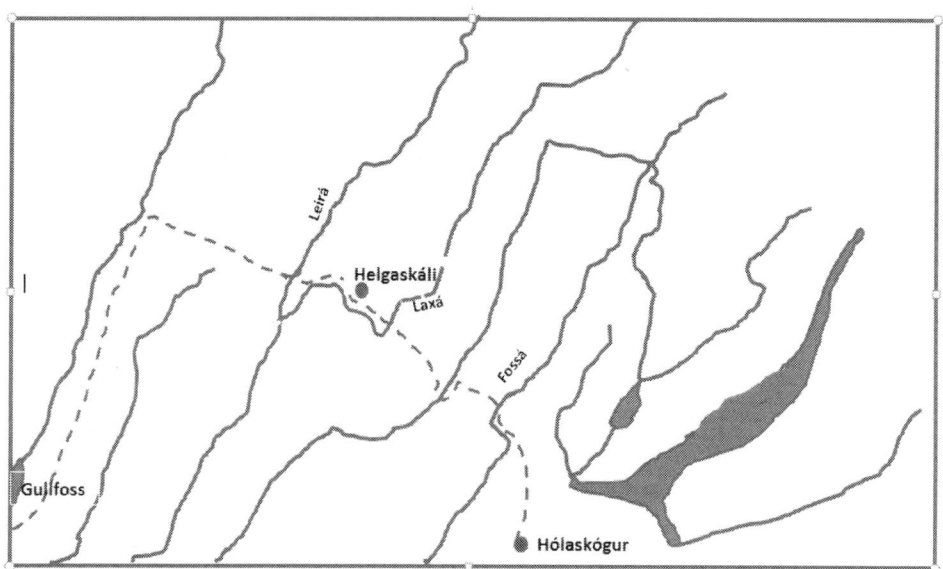

Five minutes later, another 4x4 vehicle appeared, but this one was approaching me from the direction I was facing. It was a very small 4x4, possibly the smallest I had seen, with narrow tyres and a low chassis. I waved it down and it stopped next to me, revealing a middle-aged couple inside.

"Do you speak English?" I asked.

"A little. We are from Belgium," he said.

"Are you intending crossing the river down this track?" I said pointing back the way I had come.

"Yes," he said.

"It's very deep and powerful," I explained. "It came up to here on me," and I pointed to my waist, which was almost level with the bottom of his door window.

"We will be all right," he said.

"No, I mean it," I persisted. "It's very deep. I only just managed it, "and again I pointed at my waist. He shrugged his shoulders, wound up his window and set off. I watched him disappear into the distance and round the bend. "No chance," I muttered, "absolutely no chance." Within the hour, an emergency helicopter flew very low over my head towards the Fossá. I sagely nodded my head. I was fairly certain the Belgians had needed rescuing. Why didn't they listen?

The next river appeared in front of me about half an hour further on. Once again, I removed my boots and replaced them with my river shoes. I followed exactly the same routine as before, and my newly acquired skill in river crossing stood me in good stead. I talked to myself, maintained the utmost concentration and battled across successfully. Not as difficult a river, and my confidence was now rising leaps and bounds. I could do rivers!

The rain would stop for a few minutes or so, and I would throw back my hood optimistically hoping for a change in the weather, however, within five minutes it was back again, with a vengeance, making everything grey, damp and miserable. I continued on my way, as the path zig-zagged its way either side of the power lines. These lines were supported on pylons that had two sloping legs driven into the ground, with a horizontal span across the top. Sometimes the legs sloped outwards like a foot stool, sometimes inwards. They looked quite intimidating, especially when lined up one behind the other, almost like sentinels guarding this frightening place. They reminded me of the tripod aliens in Steven Spielberg's "War of the Worlds".

It was a fair trek to the next river, with the track rising and falling, bending this way and that, contouring round various undulations in the ground. I was distinctly aware the Laxá could prove to be my greatest challenge. How would it compare to the Fossá? I desperately hoped it would not be too much for me. There was no way of avoiding it, a bit like going to the dentist knowing you have to have a tooth pulled: necessary and possibly traumatic. I stopped momentarily to have a bite to eat and recharge my batteries.

Almost immediately, the weather spitefully closed in again, and I cursed it once more. It was a filthy day and the constant deluge was doing nothing to help raise my spirits. The track continued. My mind was becoming increasingly focused; my senses sharper for I was mentally preparing for whatever river challenge lay ahead. A gradual descent led to a valley, and just before this valley, were tell-tale warning signs in yellow, informing me and other track users of deep water ahead. The Laxá was looming large and it was very near.

Upon reaching the river, I looked across and was pleasantly surprised that it did not appear to be that forbidding. It looked somewhat easier than the Fossá, so I hastily removed my boots and went through the whole plastic bag and river shoe routine once more. Thankfully the rain now stopped and for the first time that day, a patch of blue appeared in the sky above me. The Laxá split into several streamlets with black gritty sand bars between them and it was simply a matter of calculating a sensible route through them, which I did. Within a couple of minutes of intense concentration and precise application, I had traversed the river and made the opposite bank. I wondered what all the fuss had been about, dried my feet off and replaced my shoes. I was getting quite good at this river crossing malarkey, I thought to myself and set off once more.

Within moments however, I realised that I was walking, not on the track, but on a river bed, and far from having completed the crossing of the Laxá, I had only just started it! The river was actually very wide at this point and all I had crossed so far was a small portion, a mere branch of the whole river. The rest of the river had been hidden by an embankment. How I had missed it I have no idea, because I could see it all very clearly now. My heart missed a beat and I sat down, to once more put on my river shoes and go through the whole rigmarole once again. What I was faced with was indeed more challenging. The Laxá spread out in front of me for a distance of about seventy metres, almost an ocean in my eyes. With a deep sigh of resignation, I set off once more. The depth varied considerably with each step, sometimes shallow but then I would step in a pothole and be immersed up to my waist. Again I chanted my mantra: "I can see the bottom!" which wasn't strictly true, however shouting out helped me focus. I dare not slip. I dare not turn round for fear of losing my balance. All I could do was continue my sideways shuffling gait, planting my walking poles firmly. These two slim pieces of aluminium were my lifeline; without them, I would have plunged into the cold water. As I walked, I could swear the river level was rising and the volume of water increasing. The Laxá appeared to be filling up! I had read previously that on glacial rivers, glacial meltwater is often released in the afternoon, when the sun frees up the water held as ice and it then flows, almost as a mini tsunami, down the water course. This however, was not a glacial river, rather a fresh water river, fuelled by rain water. All I knew was it seemed to be of greater volume now than when I first started my crossing. What may have been happening was a surge of floodwater, from the persistent rainfall of the last twenty four hours, was now making its relentless way along the water course, just as I happened to be crossing! Impeccable timing I thought ironically. Anyway I simply concentrated harder and carefully navigated a route, attaining sand bars where possible but then plunging up to my waist in the freezing water, where the river bed dipped. Step after step, I steadily and determinedly continued on my way, talking to myself, making sure I was foot perfect. It seemed such a long way.

Eventually, I gained the opposite bank, looked on to make sure there was no more river hiding away over the next rise, and gloriously celebrated. I had overcome the last major obstacle on this section of the trek. Any other river would be less demanding, less risky. I looked back and swallowed at the sheer width of the river here. It seemed enormous. With a quaking jaw; still pumped with adrenalin, I dried myself off. That had been one wide river and I was so grateful to have made it safely across in one piece.

Laxá River

I now estimated it to be no more than two or three miles to the hut at Helgaskáli, however there was at least one significant river before that. It came upon me quite suddenly, but when I saw it, I thought I could cross it by island hopping, so there would be no need to replace my boots with river shoes. The whole routine of changing my boots, putting on plastic bags, replacing gaiters, loosening rucksack, drying feet and so on took about half an hour per river crossing, so I was actually quite pleased to find a river, shallower than the rest, which seemed to be quite easily fordable.

My initial attempt to cross the river whilst keeping my boots and socks dry, proved hopeless – the river was deeper than expected, so I ended up taking a detour along the bank until I came across a wide looping meander. I fancied my chances of crossing here but I was wrong! The water was up to my knees so both my feet were fully submerged. My walking boots were now completely wet as were my only pair of previously dry socks. Typical, despite all my best efforts to keep my footwear dry the whole day, because I could not be bothered to change into my river shoes this one particular time, my footwear was now completely soaked. I wondered how long my boots and socks would take to dry out.

I noticed for the first time some grazing sheep who looked at me somewhat sympathetically. The sky was still clear of rain and I carried onwards towards Helgaskáli. The hut unexpectedly appeared a quarter of an hour later, when I started to see a group of grazing Icelandic horses and then, within moments, a small group of people came into view, wandering outside a small collection of buildings, next to the hut, about four hundred metres away. This was an uplifting experience because the only people I had seen since Háifoss had been sitting in two vehicles. The people here were on foot and looking my way. The track curved towards the buildings and I could see a group of four men standing in front of one of them, dressed in what appeared to be, blue dungarees. They looked at me curiously as I approached them. I felt like an exhibit, being studied, judged, assessed. A quick scan of my GPS indicated I had walked eighteen miles, plus five rivers, four of substance; not a bad day's effort. I hoped there was room to stop in the hut, if not, I would camp somewhere in this area, no more than a mile or so more from here.

A woman suddenly presented herself at the door of the hut. She scrutinised me very deliberately, rather like a scientist would look at an interesting specimen through a magnifying glass, then warily approached me with hesitant steps. Finally, examination completed, she asked,

"Would you like a coffee?" I was not really expecting this offer and paused before answering.

"I would, if it's not too much trouble." She gestured to me to enter the hut. Inside I instantly felt the warm glow from a wood burning stove positioned tidily in the corner. In front of it were suspended various items of clothing: socks, trousers, shirts, all drying slowly. Next to the stove were three giant gas rings adjacent to three large Calor gas type canisters. Opposite these was a basic sink set above a unit of cupboards. Away from this kitchen area was a long table with about twenty chairs all around it. This hut had far more home comforts than I had expected. Adjoining the dining area were two doorways, leading off to other rooms.

"My name is Margrét, "she informed me.

"Mark," I replied, with a friendly, somewhat weary smile. She filled a cup of coffee with boiling water, almost as if she had been expecting me. "It's been a long day. I've been following the power lines," I informed her.

"I know. I have been watching you approaching," she said enigmatically. I then told her I had set off from Hólaskógur that morning and I was trekking across Iceland, having started a fortnight earlier. I told her of my intention to reach Gullfoss before heading onto Reykjavik. She looked at me quite deliberately and said,

"Well tonight you will stop here." She led me into a room on the left of the dining area; a bedroom stuffed with bunk beds and pointed to a narrow top bunk in the corner "You will sleep here," she ordered. I did not argue, mainly because I felt I had no real choice in the matter. She had taken control and I simply obeyed, feeling distinctly emotionally and physically drained. It had been such a long, stressful day so I was grateful to accept any welcome and generous offer.

"I've crossed some very tricky rivers today, swollen with all the rainfall," I told her.

"I know," she said. "The rivers are very high at the moment; all this rain…" She looked out of the window, towards the river in the distance. I then told her it had been quite challenging fording the rivers and I told her the battles I had had crossing the Fossá and the Laxá. She looked at me with her cerulean blue eyes and said bluntly, "Well you are not crossing the next river. It is far too dangerous. It is too deep and fast flowing. There is too much rainfall, and more is coming tonight. You look exhausted. Tomorrow I will take you across in my car, so you will be all right." This statement of intent had been delivered with such a rush, with no possibility of negotiation, however I wavered a moment.

She noted my reticence and repeated insistently, "The river is too deep for you to cross safely. I shall take you across tomorrow. " I was quite taken aback with her acute concern for my welfare.

"I'm very grateful," I said. "That's so kind of you."

"While you are here you will have to eat our food," she instructed. Now I had been expecting to eat my rehydrated chicken curry that night, so any offer of fresh food was not going to be refused.

"I'll eat whatever I'm given," I said, trying not to appear over-enthusiastic.

"And while you're here, you are my guest," she continued. "You do not have to pay." I was astounded, almost perplexed, at her generosity. I was not used to such kindness. Why should she want to help me, a mere stranger? I struggled to reply. In the end I think I just stood there and mumbled an indistinct note of gratitude, but inside my heart was screaming, "Thank you!" at the top of my voice.

Margrét explained that she was in charge of a group of horse riders who had trekked across country from her farm south of Geysir, some fifty kilometres away. The trekkers were supported by four staff also on horseback, who ensured the group stayed together. Margrét and one other followed on in the support vehicle. The riders were sleeping in the hut tonight, before returning to the farm the following day. Margrét was driving the vehicle carrying all the food supplies and equipment.

Helgaskáli itself was a shepherds' hut. Before it was constructed, shepherds used to come up from the valleys to round up the sheep for winter. This used to take several days and the shepherds would camp out in all weathers, while the sheep were gathered. Eventually Margrét's father, a shepherd himself, decided to build a purpose-built hut to house the shepherds in somewhat greater comfort than they had been used to, making their task less onerous generally. In time, the hut also came to be occupied by riding parties during the summer, so it saw plenty of usage, which was laudable.

As she spoke I noticed that Margrét did not stop working. She was preparing the meal for that evening. She was a very efficient, industrious and matter-of-fact woman with perceptive eyes. She struck me as someone who did not suffer fools gladly and procrastination was not in her mind-set or vocabulary. With that she disappeared outside, while I sat at the table drinking my coffee. As I did so, an almighty wave of fatigue enveloped me. This had been one hell of a day and my body now simply wanted to slump and unwind. I thought about the River Fossá and the extremes I had put myself through. I was pleased with my achievements today. I had learned that I could overcome my fears and deal with extreme situations, on my own. That was important to me. I did it on my own.

A door opened and in walked a group of people who looked as if they had spent a day outdoors in the wild, like me: windswept and battered. These were the pony trekkers, but when I used this term, I was quickly admonished and informed that Iceland has horses, not ponies. Well they looked like ponies to me, but I didn't mind being corrected. The group were quite vociferous to start with and when they saw me, they looked on intriguingly, wondering who on earth I was, until Margrét sprang to my defence and informed them that I was an English solo trekker walking across Iceland. Immediately, an American called Daniel struck up a conversation. Daniel looked remarkably like Paul Simon, the singer of Simon and Garfunkel fame and I commented on this to him. Others around then also saw the likeness and burst out laughing. They knew exactly what I meant because his resemblance to the American pop star of yesteryear was uncanny. An Icelandic man named Bjarni, with a quirky frizzy hair style, came and sat opposite. He was a graphics designer and cartoonist who worked for the television station in Reykjavik.

We all swapped stories about our life styles and experiences and before we knew it, dinner was ready. I wondered what food would be replacing my chicken curry. I need not have worried because over the next hour or so we were treated to hunks of reindeer, slices of goose, a pot of stew, salad, mushrooms, exquisite tasting potatoes and mixed vegetables. What a feast! I could not believe my luck! There comes a point when trekkers' noodles, chocolate raisins and cashew nuts don't quite hit the button. This meal certainly did. As for the reindeer, well I'm sorry Rudolph, Dasher, Donner and Blitzen, but you'll have to be watching your backs every Christmas Eve from now on, in more ways than one, for your kind tasted delicious.

Dessert was, amusingly, reindeer cut into little cubes and accompanied by shots of vodka. It wasn't long before a bottle of Cognac was passed round. Everyone relaxed and we shared entertaining anecdotes. My feet were still terribly cold and in the end I had to go and find the driest pair of socks I could muster and put on my river shoes, which thankfully, had now dried out in front of the wood burning stove.

Margrét told me something about herself. She ran riding tours with Sigmundur, one of the four men I had seen at the beginning. They had been organising tours here since the middle of June, when the snow had melted. She also helped out with rounding up the moorland sheep when summer was over, and moving them to lower pastures before the harshness of winter set in. She told me that her other job was as a manager for a fish-drying factory in Fludir, south-west of here. They processed stockfish which was sold to Nigeria. Margrét seemed to be a very busy lady. I liked her. A no-nonsense – just get on with it approach to life. She suggested that the following day I could join the group on their riding tour, but I declined. On any other trip I would seriously have considered it, however my sole objective remained to walk to Reykjavik.

The bottle of Cognac was Jonas's. He was a middle aged man, weathered in appearance and who apparently worked on the whale watching boats in Reykjavik. He struck me as the sort who did not say much in a social situation, preferring to stay in the background listening, but yet he missed nothing. He appeared to have worked everyone out and I wondered what he thought of me.

An attractive blonde woman called Kristina sat opposite me. She was Daniel's half-sister and she struck me to be very much an avant-garde character, not your typical thoughtful, considered Icelander. I taught her how to play the individual card game of Patience. We shared a lot of laughs and generally the evening flew by, a welcome and much needed distraction from the stresses of the day. The evening concluded with a glass of liquorice wine, something of an acquired taste.

At midnight, we all retired to our beds and I squeezed into my tiny bunk in a room containing four other beds. In the adjoining room there were eight more people all sleeping in bunks. This is what sleeping on a submarine would feel like, I mused, with no room to swing the proverbial cat. I drifted off to sleep. Sleep throughout my trip had been a difficult affair. The ever-present daylight made sleep awkward because my brain was always telling me, "It's not dark, idiot! Don't go to bed yet!" Furthermore, the sound of the wind flapping around my tent and the incessant rain hammering away on the rip-stop nylon, created a cacophony of noise designed to keep even the beautiful princess in Sleeping Beauty wide awake. Anyway, tonight I was determined to make up for my lack of sleep over the previous fortnight by getting plenty of zeds, especially having become ever so slightly intoxicated with all the alcohol...

Fat chance! Around 2.30am, I was awoken by a deep rumbling that reverberated violently around the small bedroom, shaking my bunk bed from side to side. Initial confused thoughts included:

We'd been hit by a torpedo (I was still suffering from submarine delusions);

Mount Hekla had finally erupted with an overfull magma chamber and we were all about to die;

Rudolph the red-nosed reindeer had gathered his cronies to pull Santa's sleigh over our hapless bodies as a form of revenge for having the temerity to eat some of his friends;

But no, it was none of these. It was Jonas, the whale man, who was giving it plenty in the snoring department, only it didn't sound like snoring in the traditional sense of soothed wheezing and gentle whining; this was full-blown, bronchial rattling, a sort of desperate seismic emission of viscid mucous and phlegm, that reverberated unpleasantly in Jonas's throat then subsided for all of half a second, before returning on a tidal wave of explosive throaty discharge. Not pleasant to visualise and certainly not pleasant to listen to.

I became convinced Jonas was dying, or about to die. I have seen animals on the verge of expiring make more humane noises than these. Occasionally he would pause and the room would be silent. I thought, "He's died. Such a pity, but at least we can all get some sleep," then he would surprise us all with a sudden resurgent, distasteful sound of throat-filled bile and sputum that induced in listeners, me included, a severe sense of nausea and the need to commit suicide.

This dreadful racket continued all night and all attempts I made to nullify the din – placing my hands over my head and burying my face in my pillow - were defeated. Totally exasperated, I finally climbed out of my bunk at 6am and retreated to the dining room, the scene of such jollity and merriment just a few hours previously. I now felt like death, in need of some somnolent therapy. I think I actually snoozed, with my head resting on my arms, face down, on the table. I also made a mental note to stab Jonas quite cruelly when he woke up.

18. Can't see the Wood for the Trees

If you get lost in an Icelandic forest, simply stand up and you will find your way – Icelandic Proverb

Helgaskáli – Tungufell 16.8 mls

People started dragging themselves up after eight, Bjarni the first to appear. Of Jonas there was no sign, so I folded my polar bear knife away for a short while and decided to delay my moment of savage retribution. Strangely no one else seemed to have been affected by Jonas's raucous respiratory eruptions; perhaps Icelanders are used to such seismic activity, but not me!

Breakfast was typical Icelandic fare – yoghourt of different varieties, meats, bread, oats, granola and lumpy milk – you know, the sort of milk you leave on the doorstep too long in hot weather and it turns into foul smelling cheese. That was on offer at the breakfast table and I unwittingly poured it onto my cereal. I nearly retched and gagged for I don't do lumpy, whiffy milk. All of a sudden I had no appetite, so I consoled myself with a couple of slices of bread and ham; the consequence of failing to eat sufficiently would come back to haunt me later in the day.

I had to wait a long while for Margrét to sort out the riders and it was nearly midday before we left Helgaskáli. I sat in the back of her 4x4 and we followed behind the horses before they headed for the hills and instead we followed a stony track, for a short distance. The next river, the Leirá, was indeed substantial and deep and I was so glad Margrét had offered to give me a lift across. The water was tumbling and crashing, and our vehicle roared and revved against the rage of the river, which indeed was deep and menacing. Crossing this obstacle safely would have been hugely difficult, if not impossible for me. I shuddered. What would I have done if Margrét had not have been there to stop me, back at the hut? I thanked God for small mercies, gripping the seat tightly, as I watched the water swirling high around the sides of the vehicle. Almost one river too far, I surmised. Once across, she pulled up on the embankment and looked back at me. I looked back at her - connecting. She knew what I had been thinking and I knew that she knew. Lord, I was so lucky she was around: my blue-eyed guardian angel. No words were said in this respect: there was simply no need.

She dropped me the other side of the river, and I thanked her, totally indebted to her. Me, a random trekker from England, had been so fortunate to encounter Margrét, a lovely, deeply generous, deeply remarkable woman! Her kindness, like Benedikta's, back in Seydisfjordur, almost overwhelmed me. I was finally realising just how considerate some people can be and I was truly humbled.

I climbed out of the 4x4, waving as she disappeared over the rise. The sound of the engine faded, until it was now just me and the power line track once more. I was on my own again. I now had to complete the power line walk and reach the junction with R349 above Gullfoss. Navigation was easy following the pylons, but I still consulted my GPS, basically to ascertain how far I had been walking. I placed it back in my inside pocket of my jacket and got underway. It was a bit of a pull for the next five miles, as I battled manfully onwards, all uphill and repetitive, in fact I was desperately willing the track to reach the junction and the respite of a downward stretch.

Eventually it did and I cheered quietly to myself as the road junction, defined by an ageing blue signpost indicating "Hrunamannaafréttur, þhórsárdalur and Linuvegur" to the south. My map did not include any of these unpronounceable names however I was totally confident I was in the right place, so I stopped to take a photograph of the signpost on my mobile phone, pointing the way to go towards Gullfoss. I drank a glug of water in celebration and then reached inside my jacket for my GPS, to see how far I had walked. It was not there. I checked again but it had gone. My heart sank. I now felt exactly how I had felt when my camera had disappeared and started chiding myself at my bloody stupidity, yet again! I knew exactly what had happened of course. Instead of placing my GPS in my inside jacket pocket, I had simply missed and put it down outside the lining of my jacket, where it had fallen on to the road.

"Bugger!" I shouted, acutely annoyed at my incompetence. Actually, it was not surprising that I had made such a basic mistake really, because my lack of sleep the night before caused by the Jonas Volcano, meant I was walking with my head in a daze, not thinking clearly at all. A simple mistake and now I was GPS-less. I wandered in a couple of circles wondering what to do, but I knew what I had to do; I had no real choice - so I headed, cursing my own ineptitude, back the way I had come, to retrieve the bloody thing. I did not want to lose it, for my GPS had accompanied me on every walk throughout my training regime and I had become rather attached to it. I didn't really need a GPS on this trek, because route-finding up to this point, had generally been fairly straight forward... if you ignore the incident trying to find the mountain road in the fog, on day four.

After an hour or so, retracing my steps, I spotted my GPS lying forlornly on the track, its yellow and black colouring making it fairly conspicuous. I dusted it down, switched it on to check it still functioned, and then set off back again, once more uphill, following the same blasted power lines. Such a needless waste of time and energy I thought, after such a basic mistake.

A couple of hours after I had first discovered I had lost my GPS, I returned to exactly the same spot and paused for a drink. I was not in the best of moods now, however as I turned left onto a rather stony and bumpy R349, I could see over to the right of the track the unmistakable spray cloud of Gullfoss, the jewel in Iceland's waterfalls on the Hvitá River, drifting high into the sky. What a sight! My intention was to follow R349 and look for a camping site towards Tungufell, but as I neared Gullfoss, I thought I might just drop down to the waterfall and view it more closely from the wrong side, in other words, the side not usually visited by tourists, who gather in their hundreds on the opposite bank.

This was to prove a big mistake, the biggest mistake of the entire trek. I left the road and headed across the mossy vegetation, which proved as usual, difficult to negotiate with a heavy pack, a bit like the thufur of earlier days. Various water hazards presented themselves and I had to keep changing course and direction. Gullfoss, which had appeared close, now proved frustratingly elusive. After messing around in the moss and the marsh for half an hour, and getting precisely nowhere, I changed my mind and decided I would give Gullfoss from this side, a miss, and instead head back to the road. The only problem was, I could not find the road. I knew where it should be but it had hidden itself somewhere. I was also becoming quite hungry. My lack of a decent breakfast was now starting to catch up with me, and I wearily picked my way over various bumps and rises trying to get back to where I should have been.

At last I found it, not a road in the traditional sense, basically a rocky track and once more I headed south-west, somewhat tired and sticky. At the same time, the sun surprisingly appeared, for the first time that day. After twenty minutes or so, a metal gate appeared across the route saying "Private Road. No entry". I was taken completely aback by this because this suggested I was actually not on R349, but a different road, unmarked on my map. Swearing slightly, I headed away from the river. I knew the real road must be around here somewhere, but where? I encountered some more awkward marshy stuff, so I climbed a rocky slope and headed upwards. I knew if I kept on this bearing, I would eventually hit the real R349 again. The trouble with this idea was the terrain kept rising and, without really realising it, I was headed up to the top of a very substantial hill. Upon arriving at the top, I looked around and said,

"What the hell are you doing up here?" I was so annoyed with myself because, I'd gained height unnecessarily and now I was on the crest of a long rocky ridge. The route down looked quite steep so I headed westwards along it, hoping the slope would ease off. Not a chance, in fact the further I travelled along the ridge, the steeper the descent off it became, and still there was no sign of the road. I was becoming increasingly hot, bothered and frustrated with myself for creating extra effort when all I wanted to do was to make camp and have something to eat. I had eaten very little all day, what with losing my GPS and now I was starting to fall into food and energy deficit.

It's funny how decision making is affected by tiredness; how quickly one deteriorates when hungry and fatigued, but I now started to make some very dubious navigational choices, insane really. As the ridge ran out, I found myself to be atop a small plateau of rock with steep descents all round. The only way down was a tricky scramble. Normally this would be fairly straight forward, however carrying a top-heavy pack meant this descent would be fraught with risk

"This is not a good place to be!" I shouted, sensing the danger. "Where's the road?" My voice cracked with emotion, and I felt decidedly uneasy. The only option was either to retrace my steps of the last hour, or scramble down the slope, rather precarious and cliff-like in appearance. I absurdly chose the latter option and very slowly and carefully, picked my way down. My walking poles helped somewhat, but a couple of times, I slipped on the loose surface and almost fell. I paused to reflect and take stock. This was insane and the situation I now found myself in was totally farcical and ludicrous. I was livid with myself for being so stupid, endangering myself, for this definitely was not trekkers' territory. It was all so easy to hurt myself in this situation and I was really not adequately equipped for rock scrambling. The slope took me fifteen hairy minutes to descend; every downward tread something of a gamble. I prayed that my Vibram soles now performed to their potential, gripping the rock tight. I could not see the road, even at this height and I was totally bemused. Where had it gone? It was quite clearly marked on my map. I then started to doubt where my location actually was and thought instead I may somehow have avoided the road and reached the valley beyond. Ridiculous, but I definitely was not thinking clearly. I looked down and thought I saw a way through a forest of trees to the right. This was something of a surprise, because Iceland doesn't do forests, or trees in any number at all, but right here was a forest, and my irrational mind was telling me the way to go was right through the middle of it.

The forest was made up of bushes about ten feet high, quite dense and strangely intimidating. There was no actual route through them, so I just lumbered in, anxious to break through the other side, then onwards and downwards. As I did so, the light faded, casting an eerie gloom around me. Strange shadows and dark foliage now looked distinctly threatening, causing me to feel more uneasy and anxious. The branches kept snagging on my clothing and my rucksack, pulling me forcibly backwards. They snared repeatedly around my neck and head, so progress was slow in the extreme: laborious and painful. They brushed and scratched my face and my hands, leaving thin red traces in painful geometric shapes. One particular branch caught the corner of my eye leaving a stinging abrasion that stung intently. As a result, my eye watered continuously blurring my vision, which was the last thing I wanted at this juncture. It was so difficult getting anywhere so I stopped for a breather and looked around. So dense were the trees I could not see the route I had just followed into the forest. This was quite scary and intimidating because now I was completely immersed in dense foliage and moving forward, sideways or backwards was becoming harder and harder.

"This is not a good place to be!" I shouted again, with a greater panic in my voice. By now I was becoming utterly exhausted and every step I was trying to take to extricate myself from this sylvan morass, was proving fruitless. It took on the appearance of a Harry Potter-type forest with moving, spiteful trees grabbing at me, snatching cruelly, tripping me up and holding me down. I wandered increasingly frantically for over twenty minutes, snapping branches and twigs that lay across my path, shouting desperately, but all that was happening was I was becoming more and more disorientated and hysterical.

"This is not a good place to be!" became my agitated mantra as I became ever entangled and despairing. It was totally ludicrous that a forest of this nature should prove to be such a man-trap, but it so was and I was in serious trouble. There comes a point when things become so stacked up against you, that you give up completely, and I started to think that this desperate scenario was approaching, and fast. I was at the end of my tether – hungry, fatigued in the extreme, lost, making completely farcical decisions. I started to choke with emotion; my head was burning and I was behaving preposterously.

I reached a thicket beneath which was a ditch or ravine and the trees seemed to be growing from deep within it. The ditch was steep and there was muddy black water at its base. I could not release myself by going through the forest; it was too high to go over, so what about under it? Crazy, but different. The only problem was, once I climbed into the ditch, there was no guarantee I would be able to climb out of it again. I hesitated a few seconds, then went for it. I slid down, down into the murky trench pulling branches and knotted roots aside. Above me were the interwoven roots of these god-awful trees that reminded me of the submerged red mangroves that flourish in the Floridan Everglades. It looked like a tapestry from Hell, but one which I was to thread myself through, a reluctant needle piercing a deadly stubborn canvas. With a last throw of my dice, I launched myself across the ditch, half swimming half wading through the grim liquid that felt so cold and smelt distinctly odorous: stagnant, pine scented. I gasped for breath as I plunged across, barely in control, verging on hysteria. After about thirty seconds I had covered a matter of several metres, and then I attempted to climb the opposite bank – steep, slippery and initially it appeared almost impossible to scale. My pack then snagged on an overhanging branch and for one god-awful moment I could not turn round to free myself. I wriggled this way and that like a demented puppy, grunting and gasping with fear and exertion. It took a Herculean effort to tear the infernal branch from the trunk, but this I did and discarded it with fraught relief, aside of me. Panting with exhaustion, and choking back my tears, I scrambled up the bank and in a few desperate steps I was free! I lay on a clear patch of ground above the bank and laughed. God I laughed, but that had been such a close call.

"You bloody idiot"" I chastised myself. "What the bloody hell do you think you were doing?" I slapped my face with sheer annoyance, having made some of the most stupid, irrational judgements of my life. I sat up, breathless and looked ahead. I felt as if I had used up one of my nine lives. I was mentally shot to bits. Time to reassess what I was going to do next. I munched on my last remaining energy bar and paused a while, just sitting and reflecting.

Eventually I stood up and looked around. I then spotted a grey black ribbon snaking across the landscape down below, but at this distance, I could not tell if it was a road or a river. I prayed fervently that it was my road. Picking up my pack, I resumed my journey once more, somewhat chastened but mightily relieved to be back on rather more sensible terrain. Ten minutes later, the ribbon did indeed prove to be my elusive road, though where it had disappeared to for the last couple of hours or so, I had no idea. The wretched R349, a nondescript path of stones in central Iceland was now my saviour, my route back to sanity and security. I was so grateful, I almost wept.

As I stood on the hard crumbly track, I realised I had been taught a salutary lesson. Lack of food can rapidly lead to a massive decline in all your functions. It is so important to take on refreshment to sustain your body and your thought processes.

I now set off once more, desperate to find somewhere to camp; to rest up and take on food. I walked alongside a small stream until I came upon a few buildings that marked the tiny settlement at Tungufell. Here, situated quite quaintly on a small hummock, stood a tiny church, Tungufellskirkja, no bigger than a garage, next to which was a small cemetery. A man was tending the graves and he directed me to a convenient spot for my camp. He was the first person I had seen since I left Margrét, many hours earlier.

Within thirty minutes I was eating a much needed portion of pasta carbonara. I consumed three cups of coffee, opened my sleeping bag and fell fast asleep. It was now eight o' clock and I had walked far too many miles and made far too many stupid decisions for one day. I needed rest, to recharge my batteries and refocus my mind.

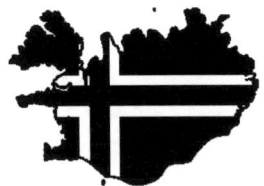

19. Tether's End

Always rise to an early meal, but eat your fill before a feast. If you're hungry you have no time to talk at the table - The Hávamál

Tungufell – Gullfoss 11.5 mls

I awoke to the sound of rain once more, pounding a staccato rhythm on my tent. The wind was also lively and my tent flapped vigorously in its wake.

"Great," I thought, "That's all I need." The weather throughout this trek generally had been quite disappointing with very few days without some precipitation, and when it did rain, it did not just drizzle, it pounded down. My kit that I had attempted to dry off in front of the wood burning stove in the mountain hut at Helgaskáli was still uncomfortably damp from the river crossings. I looked out from my tent and the rain was lashing down with a vengeance. Cooking was impossible, so the only food I had for breakfast was a packet of cashew nuts.

I broke camp as best I could in the conditions and set out once more into the grey gloom. The plan was to follow the Hvitá River to the junction with the R30, cross over the bridge and then pick up an old track leading to Hotel Gullfoss, where my next much needed food parcel awaited me. The distance was very moderate, a mere seven miles, and I hoped to pick up my food, head onto Gullfoss, then look for a campsite somewhere on the road to Geysir. All in all, quite an easy day when compared with the traumas of the previous two.

I knew however, within a mile or so of setting off, that something was wrong. The track was simple to follow, but I did not feel quite right. The weather did not help either as it battered me from all directions. It was horrendous, with unrelenting rain stinging my face and the wind trying to blow me to oblivion. I reached R30 and turned right, but I kept sighing deeply to myself and waves of lethargy and disinterest swept over me. Gritting my teeth, I headed for the bridge, a relatively modest affair and crossed the mighty Hvitá River thundering below. I had travelled a modest two miles or so. The road double-backed on itself and soon I saw the old Gullfoss road, branching off to the right, through an old farm gate. It was now just a matter of following this road up to Hotel Gullfoss. Simple. Probably the easiest route I had had to walk in days.

Only it wasn't, because I was all wrong. Every step I took became a chore and all I wanted to do was stop. What was up with me? I crested a slight rise and there, some miles in the distance, I could see the hotel. It wouldn't be long now, I told myself. I walked for an hour on a rutted and puddled stony track and then I looked ahead once again. The hotel did not appear to be any closer. This caused me a great deal of dismay, because it should have been within reach, so I battled on again for another half hour, but still the hotel remained a long way off. What was happening? My stride length became shorter and shorter until I was barely moving. I had no idea what was going on; all that I knew was, I was in trouble and I did not know why. My mind became so focused on the hotel that I could think of nothing else.

Hotel Gullfoss is a small hotel accompanied by one or two neighbouring houses and farm buildings standing in a very remote area to serve visiting tourists who want to see the magnificent waterfalls, two miles farther on. I could see its orangey roof, its white walls and its abundance of glass; it just would not come any nearer. Trance-like, I carried on, taking tiny footsteps that scrunched on the gravel. I stopped to rest for no apparent reason, then blithely continued, dragging myself forward, but still at the same snail-like pace. I felt a bit like a marathon runner who has hit the wall, and when you tell your body to get going, it quite simply refuses. My body wanted to work in slow motion, so that is precisely what it did.

I remember the track rising slightly and I also remember the large hotel windows facing me, behind which I could see tables and chairs in the restaurant. The track wound around the side of the hotel to a modest entrance with terracotta coloured doors above which was a sign saying "Hotel Gullfoss". I stood outside the hotel for a few moments, then pushed open a door which led into a foyer at the end of which was a reception desk, behind which sat a young woman. She looked at me, this bedraggled, soaked, unshaven, stinking specimen that had made an unsolicited entrance into a clean, sparkling upmarket hotel and looked somewhat taken aback. I rested on my walking poles and tried to speak but I could not. I just stood there. Silent. Shattered. My whole mind and body seized. She looked at me peculiarly.

After what seemed to be an age, I spoke.

"I think I need a coffee," I knew I was shot to bits. The woman looked puzzled, after all she was not used to vagrants wandering in, demanding a drink. Two other women now entered the foyer and they all stood around me in a semi-circle. I repeated my request for a coffee. No one moved. To break this impasse, I then said,

"Is Peter here? He has some food for me." This threw them somewhat, because I had erroneously given them the name of the manager of the hotel in Reykjahlid who looked after my food parcel, who was called Peter. The manager here was called Youenn. They now thought they were dealing with a deranged and hungry madman. We all stood looking at each other suspiciously, but I could not understand why no one was helping me. I was sure they were thinking of calling the police. I repeated, "Peter, he has my food parcel." They just looked confused. A girl emerged from the back and joined our group. They whispered amongst themselves for a while and then the new girl led me to a table, sat me down and gave me a drink of coffee. She then withdrew to the back and returned with a plate of food that I shovelled down with the minimum of decorum and etiquette, almost as if food was going out of fashion. My mother would have been ashamed, commanding:

"Chew your food completely before you swallow!" or "Don't put so much food in your mouth at one time!"

I didn't care; I was famished! The food tasted wonderful and it was all gone in less than five minutes. The girl re-emerged to say that the staff were about to partake of their lunch and would I like some? I nodded eagerly and, sure enough, a large bowl of asparagus soup appeared with crusty bread rolls. This too was consumed within an inelegant period of time, suggesting I did not stop for breath throughout.

It's amazing what a bit of sustenance does, because, within moments, I started to come to. I wiped some soup that had dribbled down my mouth, with my sleeve and fumbled in my pocket for a piece of paper. On this was Youenn's name.

"Oh," I mumbled, upon seeing my mistake. "Not Peter, Youenn. Youenn has my parcel." Everyone stopped, because they knew who Youenn was and this deranged fool was now starting to make sense. I showed the paper to the girl who had fed me, where Youenn's full name was typed.

"I posted a parcel here a month ago. Youenn knows all about it. It's a food parcel for me because I'm walking across Iceland." The girl, a German lass called Laura, pronounced ,"Low-ra-rhyming with Cow-ra"- now understood what was going on and smiled at me. "Thank you," I said, pointing to my empty plates. "I needed that."

"I know," she replied, "I could see you were done in." And that is precisely what it was. My body had quite simply run out of food, the culmination of two weeks expenditure of energy, too little food, too little water, too little salt and minerals, blood sugars lowered and my train had basically come off the rails. Thank God it happened here and not on my river walk. I thanked Laura again, and asked if there was a room here for the rest of the day. I did not want to go back out in the god-awful weather this day, or any day for that matter. Everything I owned was soaked and I needed to refresh and dry everything off.

A shower later and after several clothes' washes, everything was drying on the radiators in my rather pleasant and welcoming room. My boots and socks continued to stink to high heaven, so much so, you could smell the depressing whiff down the corridor. I opened a window wide, before I was thrown out.

The rest of the afternoon was spent recuperating, languishing in a warm bed with a soft mattress and fluffy pillows. Glorious! Mind, I was mentally exhausted and needed some 21st century conventionality. Meanwhile outside, the rain continued to lash down in a most unpleasant way. I asked Laura about the weather and she agreed it was and had been quite horrendous, and from talking with other Icelanders, exceptionally unseasonable. They felt they had not had a summer.

As for Youenn, well he was away on holiday and nobody knew where my food parcel was. I considered he may have taken it with him in a rare act of Icelandic duplicity…

The hotel was situated about two miles from Gullfoss, a short hop along the road, so I decided that evening to walk to Gullfoss, view the waterfalls and catch a meal in the café there. So, at eight o' clock I set off. This time I felt slightly more energised and up to the task, than earlier in the day, although I did take it steadily. Twenty minutes or so later, I arrived at an enormous car park. Once again, I could see the spray from the waterfall, like a mist curtain floating in the air. The weather, though improved, was still grey and distinctly murky and a fine rain made life quite unpleasantly damp.

The waterfall itself was magnificent. A spectacular cascade of the highest order, thirty two metres high with two drops. Even in the dull light of the evening, it was remarkably impressive. Tourist paths allowed me to get almost on top of the onrushing torrents, so its raw energy could be witnessed at very close hand. I was enthralled and spellbound in equal amounts." Gullfoss" means golden waterfall and I fully understood why it was given this name. The river it stands on, the Hvítá, meaning "white river" is the longest in Iceland at 185km. Below Gullfoss, it merges with other rivers to become the Ölfusá, doubling in volume and intensity. Here the water simply battered the banks and rocks as it crashed remorselessly downwards: alive, organic, nuclear.

I looked across to the opposite bank where I had found myself in so much difficulty twenty four hours earlier, losing the road and climbing the cliff. Such drama and distress literally no more than half a mile away. Here I stood, thoughtfully thanking my lucky stars for still being around. I shivered to shake the unpleasantness of the last few days from my mind, turned and headed for the café . It had been a testing day, an unpleasant day and one I would not forget very easily.

Gullfoss – the Golden Waterfall

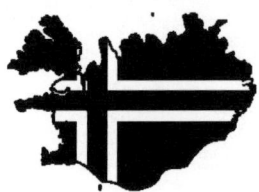

20. Spouting Poetry

His door already has the hard part of the journey behind him – Icelandic Proverb

Gullfoss – Geysir – Uthlid – Laugarvatn 24.5 mls

I made sure I had a good breakfast after the utter nonsense of the previous day. My food parcel I sent to Youenn was found, just before midnight. He had not digested its contents after all, whilst sunning himself on his hols, so he was now off the hook. I loaded my rucksack with its contents: more cashews, chocolate raisins, noodles and granola. I was becoming heartily sick of cashews, chocolate raisins, noodles and granola to be honest. I longed instead for shredded wheat and I was still totally obsessed with bread. My craving was bread was decidedly disturbing, to put it mildly.

Today was to be quite a moderate day, distance-wise. It was an easy walk to Geysir, the site of an frequently erupting hot spring, although Geysir itself, only erupts very occasionally today, leaving another smaller spout called Strokkur to take centre stage, to perform, to the delight of an enthralled audience on average, every ten minutes, disgorging a sudden jet of hot water and steam to a height of about thirty metres, though how you would measure it precisely, I had no idea.

I did not even have to leave the tarmacked road, so this was probably the easiest walking day I had had for quite a while. (Mind I had said that on a couple of occasions before!) The weather had improved overnight quite dramatically and the rain had thankfully stopped. What a difference it made not to have to bend into the teeth of a gale while being drenched right through. It lifts your whole mood and sense of well-being. I went to find Laura, and thanked her for helping me the previous day. I had asked her earlier how she knew something was wrong with me.

"I just knew," she said. "It is in my character to know."

I thought she must have seen the desperation, the hollowness in my eyes and made the connection that something was awry. Whatever it was, no one else noticed. It made me think back to Helgaskáli and Margrét. She too had looked at me as I approached the mountain hut and she too had realised I was in trouble, even though I did not seem to notice it myself. Female intuition? I was not sure. All I know was we connected; Margrét, and now Laura; both empathised strongly with me. It surely must have been the glaze over my eyes, I concluded. Perhaps I convey a look that says, "Help me!" when I am tired or under stress. Perhaps some people see more deeply into other's psyche. This had certainly been the case with Laura. Funnily enough, both Laura and Margrét had blue eyes. Now, it has come to be known that a single mutation which arose as recently as 6-10,000 years ago was responsible for all the blue-eyed people alive on Earth today, primarily those from Europe. Was there a common link, a common heritage between Laura and Margrét, my guardians, who had come to help me in these last few days, and they, in turn had connected with me?

I gave Laura a grateful hug and set off renewed, on my way once more. The walk to Geysir was very straightforward. I simply turned left out of the hotel

Laura, my guardian

and headed along a very straight road, that declined at a gentle angle, for two miles or so. Either side of the road, agricultural land with grazing horses and cows, reflected a minor seismic shift in land usage. Less lava, more soil and as I walked, the sun grew stronger, and as it did so, it felt as if someone had lifted a huge veil from me, so that my spirit of despond, so evident in recent days, evaporated and dispersed skyward. For the first time in a long while, I felt pleased with myself; free of the stresses of uncertainty; more energised and optimistic. It had been a long time coming! No more dangerous rivers! No more lava deserts!

The last leg of my walk – from Gullfoss to Reykjavik was hopefully to be the friendliest and easiest. This part of Iceland is the part mostly populated by its citizens and the nearer you get to Reykjavik, the greater the demographic density, in fact Greater Reykjavik itself is populated by 62% of the whole Icelandic population. I expected therefore to find it busier in terms of people, traffic and services. Tourism too, particularly around the "Golden Circle" of Gullfoss, Geysir and Thingvellir is particularly popular and prevalent. Strange to think that just two days earlier, I had walked from the mountain hut at Helgaskáli and seen practically no one all day.

As I walked, the sun decided to put in a rare appearance from between the clouds. I shouted, "Yes!" and punched the air. It had been a long time coming and hopefully it would hang around for a while. It gathered in strength and intensity. I wasn't used to having to squint because of the brightness, but I was not complaining, no, I certainly wasn't complaining!

As the road fell away, I suddenly saw a large white plume of steam diffuse into the sky about a mile and a half away. I knew immediately what it was. Against a backdrop of an imposing hillside, Strokkur was showing its mettle, spurting water skyward, some twenty metres or so. Even at this distance, it was wondrous to behold and my pace quickened. I could not wait to get there.

And get there I did, however I was confronted not only by a drastically striking water feature, but also, regrettably, by hordes of people, in fact more people than I had seen for what seemed an awfully long time, and I actually felt quite disturbed by this, quite uneasy, almost as if they were intruding on my world, on my patch so to speak. I held back hesitantly at first, my social skills having deserted me. I felt to be on edge, out of my depth, not feeling I could walk among them as they gathered in excited confusion around the base of the water spout. I felt highly conspicuous with my large rucksack, laden with all my essentials. I became self-conscious of my appearance for the first time – ridiculous really. They poured out of the many tourist buses in the car parks accompanied with cameras and tripods of every description. I, of course, did not have my camera, and I seethed once again at this unfortunate aberration. They stared at me as I approached, well it felt like they were staring at me. I just wanted to ignore their unwarranted scrutiny and remove my rucksack, which I perched on a nearby bench and went to stand expectantly at Strokkur's edge.

Waiting for a geyser to erupt is quite an exciting and unpredictable activity. You stand around full of anticipation and nervousness. As the square-shaped puddle of water heaves and pitches, it generates several false alarms, as it threatens to explode into the air, but then subsides once more, to an accompaniment of nervous giggling and laughter from the watching throng. You can wait a full ten minutes, watching the puddle churning and rolling in a mild agitated state, and when you least expect it, it bursts with a sudden detonation and a spritz of super-heated water and steam that soars like a jet into the air, right in front of you. The release from your nervous suspense as you duck out of the way of the descending, cooling water droplets, conjures instant cheers and whoops of laughter. You scream with delight and the whole charade is accompanied by a cacophony of hundreds of Japanese camera clicks and shutter releases. The falling spray then drains back into the square hole once more, a bit like an emptying bath, and the whole process begins again. There are not many better ways to spend ten minutes of your time.

After enjoying the geyser show for half an hour or so, I knew it was time to get going. Time to stop being a tourist and time to become a trekker once more. After all, Reykjavik was my true objective and that lay west of here, a hundred miles or so.

Stokkur

The sun continued to shine and I carried on along the tarmac road that cut a course through the farmland. Icelandic horses were now in great abundance in the fields in their various paint box shades such as: black, silver dapple, yellow dun and bay roan. They appeared to be a hardy breed, putting up uncomplainingly with the vagaries of this summer's unseasonably atrocious weather. They all possessed a calm temperament and a serene disposition. I watched them as they quietly fed and browsed on the thick grass beneath their hooves.

Aside from that, there was little to capture my attention. My thoughts drifted back home. I had sent various texts to family and friends and everyone responded with great enthusiasm and noticeable pride. They were following my progress through the GPS tracker locations I relayed to them on a daily basis using my Spot Satellite Tracker. Each night they received an updated precise location of my whereabouts and could even get an idea of the terrain I was walking in thanks to google maps satellite images. Brilliant technology that allowed me to connect with them.

Generally, this was a laid-back day. Occasionally I would come across a backpacker or two overladen with non-essentials for their journey. It never failed to amaze me the ridiculous loads backpackers will attempt to carry, expending energy as if it was going out of fashion. Huge rucksacks extending far above their heads, as they totter like drunken Quasimodo Friday-nighters, on an English city street. They looked like they were taking part in an enormous house clearance. One backpacker was carrying a radio of ghetto blaster proportions, clamped to his head like a bazooka. I simply asked myself, "Why?" Another was carrying a brass trombone, slightly battered and misshapen. Lord knows where he was going to play that, if indeed it was capable of being played. Not next to my tent, I hoped. My pack weighed anything from 18 to 20kg. Theirs weighed, I estimated, up to double that. I felt sorry for them, that no one had taken them aside before they started out and had a quiet word to leave all this superfluous stuff behind. They were going trekking, not attending an open-air pop concert, for God's sake. One trekker was struggling with a wooden elephant sculpture, strapped to his sleeping bag, probably something he'd picked up in town and now he was having to carry it everywhere with him, a mistake of pachydermal proportions if ever I saw one. Why would you want an elephant as a memento from Iceland? Myself? I would personally plump for a fluffy puffin. Souvenirs were definitely for the homeward stretch.

I was heading for Uthlid, a farm community next to an extensive lava field. There was a campsite here, opposite a golf course. Now I had noted this sporting oddity several times on my trek – that is, the sheer number of golf courses that exist right in the middle of an Icelandic nowhere. The one at Uthlid was not as remote as some, but I just wondered how the golfers coped with the vicious prevailing elements: the snow, the rain and yes, the wind.

I was reminded of a time I journeyed to Cyprus to the Greek occupied southern sector. A friend invited me to play golf at the RAF base at Akrotiri, on the south coast. Now I'm not much of a golfer, but I own a cheap set of clubs, and at the time, I used to hack my way round my local municipal golf course in Nelson, Lancashire in something like 110 strokes and felt very pleased with myself. Playing golf filled an afternoon, and for a while I became quite obsessed, morbidly so, in my frantic attempts to break a hundred. I never did; the closest being when I four-putted the last to make 101.

We arrived at Akrotiri as a slight breeze was blowing off the sea, well, not so much a slight breeze, more a full-blown gale. Already I was a little dubious as to how I would perform. The course consisted of quite barren, dusty fairways littered with evil-looking rocks and neglected sand bunkers. The greens themselves were a sight to behold; in fact, in Akrotiri, they did not call them greens, they called them "browns", due to the reason there wasn't a single blade of grass on them and were simply small plateaux of sand, bound together with engine oil, probably the aeronautical variety. A stench of kerosene accompanied every short putt for par. So different from the fragrant smelling, ornamental rhododendron bushes that line the course at the Augusta Masters, with their beautifully tended fairways. Here you were having to compete with sand, deeply impregnated with the equivalent of good ol' four star.

I remember I teed off at the fourth, with the wind whipping across the desert-like fairway ahead of me. My shot, a three iron, connected sweetly and flew like a bullet on a low trajectory, until the ball hit a protruding rock, half submerged in the sandy soil. It ricocheted with such force at right angles, across the fairway and into a dense copse of gorse, never to be seen again. Claiming a lost ball, I repeated the shot, with quite a degree of athletic finesse and a technique borrowed tentatively from Bernhard Langer, albeit in his later years, and exactly the same thing happened, different rock though. This time the ricochet hit another rock, strategically positioned for this very situation, sending the ball quite deliberately back in my direction, where it landed a short distance from my feet. I could have reached out and placed it in my pocket. Discreet gnashing of teeth was heard, followed by a less discreet, singular expletive. It was like playing in a shooting gallery or on a pinball machine.

On the ninth, another shot, a seven iron, soared high, dead straight and on line for the oily "brown", surrounded by bunkers, like hungry, expectant fledglings in a bird's nest, with mouths agape. The wind simply caught my ball, an unruly Frisbee, one-handed and carried it away into the sea, a distance of some ninety metres or more. The course was simply impossible to play. I think I got through eighteen golf balls, one for each hole, and an excessive amount of swearing. I was not invited to play again.

Now, I think playing in Iceland would be similar. A technically proficient shot would be rewarded with an inopportune ash cloud descending from a nearby volcano, stifling its velocity so the ball would drop into a bubbling pool of lava. Try chipping in from there! Shanks would disappear into unforgiving icy crevasses or saturated fields of thufur. Putts would be blown back past their point of origin much to the chagrin of the hapless players. Yet, these golf courses were springing up everywhere with locals playing 24 hour golf in summer, and at the last count, Iceland boasted over fifty golf courses situated across the country. As I considered what it would be like to play a nine iron from a bunker filled with black sand, at three in the morning, a sign indicating Uthlid Golf Course came into view, right next to the R35. This 9 hole, Par 35 golf course came into being in 2010. I wondered whether I should consider hacking my way round, but decided I had walked far enough already that day.

On the other side of the road was my turn off for the campsite, but my initial pleasure was dampened, as the reception block for the site lay at the top of a steep hill. This annoyed me greatly. Having walked twelve miles, all right, not the greatest distance, but a reasonable effort nevertheless, one does not expect to have to walk to the top of a hill in order to pay for the privilege to camp there for the night. I arrived sweating and breathless at reception and vented my spleen.

"Bloody hell," I complained. "Whose idea was it to build the reception right up here?" My question got short shrift and when I ordered a pizza from the adjacent café, it was distinctly average and cold.

"You can camp on the left hand side of the track," I was instructed. "Normally the tents go to the right, but because we've had so much rain, the field is rather boggy." This comment did not fill me with glee as I observed the modest pond in the middle of a water-logged field away in the distance, but I did as I was told and pitched my tent in the field on the left instead. This too was very soft and spongy, and I'm sure, during the night, my tent sank by several inches. It felt like I was sleeping on a water-bed or aboard a slowly descending submarine. My mood during the twilight hours became quite belligerent and cranky because a group of Danish girls in the tent next door decided to party, with absolutely no consideration for a serious, sleep-seeking backpacker like myself. I couldn't wait to leave the following morning. They continued their drunken revelry throughout the night shouting and singing seemingly unaware of the other campers roundabout. I fingered my polar bear knife stashed safely away in my trouser pocket from time to time, as my ire rose to breaking point, with the reckless thought to confront the Danish party-goers with a bit of cold British steel, however I decided I was heavily outnumbered and I would probably have had to flee the campsite minus all my belongings. Instead I seethed from one hour to the next, as the interminable night stretched on and on till breakfast time. I finally fell half asleep as a nearby cockerel announced the start of a new day.

I awoke feeling quite groggy and irritable due to my nocturnal interruptions. The Danish revellers were now silent and rather annoyingly, fast asleep. I crashed about loudly on purpose, bashing my two camping pots together as a vocal protest to their anti-social behaviour. The sky was very grey and the whole scene quite subdued. I dug into my rucksack and found a dehydrated meal called "Expedition Breakfast". This raised my spirits somewhat as it would make a change to my usual miserly portion of granola. I was expecting it to consist of dehydrated bacon, dehydrated egg, sausage, baked beans, a mushroom or two and maybe a slice of dried tomato – that sort of thing. I could almost smell the aroma of bacon fat pervading the morning breeze. What I got however was not a dehydrated version of a full-English breakfast, but a portion of rather stodgy, insipid porridge, laced with pieces of stale apple. It resembled something normally emitted by drunken revellers after a late night boozing, Danish style. I was singularly dismayed, if not a trifle hacked off, by this unfairness. It tasted foul and I gagged upon every other mouthful. This was not a good start to my day. I continued to crash my rucksack about and I also turned on my pocket radio. I had brought this along to listen to, in my quiet, reflective moments. Right now, I was going to be anything but bloody quiet and reflective, as I picked a piece of dried apple peel from between my teeth. The only stations I could pick up were Icelandic ones playing pop from the 1970s, when Mungo Jerry, Donny Osmond and Lieutenant Pigeon were at their peak. Anyway, I turned this on as loudly as I dared, with Carl Douglas belting out "Kung Fu Fighting" - summing up my mood somewhat - facing it towards the Danish tent, while I decamped at a gentle, somewhat sedate pace and then set off, singing Rolf Harris songs at the top of my voice.* I was headed for the town of Laugarvatn thirteen miles away.

Laugarvatn stands in an active geothermal area and historically became well known as the place where Icelandic chieftains were baptised, preferring being dunked in the pleasantly warm waters of the hot springs located there, rather than the distinctly chilly waters of Thingvellir, home of the Icelandic government. Otherwise, Laugarvatn's claim to fame is being a staging post between Geysir and Thingvellir, as tourists journey in their thousands each year round Iceland's most famous natural attractions.

This was to be another easy day and as I walked, like yesterday, the sun got brighter and stronger. The scenery was also similar; wide agricultural land with even more contented grazing horses and cows; extensive views to the south and imposing hills to the north. As I walked I was becoming aware of a gradual increase in the number of flies buzzing around me, to such an extent I had to put my head mesh on, for the first time since Kidagil.

It was not long before I approached a large aluminium chimney with steam belching profusely from it. This was the geothermal area of Reykjavegur. Basically, the heat within the earth's crust heats subterranean water, which is then piped into homes as a cheap form of energy. It is used also to heat swimming pools as very many Icelandic villages have their own naturally heated outdoor saunas.

* The reputation of Rolf Harris was still untarnished at this time.

Not a bad form of compensation for living in a place which is dark over half the year. I did not stop because I wanted to reach Laugarvatn as soon as possible, and it was not long before I could see the small settlement, two miles distant.

Unfortunately, the road at this point swept in a wide arc away to the right and Laugarvatn was actually still over seven road-walking miles away, a distance that took me more than two hours to cover.

On the way there, just out of Uthlid, with my irritation at the Danish party revellers still very fresh, I heard voices behind me, so I glanced back over my shoulder, to see if the angry throng were pursuing me, adopting kung fuish stances, riled beyond reason for having been woken up, but to my surprise, I saw no one. I shrugged my shoulders and continued.

Three miles down the road, I could once more hear someone behind me, talking away. I could not quite discern what they were saying , but their tone was calm, rather than agitated, as if they were having a discussion. Again, I looked back but no one was there. Mystified I carried on, but the voices ceased so I thought nothing more about it. Another ten minutes or so later though, I could hear them again, not distinctly but definitely voices, so I stopped, scoured the road behind me, the fences, the ditches, the trees, but nothing. Now I knew I had walked a long way, but I was now hoping I wasn't starting on the road to insanity, and the arrival of the men in white coats to cart me off to the funny farm, but I could clearly detect someone speaking. I could not tell what they said, but they were saying something. I shook my head and immediately the voices disappeared. I put it down to my age. Or over-exertion; something like that. Ah, life in my sixties promised to be exciting, if I was going to hear voices at regular intervals. At least I would not be lonely, I thought reassuringly. Actually loneliness had been an unwelcome factor on this walk. Before I set off, I considered that I would have very little time to feel alone. Basically I would walk all day, then have my tea, after which I would collapse exhausted in my tent, sleep the night away and get up somewhat refreshed, ready to start all over again. Unfortunately, this was a very simplistic and rather short-sighted view of how I would fill the evening hours. I actually had come to dread the evening. I was happy enough spending the day walking for hours at a time. Placing one foot in front of the other, mile after mile, was enough to pre-occupy me and prevent feelings of loneliness rearing their ugly head. When I was cooking for myself, washing up, carrying out menial tasks, I still did not feel lonely, however when I had done all that and finished for the day, I was faced with a massive void of several hours before I went to sleep, which came to be a terrible obstacle for me to overcome.

Quite simply, I found my own company insufficient to bear; I craved company and social interaction of some description. I needed my daily fix of exchanging platitudes with anyone who would humour me. I typed for hours on my word processor, consulted my maps so that I knew by heart every last detail and contour. I listened to my i-pod nano but now the battery was running low and I had barely enough power left to listen to the remainder of my Mark Knopfler tracks. What I tended to do was to go to bed early, but if I could not sleep, I just lay there, in my yellow-lined nylon bubble, feeling detached, distant, desolate. All thoughts became exaggerated and a trough of despond became a nightly feature. This occurred almost from day one of my trip, and it was something I found increasingly difficult to deal with. Funny to think that I had trained sufficiently to walk the long distances, but how on earth do you prepare for solitude? I had no idea. Thankfully, once I fell asleep, even if it had only been fitful, I was able to bounce back each morning eager to take on the challenges of the new day. But that summed me up to a tee. I had always been a morning person. My batteries always ran down as the sun lowered. Perhaps I should have lived in more historic times, when, as the darkness came, everyone went to sleep.

Anyway, it was not night time, it was early afternoon. As I reached Laugarvatn, I was aware of the increase in traffic volume and a great increase in traffic noise as tyres rumbled over tarmac, after all this was the main tourist route to Geysir and Gullfoss. A chic café lay to the left with my campsite opposite to the right. The reception area was thankfully situated at ground level, very un-Uthlid-like and the campsite consisted of neat rows of raised grass terraces. I chose a location away from other tents but not so far away from the shower block and pitched my tent. I then showered, partook of lunch at the chic café and relaxed. God, I was acting like a damned tourist!

One Hilleberg tent and the contents of my rucksack

Having time on my hands, I wandered into an art gallery next to the campsite and quickly struck up a conversation with its proprietor, Jon and his partner. There also was an American here too, a musician, who had come here to write musical scores based on Iceland's natural aura and energy. Jon, apart from running this gallery, was also a teacher who worked here in his holiday breaks, converting a former hotdog establishment into a place that exhibited vivid Icelandic landscapes and creative, thought-provoking sculptures. Apparently workshops were run here for artists from all over the world. This was a place in which they could absorb themselves in the raw beauty of this wonderful land of ice and fire.

I mentioned to Jon that I had been given an Icelandic poem earlier in my trek and I wondered if he could translate it for me. The poem was given to me when I stopped at the mountain hut at Helgaskáli, the place where I so enjoyed the reindeer banquet. Jon was happy to oblige and we spent an enjoyable, laugh-filled half hour deciphering a little piece of Icelandic literary culture.

The poem went:

> *Undir fellinu er friðsæll klettur*
> *Þar fellur hún Laxá í hyl*
> *Þar er fáskrýddur fjallmannaklettur*
> *Og fossandi brennivínsgil.*

Which roughly means:

> *Under the mountain there is a tranquil river*
> *Where the River Laxa runs deep.*
> *Here simple shepherds stay*
> *Drinking the waters of the waterfall.*

I had been curious to know what it had meant, having carried it with me for so many miles since Helgaskáli and I was grateful to Jon for enlightening me. Simple words conveying a simple message, definitely not of the calibre of Wordsworth, but quaint nevertheless.

I now returned to my tent and reflected on the past week. My trek had evolved and was now vastly different in nature to the trek I had set out upon way back in Seydisfjordur. Gone were the challenges of the moors and the mountains. Gone were the river crossings. Instead the challenges were about mileage, about distance. It was now just a matter of following the road to Reykjavik and it was here that I would eventually be met by my family. It seemed to be an age since I left them back home, many, many miles ago. I wondered what they were doing and how they were coping with my absence. I had received one or two texts from my wife but generally there was scant communication between us. Swiftly my mind switched to other thoughts. I considered what lay ahead on my journey. The only real obstacle in my way was Thingvellir, itself a National Park and the last real wilderness to confront me before the finish. I was looking forward to reaching there the very next day.

That evening I walked into Laugarvatn, a small town made up of several hotels and schools. For its size, Laugarvatn had a surprising number of facilities including a petrol station, several restaurants and a supermarket. I treated myself to a pizza, that tasted delightful. Fast food had never tasted so good! This was followed by an apple pie pizza for dessert, A weird gastronomic concoction and a dietary excess I somewhat regretted, later on.

After a lazy day, I retired to my bed. Unlike most people who take their clothes off to go to sleep, bedtime for me involved getting dressed, in order to prevent the coldness of the ground penetrating my underwhelming sleeping bag and keeping me awake through the small hours.

On my top half I wore my base layer, usually not the soaking wet and sweaty one I had worn throughout the day, but rather my spare one, usually slightly damp and festering. I then put on top of this a somewhat whiffy midlayer that had not been washed since... well since April, I think. On top of this I wore my two insulating tops purchased in Egilsstadir, followed by a duvet type jacket. On my head I wore a woolly hat, that also smelt slightly rancid, but I reckoned better to have a warm head and reek a bit, rather than stay awake all night. On my lower half, I wore a pair of grey long johns which kept my bottom and legs warm and on my feet I wore a pair of inner socks and my remaining pair of walking socks. Over my sleeping bag, I usually draped my jacket and any other clothes I was not wearing. The consequence of wearing all this night garb was, I found it difficult to move or turn over, but at least it did keep me warm.

As I shuffled about in my sleeping bag trying to get comfortable, blow me down, I thought I heard the faint sound of talking, similar to the voices I had heard earlier in the day. I froze, because I knew there was no one near my tent, but there it was again. Damn! I was clearly hearing voices in my head. Was I going mad? I knew I had talked a lot to myself lately, but that was because I had no one else to talk to. When you are stuck in the middle of a lava desert, miles from human habitation, you do tend to strike up quite a conversation with yourself, sometimes quite animatedly. Well, why not? The voices continued: soft, calming, unequivocal.

"It's completely normal," I convinced myself aloud. "You are not going mad, you're just rather tired and a tad lonely." As I thought this, the voices persisted, almost joining in my conversation; gentle whispers intoned in a soothing, relaxed style. I felt anything but soothed or relaxed. I was now on the steep, slippery slope to insanity, skiing my way to certification. This was not a healthy situation to be in.

"I'm not going mad," I said defiantly, but I felt rather uneasy, to the extent I broke out into a clammy sweat. I giggled a trifle hysterically and tried to ascertain exactly what the voices were saying. Not English voices definitely. No Queen's English, that was for certain. I wondered if the apple pie pizza, containing bits of cinnamon, had anything to do with it. "That's it!" I thought. "The pizza! Cinnamon always did disagree with me. Perhaps it was off! But I instinctively realised that eating iffy food did not result in you hearing persistent noises in your head, so I lay there quite agitated, nervously laughing one minute; at my wits' end, the next. Not one to simply do nothing in a crisis, I decided action was required so I thought it a good idea to take a paracetamol, to cure my dire state of malaise. It was either that or one of the antibiotics I had brought with me in case of toothache. Trouble was, it was not my teeth that needed relief, but my brain, now clearly on the path to rack and ruin. Hands shaking, I sat up and rummaged through my rucksack for my first aid bag. As I did so, my pocket radio, the one I had turned on to awaken the noisy Danish that morning, tumbled out and from it, very faint voices were forthcoming, dulcet tones in unrecognisable Icelandic.

"You bugger," I cursed. "Worried me there for a minute, you bloody did," and I turned the volume control to "Off" with an abrupt click. "You're seriously losing it, you twit," I admonished myself. "Jesus, you're a TWIT!" I shouted, waking up half the campsite. Dogs began to bark and babies started to cry, but I didn't care a jot. My sanity was still intact. Heaving a huge sigh of relief, that Alzheimers had been put on the back burner for a little while longer, at least for the next year or two, I snuggled into my sleeping bag, and thought tomorrow is another day.

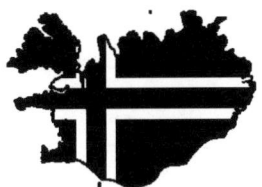

21. Lord of the Flies

More flies mean more food – Icelandic Proverb

Laugarvatn – Thingvellir 16.8 mls

The Chironomid Midge measures up to 2cm and is often mistakenly, although understandably so, confused with a mosquito. It has a slim dark body and usually likes to rest its forelegs in front of its head, similar to the posture of a footballer celebrating a goal. Fortunately it is non-blood-sucking and therefore does not bite, preferring instead to nibble, defaecate and lick. It frequents freshwater habitats including lakes, rivers, ponds and temporary pools, especially, vindictively so, the Icelandic ones, all along my blasted route of travel. O yes, it also had a tendency to hitch a ride on my sleeves with all its friends, taking part in an insect version of "Strictly Come Dancing", stomping out the beat to a cover version of "I believe I can fly", sung by Midge Ure, and, where possible, walking around on my stubbly face, uninvited, completely exasperating me in a exo-skeletonly, plaguey sort of way.

This annoying arthropod does not taste particularly pleasant, but consumption of this creature is, I'm afraid, quite inevitable. Crossing Iceland, it had a suicidal tendency to fly banzai-like into my mouth, uttering a final, frantic buzz of doom, at annoyingly regular intervals. Whilst I appreciated its undoubted protein content, it often stuck stubbornly at the back of my throat, tickling my uvula and causing me to convulse and choke violently, making ingestion of said midge, somewhat of a dispiriting and quite unpleasant chore. Unsolicited visits up my nose resulted in me sneezing frenetically, shaking my head and waving my arms moronically, like a whirling Dervish who has surreptitiously inhaled too much sherbet powder. The latter half of my Icelandic transverse was dominated by the inopportune and unwelcomed arrival of planet's entire population of the Chironomid Midge. I am not one to make enemies, however half a day with these minute brutes changed my outlook quite severely. Exploration of my ears was a pastime it undertook with sadistic relish, and subsequent temporary deafness an outcome that was frankly, bloody aggravating! It shared the same sadistic sense of humour with the notorious Scottish Black Fly and it probably had its own bleeding facebook page and twitter account. It was precisely at 9.30am on Day Eighteen that I encountered the Chironomid Midge along with at least seven billion of its irritating little bastard friends.

I had come across some other pesky flying insects previously, whilst wild camping next to Kálfborgarávatn, east of Kidagil, perhaps distant cousins of the Chironomid. Back then, I avoided too much conflict by dextrous use of my head mesh and precision swatting with my hands. But here, in Laugarvatn, the wretched critters came with such purpose, such evil intent, that my life was made a misery at the outset.

After a good night's sleep, I breakfasted at the chic café over the road from the campsite. Here I spoke with a charming American who had himself completed several long distance treks. We compared notes on crossing deep rivers and I was impressed with his knowledge and know-how. Following a substantial continental breakfast, I set out for Thingvellir, fifteen miles or so away. Almost immediately, squadrons of flies descended on me en masse, so I quickly pulled out my mesh to thwart the little blighters.

Laugarvatn is home to several large hotels and I passed quite a select one, the Héradsskólinn Boutique Hostel, before reaching a roundabout from which branched a brand new thoroughfare, in fact it looked so new the tarmac was probably still hardening. R365 was to lead over an isolated highland route towards the largest lake in Iceland, Thingvallavatn. Initially the climb away from Laugarvatn was quite steep and unrelenting, as I slogged up it accompanied by my own personal midgy cloud of fluttering disciples. The road swept upwards in a protracted curve, a parabola onto an expanse of uninhabited heathland. I had been travelling for twenty minutes or so, when a car pulled alongside me. It was my American breakfast friend.

"Would you like a lift?" he shouted, temptingly.

"No," I yelled back, "I wouldn't."

"Why not?" he asked, in his American drawl grinning away, already knowing the answer.

"Because I haven't walked all this way to start cheating now," I explained.

"You mean, you will not compromise your principles and climb into my car?"

"No, I bloody won't, so sod off."

We both laughed and he roared off into the distance. Actually it would have been quite tempting to hitch a ride, because the bastard flies were starting to get on my nerves, mesh or no mesh. They were everywhere. If you have ever seen pictures of Muslims congregating at Mecca for the Hajj when they encircle the Masjid al-Haram, you have some idea of the sheer insect numbers packed into every square inch of space around here. I was stunned at their persistence and gung-ho attitude as they attempted to colonise my jacket. It was quite warm at this juncture and progress was sticky and hot. I was undoubtedly secreting a sweaty odour that was particularly attractive, almost sexually inviting, to Chironomid Midges, because they began to actively encourage each other to crawl lustily up my sleeves into my armpits looking for their copulatory fix. Doing my best to ignore this invasive promiscuity, I maintained a resolute rhythm across the heathland, with dramatic views to the right of the lofty Kálfstindar Mountains rising to a heady height of nearly 2700 feet. Eventually I stopped for a rest at the side of the road, flies dementedly circling my head like passenger planes stacking over Heathrow Airport. I sat on a sandy ridge, legs splayed out in front of me. A solitary phone mast, about ten metres tall, kept me company along with ten million flies. Almost immediately another car pulled up alongside me. A woman driver wound down her car window and asked,

"Are you all right? Do you need any help?" I nearly replied, did she have any effective insect repellent, and if not, would she help me to commit suicide, but I desisted and said demurely,

"Thank you very much, but I'm just taking a breather. I'm walking to Thingvellir."

"You're sure you'll be ok?"

"Yes thank you. Thanks for stopping anyway." She nodded, swatted a fly or ten away from her attractive face and pulled away. I watched her ageing Peugeot disappear up the road pursued by an enormous misty swarm of flies that traced pleasant cloud shapes against a cornflower blue sky, a bit like starling murmurations wheeling this way and that, before a night's roost in the marshes. From a distance, it looked quite aesthetically pleasing. I then reflected once more on the kindness of Icelandic folk. I could now number all sorts of instances where people had gone out of their way to help me. Perhaps this is what happens when you live on a small island. You develop a strong sense of community, consideration and togetherness.

I continued on my way, and amazingly the flies still grew in vast numbers. Swarms developed into plagues. The air was thick with them, whichever way you looked. To walk with your mouth open would have been utterly foolhardy – instant arthropod asphyxiation! I have never seen such an agglomeration of flies, seething and teeming in such a confused and jumbled mass as they did around this particular region of Iceland. I hoped sincerely that they would not bite their way through my fine nylon mesh. I would have gone insane in seconds.

I paused awhile at a remote viewing point and watched several vehicles pull up in order for their occupants to take advantage of the photogenic panorama below. As each vehicle stopped, the engines were switched off and people emerged to appreciate the vista. This was then followed by a few seconds of frantic swatting, with looks of sheer panic and horror creasing their faces, before they beat a hasty retreat back to their cars, reversing at speed, crunching their gears and then roaring off maniacally into the distance, swerving this way and that, windscreen wipers going full blast as the pesky creatures attempted to hijack their vehicles. I watched this happen five times, with a certain sang froid, generally content with my head protection. Whilst I stood there, I considered I had missed a trick. I could have made an absolute fortune selling fly meshes in this particular location, so I made a mental note to return to Iceland next time with a bulging suitcase full of them.

I suddenly noticed a glimmering strand of water to my left ahead of me and my spirits rose, because it was my first sighting of Thingvallavatn, the lake by Thingvellir. I therefore assumed I had broken the back of today's walk and set off with renewed motivation. The road started to descend, however the numbers of flies now started to increase even more, quite dramatically. I attempted to count the flies on my mesh. Obviously they weren't for standing still while I carried out my fly census, but I totalled at least sixty.

Contemplating life beneath my fly mesh

My sleeves and cuffs were covered with hundreds of them, all milling about, discussing the news of the day and putting the world to rights. One fly had successfully got under my mesh and was carrying out a sneaky survey of my nose. An inadvertent sneeze put paid to him. Another fly had also sneaked under my sleeve and was tickling my forearm. The resultant smack flattened him instantly so he resembled a small grisly, thin-based pizza, topped with tiny pieces of green pepper and black olives. This insectoid conflict carried on all the way to Midfell, a prominent landmass at the side of the lake. Here, thankfully, the insect swarm abated awhile, in fact, I hopefully concluded that that was the last of them. Not a bit of it! They were simply getting their second wind before driving me to distraction, all the way to the northern shore.

I stopped to study my map. I was not quite sure which way to go, but I need not have worried, because a National Park Ranger's vehicle pulled alongside me.

"Need a lift?" asked the ranger with a Scottish accent. I wondered if it was a compulsory question that was asked by all drivers, of pedestrians waiting by the side of the road around here, after all it was the third time I had been asked this, in just a few hours.

"No, I'm fine," I assured him. "I'm walking to the Visitors' Centre at Thingvellir." We got chatting. He obviously had little to do and I obviously needed a bit of social interaction.

"The flies," I complained. "What's going on?"

"Yes," he agreed. "This is the worst they've been for many years. It's the damp conditions, see. We've had so much rain this summer, it's been ideal breeding conditions for them and now they're everywhere."

"I know," I replied, picking one out of my teeth. Prawn flavour, I reckoned, with a hint of oxtail. He asked where I had walked from and, when I informed him I had set out weeks earlier from Seydisfjordur, he was distinctly impressed.

"Not the best weather to walk in," he said stating the obvious. He told me it was about an hour's walk to the Visitors' Centre. He again asked if I wanted a lift, but again, I turned him down. He was going to check on the fishing licences of the anglers along the banks of the lake, who were trying their luck at catching various varieties of trout, and away he went. I heaved my rucksack on my back once more, spat ten flies out of my mouth and headed off.

It took me an hour and a half and, as I neared my destination, the number of people here increased dramatically. Whole busloads were wandering around taking in the unique geology of the area. I wondered how they were dealing with the flies, because no one appeared to have a mesh. My question was answered as I observed them thrashing the air around them almost like demented semaphore operators. This was not the tranquil, reflective place it was meant to be. Instead the whole sky was full of infuriating winged beasts making everyone's life a misery.

Thingvellir is indeed an impressive place. It lies at the junction of two tectonic plates, the jigsaw pieces that make up the earth's crust. Here the North American plate and the Eurasian plates are pulling apart at the rate of two centimetres a year along the line of the North Atlantic Ridge. Between them is a rift valley, gradually subsiding as the gap between the plates widens, and within the ridge valley, cracks and fissures populate the area, some filled with water and others lined with birch and willow trees. On one side of the valley is a huge basaltic cliff that runs for several miles here. You can see the giant tears in the ground as whole blocks of lava have been pulled away. Down at the base of the rift, pools of water collect in the cracks forming a quite wonderful natural landscape, a natural tessellation of water and rock making the whole area a photographer's dream. This place was completely unique and even though I was tired after walking seventeen miles, its aura transmitted itself to me in quite a surprisingly spiritual way.

Strangely, the flies now declined in number and activity, so for the first time today, I could remove my mesh and fully absorb the sights around me. Little islands punctured the surface of the lake whilst birds enjoyed the feast within its waters and in the sky above. I was enthralled, well as enthralled as it is possible to be when you are hot and sweaty, with aching legs and sore shoulders and in need of a good meal.

I strode up a stepped path at the base of the cliff and reached the Visitors' Centre. I inquired as to the whereabouts of the campsite, which I knew had a cafeteria adjacent to it.

"It's about four kilometres away," said a member of staff, giving me an answer I did not want to hear.

"You're kidding," I replied exasperatedly. "I was told it was by the Visitors' Centre."

"I'm afraid you were misinformed, sir. The campsite is just here," and he indicated its position to me on a map. I looked heartily aggrieved.

"You mean to say, I've just walked over twenty five kilometres through swarms of flies, all the way from Laugarvatn and now I've got to walk another four?" He looked at me sheepishly. I don't know why. It wasn't his fault I had been harassed and bedevilled all day. "I mean," I continued, "look at me. Do I look like someone who can walk another four kilometres?"

I knew I looked wrecked, because I always looked wrecked after a walk. Sometimes I looked near death, and it was this look of someone potentially about to expire in front of his eyes, that softened the man's attitude to me. He looked at me sympathetically.

He paused a moment and then said, "I'll tell you what. I'll take you round to the campsite in my car. How about that?" I could have kissed him.

"What's your name?" I asked him.

"Einar," was the response.

"Well Einar, I am now going to put you on my Christmas card list, forever." I was chuffed to bits he was helping me, another example of the kindness of these people on this little volcanic island. He grinned at me and we shook hands. My arm nearly fell off, but I didn't care. Einar was giving me a lift.

We arrived at the campsite, basically a large exposed field with an undercover kitchen area and toilets. Next to this was a café and information centre. At that moment it decided to rain, so I rushed to erect my tent. One blessing was the flies had died down, not completely, but no longer of plague proportions, more a slight swarm, a drizzle of insects to keep you on your toes. Right now, my toes were sore and I needed a rest. Thingvellir was going to be my home for the next day or so.

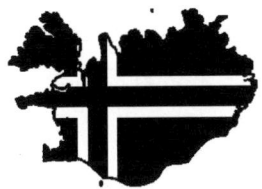

22. Thingvellir Contemplations

"I have seen what I want and I know what I'll be. I've seen it all, there is no more to see."-
Bjork

Morning arose and I opened my tent flap and swallowed a fly. Not a particularly pleasant way to start your day but at least it had the effect of waking me up and clearing my head. Today was a day to explore, a day to get to grips with this place. My legs were aching slightly after the trials of yesterday but I put the aches aside and made my breakfast of granola, once more, and chocolate. At this rate I would look like granola, gnarled, slightly brittle and dry to the touch. Well at least until the next rain shower! It took me exactly three minutes to brew a cup of coffee on my petrol stove, which is just as well really, because the flies had come out to play and so, cup in hand, I retreated to the kitchen area, a covered but not fully enclosed shelter a few metres away. Here, the flies kept out. I've no idea why; there was nothing to stop them flying in. I looked around and beyond the camp site rose the magnificent form of Ármannsfell, a heady mountain of nearly 2000 feet made of tuff, a rock comprising consolidated volcanic ash. To the east I could see lines of fissures that scoured the landscape like a lion dragging its claws into the ground, exactly as my primary school teacher, Miss Bartlett, used to drag her fingernails down the blackboard to get the children's attention. Such a remote, beguiling place. Without this campsite establishment around here, this area would indeed be utter wilderness.

After breakfast I followed the signs to Thingvellir and walking at a very sedate and thoughtful pace, arrived an hour or so later. Once more I climbed up to the Visitors' Centre and looked down on a row of attractive cottages, next to which was a tiny church, built in 1859. These cottages are now used as holiday homes by the Icelandic president. "Chequers" – country home of the United Kingdom Prime Minister - would probably be its equivalent. Further along flew an Icelandic flag marking the probable site, though it is not certain, of Lögberg, the rock where important governmental speeches were made back in time and Iceland's ancient laws were recited to anyone who cared to listen. This rock was the focal point of the Althing, the legislature that met to hand out the laws of the land. Iceland is very proud of this place and its importance is reflected in the vast numbers who come to visit here each year. This year it was my turn and I was duly impressed and wowed. I sat on top of the viewing platform, my legs dangling over the side and contemplated the wealth of geology and history in front of me; a truly magical place.

I must have sat there for a full half hour and various busloads of tourists bustled around me as they took their pictures of the scene below. As I sat there, however, I became increasingly and surprisingly somewhat dispirited, somewhat down, a mood totally at odds with my surroundings, but I could not help it. I was feeling lonely. It was all very well seeing and experiencing these magnificent sights, but I had no one to share them with. I was lonely in a crowd but no one noticed. The brutal reality was, I had been on my own for nearly three weeks, but now it was all starting to catch up with me. A sense of torpor, of melancholy filled me and I would have given anything for a hug or embrace right there. I continued to sit, feeling very sorry for myself for a further quarter hour, before dragging myself to my feet and shuffling down the hill towards Lögberg. I barely glanced at this historic significant place and carried on head down, along the path alongside the fault line, back to the campsite. I felt mentally exhausted and immediately took to my tent upon my return.

Thingvellir

My whole mind and body felt sluggish and lethargic; a lassitude that sat heavily on me and I was not sure why. Yesterday had been a very long, testing day, but no longer than some other days. In a way, I had felt something like this when I ran out of steam at Gullfoss, not physically but mentally. A world weariness that hung like a cloak and all I wanted to do was lie down and sleep; rest and do nothing.

So that is what I did. All afternoon, I lay in my tent, dozing lightly, feeling the warmth of the day on my face, not moving, just keeping still, recovering, recuperating from the excesses and challenges I had placed on my body and mind from the very start. I reflected on the day I arrived in Reykjavik and went for a coffee at BSI, the bus station and remembered how I had been completely intimidated by the scale of what was facing me. I had felt scared, too scared in all honesty, but I had, thankfully overcome my fear and got on with it.

I thought of my battles through the rain in north-east Iceland, the fog and the mist, when I was lost looking for R901. The traumas of the river crossings, when I thought the next step might be my last. The struggles through the thufur – how I hate that word and all it represents. The uncertainty of walking down Sprengisandur, losing my camera, thrashing around in my Harry Potter Forest, coming to the end of my tether at Gullfoss. All these events sprang into my mind as I lay there in my tent. The sheer thought of them exhausted me, drained me. I was completely spent.

I then turned my attention back home and thought once more about my family. I thought about my son growing up so very quickly. I thought about my wife and how we seemed like remote islands so much of the time. In a way, my self-enforced isolation out here just seemed to confirm this. I was doing my thing, she was doing hers. It filled me with a stark sense of dismay, a general unease and an increasingly nagging sense of dread – the realisation that things between us were not as right as they should have been. Retirement was changing me, getting older was changing me, Iceland was changing me. I had been seeking to challenge myself in a remote environment and that I had almost done. I had learned to respect this place and I had discovered that I could walk a very long way, but I could not really cope with myself. I needed people around me through whom and to whom I could convey my aspirations, emotions and opinions. But not just any old people, I needed special people who respected and admired me just for being me and who in return I could admire and respect. Although I was now certain I would complete my trek, the future from a personal standpoint looked uncertain and fraught. My journey into the wilderness seemed set to continue way beyond Iceland and it was a journey I was in no way prepared for. I squeezed my eyes tightly at the sheer thought of the desolation that lay ahead and shuddered…

It must have been about six o' clock that evening when I finally emerged from my hidey hole, hair tousled, unshaven, bleary eyed. My legs had stiffened up and I creaked my way to the toilet block and then back again. I felt slightly better but emotionally fragile, however I considered if I ate a good meal I would feel much better, and so it proved. I ate a bowl of thin soup, asparagus I think, but I couldn't be sure, a hotdog, pretty good, and a chicken and bacon roll, very good. These were accompanied by the usual cups of coffee.

Two fresh-faced young students were sitting outside and I went to join them. Their names were Nina and Laura, the second Laura I had met this trip, although these two were Dutch, not German. They were hitching their way round Iceland. They had no particular agenda because hitching did not allow them to work to a fixed schedule. Instead they were exploring Iceland ad hoc, impromptu and they sounded like they were having a whale of a time. They asked about my trek and I told them of my physical and mental ups and downs, the places I had visited and the people I had met. Nina was a psychology student who had travelled to India. She obviously had the travel bug and I could not see her settling down to a conventional life style for a long time, if ever. Laura was a financial buff, into econometrics, which I gather is mathematics, statistics and computer science all merged into one. We talked for hours about our families, our culture, our backgrounds, our politics and our aspirations. The evening went so quickly it was almost ten o' clock before we went our separate ways. The conversation was just what I had needed. A trampoline off which I was able to bounce comments and ideas, and after three long weeks, I had been in dire need of a trampoline. I hoped I would bounce back to my former self completely the next day.

I retired to my sleeping bag. My air mattress beneath had sprung a slight leak so I had to rouse myself during the night to restore a semblance of springiness keeping my weary legs and back away from the coldness and hardness of the ground. Half a dozen breathalyser puffs later I dropped off to sleep once more.

A new morning, a revitalised spirit. I had decided to return to Thingvellir Church that morning at 10 o'clock because I had heard there was to be a guided tour in English around the area starting from here and I fancied a bit of culture and education for a change. I arrived shortly before ten and was surprised to see the Scottish ranger who had offered me a lift two days earlier.

The tour was joined by about ten people and we wandered around the church and in the environs of the Lögberg. We stared into various fissures filled with crystal clear water. I learned that the original Vikings had left their homeland in search of new lands, because fathers had to bequeath a patch of ground to their sons on reaching adulthood, and such was the shortage of land back in Norway, there was no more land to bequeath, hence

Looking across Thingvallavatn

the invasion of other territories. Whether this was true or not, it seemed feasible and gave me something to think about. I learned too that the transparent waters in the fissures around here were made that way because of the natural filters in the rock that the waters passed through. All impurities were simply filtered out. I also learned that one particular pool of water never froze in winter, when all other pools did, because of the unique insulative properties of the surrounding rocks. I felt well prepared to take my exam in Norse History and Geology! It was good to just meander around, instead of striding out from A to B, as had been my wont of late. This day was really about washing clothes, cleaning equipment and recovering really.

I was considering heading off the following day, partly because the weather was still iffy and partly because I wanted to get under way once more. It was strange becoming so restless after just a day or two in one place, similar to my frame of mind back at Reykjahlid. I never realised I was so nomadic!

It was while I was pottering about, going through my equipment, I reflected rather carefully on various items I had carried all this way with me. I had a comprehensive first aid kit in an aptly coloured green bag inside which were numerous sized plasters and bandages. Up until this point I'd only used an elastic bandage for an aching knee and a single small plaster when I tore a nail badly, erecting my tent. Otherwise the remaining ten bandages and plasters had been unused. I had however, used several Compeed anti-blister plasters, but generally my feet had held up very well, although several toenails had gone black with the constant pounding inside my boots. I had optimistically brought sun cream factor 30 along with me, which, considering the appalling weather conditions I had suffered at times, meant this stuff had been redundant and a total waste of space and weight. Antibiotics, which I had brought along in case of toothache, were not needed thankfully. My soap had pretty well run out quite quickly as had my shaving gel so I used shampoo quite often for cleaning and shaving purposes. Instead of being called "Head and Shoulders", it could easily have been called "Groin and Backside" or "Face and Armpits" because it worked equally well everywhere. I also carried a comb, that went largely unused and so I had developed a pretty tousled look that was probably rather unbecoming, more suited to that of a homeless vagrant really. I had also chosen not to shave very often. It is amazing how quickly simple chores connected with personal hygiene and appearance get neglected when participating in a long trek. Instead one's attention is focused on food consumption, clocking up the miles and keeping warm and dry. Because no one knew me way out here, I did not have anyone to impress really. Currently I had a week's growth of itchy stubble that made me look like a petty criminal, you know the sort who robs old ladies of their handbags or picks pockets in Piccadilly Circus. I was amazed that anyone had actually ventured to help me out on occasions, let truth be told. If I had met myself, I think I would have crossed the road as quickly as possible and then looked up my face on the internet to see if I was wanted for any particular heinous illegal activity.

I had carried various batteries as back-up power for my GPS, camera – argh my camera! – my satellite tracker and my word processor. Actually I probably overdid the number of batteries I needed because I was probably carrying around more electric current capacity than the whole of Iceland's National Grid. If someone had plugged me in, I would have lit up the Icelandic sky like a compellingly realistic version of the Northern Lights. Strangely, I had rarely used my Silva compass to find my way. Route finding had been easy, much easier than navigating a trail through the Forest of Bowland or the Yorkshire Dales. Basically there were so few geographic features to confuse me, it was easy working out what was where. Walking back home, the clutter of natural and man-made features caused me to go the wrong way on a regular basis, but not here, thank goodness. My maps too, had been easy to follow and were well worth the £80 I had spent on them. I always wore a pair of sealskin gloves when walking but they were now suffering somewhat. Their constant saturation meant they were now unpleasantly slimy and extremely pungent with a pong similar to that of a sweet, festering stilton cheese that has been left rather too near a hot radiator for several days. Two of the fingers appeared to have fused and a strange webbing had appeared between several other digits – a form of Trench Foot for gauntlets. Inserting my hands into these on a daily basis was probably similar to a vet (providing he put a peg on the end of his nose) artificially inseminating an obstreperous dairy cow in a damp, muddy field – moist but surprisingly warm, slippery but reassuringly snug. My walking poles I loved, my constant metalled companions who supported me every step of the way, ensuring I did not fall over. How I had needed these when crossing the rivers, descending the steep slopes east of Kidagil and again at Gullfoss. At the end of each day, the poles changed role and became supports for a rudimentary washing line from which I attempted, usually unsuccessfully, to dry out my saturated base layers, bedraggled baseball cap and mangy socks. A cold Arctic breeze was fairly useless for drying, however when the sun did shine in the evenings, I managed to evaporate some of the perspiratory excesses of the day from my kit. My tent was a godsend; very light and strong. It had protected me throughout the worst of the weather. My cooking stove too, had performed in exemplary fashion, roaring noisily away with unabated enthusiasm in the stiff wind, boiling water for my coffee and dehydrated meals with consummate vigour. My Osprey rucksack that I had had to fit all these items in and carry across the country, had been a very faithful servant. Although my shoulders and back ached most days, without this particular rucksack I would have been in a much sorrier state. How I appreciated my hip belt! Furthermore, I was happy with my boots that had slogged across the sharp lava, uncomplainingly protecting my feet in all-terrain comfort. My waterproof jacket too had stepped up to the mark and kept most of the rain off me. As for Marti's waterproof trousers – well, she had been proved right. I had worn these every day since day one, so I almost regarded them as a second skin. They kept me dry, warm and swished silently as I walked. I so loved my trousers, almost as a personal friend. We had bonded – emotionally and, I'm afraid, almost literally. The end of the trip would either see them condemned to the tip, set on fire or else subjected to a deep cleaning procedure usually reserved for the most soiled carpets and upholstery. I congratulated myself on my equipment choices, at which point an unexpected gust of wind caught my drying clothes on my makeshift washing line and dumped them all unceremoniously in a wet, muddy patch.

My attention was then caught by a passing backpacker arriving at the camp site burdened with a rucksack of gargantuan proportions. He collapsed in a heap near me and lay groaning with exhaustion. It transpired that he was called Ruvn, from Hamburg in Germany. He was a seventeen year old Psychology student on his gap year and this was his first time unaccompanied away from home. He had decided, on a whim, to visit Iceland with the intention of following the Kjölur route along R35, connecting north and south Iceland across the interior, a watered down Sprengisandur, so to speak, connecting Akureyri with Gullfoss running between the glaciers of Langjökull and Hofsjökull, a distance of over 150 kilometres. It also transpired his pack weighed 38kg, way too much for a trek of this nature .

As he rested in front of me I detected an air of desperation about him and he struck up a conversation with me. After a lengthy discussion, he agreed to jettison the bulk of eleven days supply of food, half his clothing and all of his water, reducing his pack to a more manageable 25kg, but still overly heavy. I did not envy him carrying that load day in, day out. We spent an enjoyable evening chatting to each other and he proved to be really good company, however I needed to get away early next day, in the direction of Reykjavik, so we said our goodbyes and retired for the night.

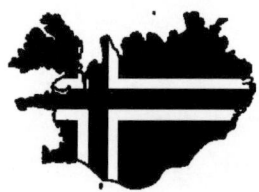

23. Guardians of the Sky

Young and alone on a long road, once I lost my way: Rich I felt when I found another; Man rejoices in man – The Hávamál

Thingvellir – Mosfellsdalur 19.6 mls

O nce again, the weather was not being kind and a particularly gloomy morning greeted me as I peered out of my tent. The dampness did not dissuade the flies from putting in an appearance, so once more, my mesh was worn to keep me free of unwarranted distractions.

It seemed a long time from when I arrived here with Einar, but that was all in the past. It was now time to go. I paid a last visit to the café, then looked over to Ruvn's tent, but, like all teenagers, he was dead to the world at this unearthly hour – it was nine o' clock – so I quietly left the scene and headed off on the R36. My mission over the next two days was to finally reach Reykjavik. This promised to be quite an emotional day really, the end being in sight, and with it, vast changes in my daily routine of the past month, but, not yet. "Not yet," to paraphrase Juba, the black slave who fought alongside Russell Crowe in the film "Gladiators" when contemplating when he himself might die, after witnessing Crowe's character Maximus dying. "Not yet." I still had over a day's walking to go. The sky was darkening and the clouds building. I knew I was in for a long, difficult day; the end was approaching, but not yet.

Skirting the northern perimeter of the lake the scenery changed very little. Lake on the left, moorland ahead of me, mountains on the right. I was quite pleased to be on the move again. These long distance treks are all right while you're on the go, it's just the stops in between that I struggle with rather more. But right now I had a purpose and that purpose was to travel about thirteen miles across the heath and wild camp, then push on to Reykjavik the following day. There was a large lake called Leirvogsvatn, roughly halfway to the capital, so that was my objective.

I had only walked a couple of miles and the cloud descended almost to head height and the rain poured down, rather excessively and unkindly I thought. Walking in those conditions was dire and it was with great fortitude that I trudged on, droplets dripping off my hood. The flies were everywhere despite the rain, so I had to wear my mesh inside my hood to make life as easy as I could, while the miserable blighters performed a rain dance atop my head.

Time for the rhythm of four. Time to count to distract myself from the utter misery of the day. Four paces …one; four paces…two, over and over; four paces… one hundred and twenty six; four paces…one hundred and twenty seven. I took a certain comfort from the familiarity of number, saying the number aloud seemed to reassure me that this long, timorous journey was gradually, progressively, unhurriedly coming to an end. All the while, drops of water trickled from my hood and the blue brim of my cap like an intravenous drip; a steady drizzle, in accord with my footfall, in time with my breathing. It induced in me a stupor of soporific quality, almost a hypnotic trance as I ate up the miles, splashing through puddles resembling vast lakes and oceans. This was not the Iceland you see in the brochures. This was primeval privation; a type of squalor that made me sigh and despair. The wretched weather seemed determined to break my soul, but I was not for breaking. I was made of stronger stuff, and since the start of this trek I now felt more resolute to deal with the vagaries of the god-awful climate. Conditions were so foul, so miserable I almost laughed at my unmitigated suffering. Dreadful was the day and it was only part done.

I walked for two and a half hours and frustratingly, Thingvallavatn was still stubbornly on my left hand side, refusing to go away. I had expected it to be well behind me by now, as I headed westwards over the heath. Cars and 4x4s splashed tentatively by, their occupants staring inquisitively at me, wondering what on earth I was doing out there in that monsoon. I did not care. I was past caring. I just placed one foot in front of the other and ploughed a sorrowful furrow in the direction of Reykjavik.

Two cyclists sneaked up and frightened me to death on one steep climb, their headlights fuzzy and dim in the cheerless weather. They were competing with a stiff wind that was blowing into their faces. They drifted past me, unspeaking, focused, intent on finding a way out of their saturated misery. The appalling wretchedness carried on for several long, demanding miles. I have rarely walked in such uncomfortable, dreadful conditions and I have certainly walked many miserable miles in all seasons in all types of weather, but this really took some beating. It was as if Iceland was saving its worst weather until last. A sense of resignation hung over me, but fortunately my sense of purpose in reaching my destination outweighed the negatives. On and on I went.

I reached the junction with the R360 that ran down the western shore of Thingvallavatn. Above this was an incline to a parking space, where several cars were gathered. Ten minutes later I was there myself and I could now see why the cars had stopped. In a field at the side of the road, people had created basic sculptures and constructions out of the small pieces of lava that were scattered around. It was a playground in stone, with fanciful and elaborate igneous compositions balanced precariously. You know, the sorts of things you used to make at school out of plasticene, and in miniature.

It was here I ate the first of my sandwiches in the pouring rain. I sat on a bench – my trousers still retaining their superb waterproof qualities - well done Marti back at the outdoor shop in Long Preston - and devoured my meal quite passively. I was considering my original objective – to wild camp up here on the heath. It did not, as the rain tippled down, somehow seem such a good idea, right now. Firstly the ground was so waterlogged and secondly there was no shelter from the strong, unrelenting wind rushing by. I needed a Plan B.

After a few minutes peering at my map, I came up with a solution. Instead of stopping at Leirvogsvatn and enduring an unpleasant night out on the moors, I would instead keep going all the way to Mosfellsbaer, on the outskirts of Reykjavik. This was a challenging objective, basically a day's walk of twenty miles plus, but I had discovered previously that there was a campsite there. It had to be better than my original plan to camp on the heath which no longer seemed plausible.

The interminable climb towards Leirvogsvatn subsided and the road flattened out. It was now a case of following some more power lines, and as I did so, the weather finally started to improve. Patches of blue sky appeared for the first time that day and I thanked God for small mercies. It had been such a torrid, unpleasant day's walk so far and I was due a bit of respite.

Leirvogsvatn eventually appeared, an elongated stretch of water aside the road, as did a large basalt landmass to my right. I knew immediately that this was Mount Esja, and it comprised not one, but a whole range of mountain summits, the highest being nearly 3000 feet above sea level. On observing this, my spirits lifted dramatically because this was the first visual indicator that I was nearing Reykjavik. Mount Esja dominates the skyline north-east of Reykjavik and now I could see its vast mass. Niggles that had been bothering me were now starting to reduce; my mood was getting brighter!

I turned a corner and gazed far into the distance. The sky thankfully had cleared substantially and, between a small dip in the hills on the horizon I stopped with a start and squinted. What was that ahead? I focused my gaze on a tiny blue-grey ribbon that sparkled occasionally as it caught the sun. It then dawned on me what I was actually seeing, and my heart missed a beat, then leapt skyward. What I was seeing was a narrow horizontal patch of sea, the simply wonderful, the simply incredible North Atlantic! When you have walked for so long in such appalling conditions and you unexpectedly come across something that represents an ending to your tribulations, you basically go nuts.

"Yeahhh," I screamed. "The sea! I can see the sea!" I sounded just like a small boy from the city on his first day trip to the seaside, but I could not have cared less. This sudden and unexpected sighting of the sea meant so much to me. My heart was dancing, my whole body was dancing. The sea, what, five miles or so distant? I do not know what it is like to win the lottery, but the emotional rush one gets at times like this is compellingly intense and strong. I felt euphoric, triumphant, elated. Cloud nine was right there in front of me to walk on – and so I did, for several wonderful, ecstatic minutes. I could almost smell and taste the unique briny freshness that is the sea. Wow! What a moment!

Eventually I calmed down somewhat and contemplated that I still had plenty of walking to do. I was not there yet, but this blast of encouragement would see me to the finish. As I stood there, three birds flew low overhead. It had been a while since I had seen the birds, and it seemed an age since they hurled abuse at me for all my shortcomings. I looked at them as they flew lower, then settled down on a patch of bare grass to my left. They all had downturned bills so I knew they must be spóa, or curlews. They milled about for a while and I looked at them, waiting for the insults to start. I settled on a gravel pile, eating a nut bar, aside the road; part of an abandoned building project, I guessed.

"What do you have to say for yourselves?" I shouted, rather aggressively towards them. "I know I'm pretty well done for, but at least I can see the sea! I'm nearly there!" I waited for the usual tirade of derision to come my way, after all, I had got quite used to the birds' barracking, from when it first started on Route One coming out of Egilsstadir, and then continuing all the way across the country. "Go on then, give me your worst!" I taunted them. One of the birds sauntered right up to me. I could almost touch it, its feathery back smooth and silken, as it walked onto the tarmac, by one of the roadside yellow marker posts, a mere metre away. It rubbed its bill against the ground and then stared at me, cocking its head to one side. This was the closest encounter I had had with the noisy birds the whole trip. Usually they walked ahead of me, keeping a safe distance, before uttering contempt for my ineptitude. What happened next caught me by surprise, so much so, my jaw nearly hit the floor. The bird spoke, but not in its usual unruly tone, but in a harmonious, conciliatory register.

"Well done Mark," it intoned, "you're nearly there. We have been keeping an eye on you the whole way, and now the end is in sight. Don't mess it up now!" My heart missed a beat; I had not expected such a turn of affairs and just stared, trying to take in what this solitary bird had just said. It looked at me, retreated a short distance, then continued, "You needed us. We have been your benefactors on this journey, looking after you when you needed looking after, all the way from Seydisfjordur. All right, we may have moaned at you a bit, but you really needed moaning at. This country is not one to be taken lightly, for it comes with a vicious bite that can destroy you if you are not careful. One more day to go, one more day for you and for us. Good luck and…well done." And with that short homily, it turned and rose up into the air, where it was joined by all of its companions. Together they wheeled round once more, keeping me within their watchful gaze. They rose skyward, higher and higher, viewing me from afar. It was at that point I truly understood. These moorland birds who had seemingly tormented me endlessly for nearly three hundred miles, were, in fact, my guardians, my "angels of the sky." They had berated me initially, picking faults with my indecision, my ineptitude, but they had looked after me when I got lost in the fog, when I crossed the rivers on the power line walk and when I struggled around Gullfoss and Tungufell. They had seen me through the foul weather that befell me day after day, and because of them, I was now nearly there. Sentimental mush maybe, but at that precise moment I truly wanted to believe it.

A pylon that I had been trying to reach for a couple of hours was now behind me and the road started to dip. Scanning the valley ahead of me, I could discern the road snaking through a gathering of buildings. In fact, buildings, of which there had been none up on the moors, were now becoming more evident. Isolated farm buildings, houses, barns; all were coming towards me, firstly as a trickle and then as a steady flow. The sun now grew stronger and it was around this time I started to feel peckish. I think I had a bag of granola for tomorrow's breakfast, but nothing else. The trek over the moors had emptied my larder. It just meant I would have to find somewhere to buy something to eat.

Unfortunately Mosfellsbaer simply refused to appear. It dug in its heels and stayed infuriatingly out of sight. I must have walked at least eighteen miles, all of it into the wind and my body was now feeling the effects. The initial surge of excitement upon seeing the sea had worn off to some extent and all I wanted to do was to find the campsite, but the campsite was not there. In fact, I had no idea where it was at all. It was not indicated on my map. I had just heard something about there being a campsite in this location when I was back at Thingvellir. I now wished I had been more thorough in my planning, because it could be situated either this near side of Mosfellsbaer, or on the far side, I had no idea. Did it lie on the main road, or was it secreted away, over the brow of a hill? Wherever it was, I needed to find somewhere to rest and eat.

The road finally stopped descending and instead it stretched horizontally for about two miles, straight as an arrow. I calculated that to reach the end of it would take me forty minutes. My legs were now starting to seize and my ankles were complaining bitterly too. This was going to be a difficult last leg of my walk. I plodded on, muscles tightening, facing oncoming traffic at the side of the road, when I suddenly came across a pavement. Now I had not walked on a pavement for over 250 miles, but here was one; a real life pavement - right in front of me and I stepped onto it, as an alien would step onto the surface of a foreign planet. It felt weird but also pleasingly familiar. Civilisation was approaching and the next piece of evidence for this was a remote and tidy bus stop and shelter. A bus stop? Out here? I nearly sat down inside it to hide away from the wind, but resisted the urge and carried on. There was a sign in the middle of the carriageway ahead of me. What were the odds of this directing me to my campsite? I screwed up my eyes to read the uneven writing, and, to my delight, in faded letters I could pick out the letters that made up the word, "CAMPING" and an arrow pointing left. The relief was huge, and within 200 metres, I turned off the pavement onto a small dusty track. Three flags of different nations fluttered atop tall masts.

The campsite at last, at a place called, not Mosfellsbaer, but Mosfellsdalur, a satellite of the former.

It was a very modest affair, with very few residents. I could see one or two camper vans but that was about it. No tents, no people, just a small house next to a field and some plastic tunnelled greenhouses. A man approached me. He spoke in broken English and I thought I detected a French accent. He told me I was welcome to stay here and showed me around the facilities. This took all of ten seconds because basically there were very few. A single toilet, a sink and next door, two showers, open to the sky. Al fresco showers inside flimsy plywood partitions. I did not think they would be able survive a storm, but anyway, this campsite was better than wild camping up on the moors. There were sheltered camping pitches and the ground looked relatively firm, well as firm as you could hope for, after a deluge.

Having pitched my tent, I looked for the Frenchman but he was nowhere to be seen. Instead another man appeared with a beard. He spoke with an Icelandic accent and I asked him if there was a shop nearby. He informed me rather brusquely that the nearest shop was four kilometres away. My heart sank, because I was relying on that shop for food for that evening and there was no way I was going to walk an extra four kilometres on top of the thirty one kilometres I had already covered, plus four kilometres back. My legs would rebel. There was nothing for it but to retire to bed early. I have always found that if you are hungry or have a headache or some other malaise, the best solution is to sleep it off. In the morning you'll be fine... or dead!

With a grumbling stomach in dire need of filling, I climbed into my sleeping bag. Actually I was quite grateful to be lying down, resting my legs. My eyes were tired, my leg muscles aching and throbbing; everything was flagging, however I knew I could replenish my engine and get something to eat in the morning. As I settled down, I started to drop off, but I became vaguely aware that there was a shuffling sound outside my tent. Then my stomach rumbled rather impolitely, as if to say,

"Oi! What about me? Aren't you going to look after me?" I ignored it and turned over. The shuffle became more pronounced and distinct. It seemed to be right beside me, outside my tent. Then a voice, a deep voice, boomed,

"Englishman! Come out of your tent!" I froze in terror. Then I convinced myself that the command was not directed at me, but someone else, which was plainly ridiculous because I was the only tent on the campsite and the only person for miles around with an accent originating in the Shires.

"Englishman! Come out of your tent!" boomed the gruff, rather threatening voice again. I had two options. I could reach quickly for my polar bear knife, so far unused, and take the initiative and plunge it through the rip-stop nylon in one deft sweeping thrust, right into the heart of the assailant, killing him instantly, or I could meekly unzip my tent and await whatever fate befell me. It took me one second to decide. I reached up with my arm...and unhurriedly, so as not to induce a mad frenzied attack, slowly unzipped my inner tent, with a rather soothing reassuringly non-violent zipping sound. There before me stood the bearded Icelandic man I had spoken to earlier. I cowered and waited for the first fatal blow to land.

"I've brought you this," he snarled. I thought he initially said, I'd bought it, as in, I was about to die. "Take this," he rasped, and in his hand he was holding a large piece of stiff white plastic upon which was placed a doorstop of a sandwich, filled with a slab of cheese and salad vegetables. I was stunned. In his other hand he held what I was later to find out, was a glass of gin and tonic. The whole scene was quite surreal. There was me expecting my brains to be dashed with a heavy cudgel, when all the bearded man wanted to do was feed me. My mind was scrambled. Was this a nightmare?

Had I dropped off to sleep and I was now existing in a bizarre Alice-in-Wonderland fantasy? I did not know what to do, however I managed to say,

"How kind of you. That is really kind of you! Thank you so much."

"You're welcome," he snapped. "I thought you needed this!" and he thrust the sandwich and drink towards me, in a stabbing sort of gesture. Without a further word, he turned around and marched off. I was truly gobsmacked, shocked, stunned. I had not expected this! My starving stomach could now be rewarded with this gigantic hunk of bread. As I looked out incredulously, towards the spot where he had now vanished, I was sure I spotted a mottled bird-shape in the undergrowth, silently watching me...

I withdrew into my tent not really knowing which emotion to express. There was I, a few moments earlier, contemplating my premature demise and now, I was stuffing my face with the Icelandic equivalent of Cheddar. The G and T tasted divine too. I hadn't tasted gin since college, and I'd only given it up because someone said it was a woman's drink. Well, at that moment, I honestly didn't care if I was a man's or a woman's drink, I was going to sup it and enjoy it. My stomach appreciated being taken care of, but I could not get over how considerate this man had been to me, but how did he know I was starving hungry? How did he know? Then I thought back to the bird outside, and I had my answer.

Now I had something in my stomach I felt a lot better. All was now right with the world. The G and T made me feel slightly giddy and distant, but that was just fine. I smiled contentedly and within seconds, I was asleep.

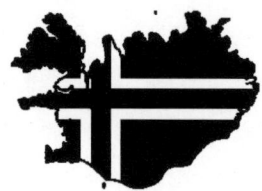

24. Solfar So Good

He who has seen and suffered much and knows the ways of the world,
Who has travelled, can tell what spirit governs the man he meets - The Hávamál

Mosfellsdalur – Reykjavik 11.8 mls

During the night various other campers had arrived and pitched their tents, so when I awoke in the morning, my solitary tent now looked to be a minor structure in a massive refugees' shanty town. I almost had to fight my way to the toilet, tripping over numerous guy lines criss-crossing my path. Because it was early, no one else was awake so I had exclusive use of the showers, which was just as well, because the lock on the flimsy plywood had failed. It is a weird experience taking a shower when there is no roof. It's even weirder when the shower is cold. Why didn't I just wait for it to rain and then stand there in the buff, soaping myself all over? Anyway, I jumped about, issuing sharp involuntary breaths in response to the ice-cold, bracing water that poured from the showerhead, that was reviving my tired muscles and joints. I then dried myself on my special microfibre camping towel. If ever there was a contravention of the Trades Description Act 1972, then this was it. My dictionary defines a towel as: "A piece of absorbent cloth or paper used for wiping or drying." Well, my microfibre thingy clearly did not meet the basic criterion to even be called "a towel". All it proceeded to do whenever I had emerged dripping, usually freezing to death on this trek, was to spread the water around my body without actually absorbing any of it. I might have well have dried myself with a plastic bin liner; the effect would have been the same. So when I came to put my socks back on, the task was nigh impossible. Wet feet do not slide easily into chunky walking socks. And placing one's damp backside into a pair of briefs is not the most pleasant experience I have encountered either, as they tend to cling in just the wrong place, annoyingly and discomfortingly so. After fighting with my clothes for a goodly ten minutes, I emerged fully dressed, just about, and started to decamp. I wanted to get underway and find a shop where I could purchase breakfast. I was now fairly good at decamping, even in the rain. I had had plenty of practice stuffing a saturated tent into a bag several sizes too small. I was good at deflating my air mat by lying on it prostrate: face and groin down in the mud, rocking gently towards the valve end. It always looked a bit dubious and perverse, so I tended to deflate it inside my tent, away from public gaze. I used ten tent pegs to put my tent up and generally I counted ten pegs back in, but occasionally one tent peg would take it upon itself to play hide and seek and would disappear into the long grass sniggering.

Once packed, I walked round to reception, well the house next to the field actually, and knocked on the door. The gruff, bearded man appeared suddenly from nowhere and peered at me closely. Close behind him was a black and white collie dog. I said timidly,

"I've come to pay. How much is it?" He thought for a moment then bellowed,

"One thousand," which I took to mean one thousand kronur which is about five pounds, and actually very reasonable, even if the shower did not have a roof. There had been loo roll in the toilet cubicle after all.

"Thank you so much for the sandwich last night," I gushed, but I really meant it. His kindness had had a chastening effect on me, even if I was frightened to death of him.

"You're welcome," he said, slightly less aggressively, then almost as an afterthought, "would you like a coffee?" I considered this generous gesture for a second, then replied in the affirmative, after all, I had had no breakfast and this coffee would at least help get me to the shop four kilometres further on. Mind, I mused, I dare not say no really. Once I had taken a few sips of a mug of filtered coffee, I visibly relaxed, especially when I saw there were other family members out the back. He must have had a gentler side after all. I discovered that he was a gardener who grew vegetables for sale in Reykjavik. The campsite was a side-line. The Frenchman who I had spoken to the previous day, then put in an appearance. I discovered that he was a student from the Vendee who had come to study gardening as part of a work experience programme here in Iceland. The gruff gardener was called by the nickname "Nonni". He actually said very little – a man of a few gruff words - but his kind and welcome offering of a cheese sandwich the night before would remain in my memory for a long time. I finished my coffee, looked Nonni in the eye, bade my farewell and shook his hand. Mistake! I could still feel my arm muscles spasming two hours later, as he nearly wrenched my upper limb off at the shoulder, probably to feed to his dog.

Hitting the pavement once more, I headed for Mosfellsbaer, just outside Reykjavik. This was going to be a strange day, an exciting day. The first thing on my mind however was still to find something substantial to eat, so I headed into town for sustenance. R36 would run out shortly and I would rejoin Route One, Iceland's ring road that I last walked along in Reykjahlid, nearly two weeks earlier. The murky sky merged with the grey patches of sea I could spot to my right. A light drizzle was falling but it would take more than that to dampen my mood. I gradually drew nearer the roundabout that marked the end of my countryside excursion and the beginning of the urban sprawl that was Mosfellsbaer.

I reached the roundabout just after 9.30am beyond which lay swathes of sea running across to Reykjavik harbour, still out of sight. Construction workers were busy installing cables at the roundabout, too busy to notice me with my weighty blue rucksack, waterproofs and walking poles. Pausing briefly at the roundabout, I looked around and considered the sheer normality of it all. Gone were the windswept moors, gone the single road meandering into the distance and gone my guardians of the sky. Now it was industrialisation, urbanisation, yellow buses, traffic lights and apartment blocks.

It felt strange, almost as if I was intruding on someone else's life, peering in the front window of a modern sophisticated society, whilst I stood detached, outside in the rain. People actually lived here and I had wandered in, almost like a gate crasher at a party.

Turning left onto Route One, the volume of traffic increased significantly, but what struck me most, was the noise, the rumbling roar of car engines and tyres thundering over smooth tarmac. Quite a culture shock. The pavement dropped down to a pedestrian crossing – my first pedestrian crossing in the best part of a month. It is strange how quickly everyday features of modern living become alien, almost forgotten.

The road wandered upwards and to the right and then came my first problem of the day. The pavement had run out on Route One and I found myself being led towards a tunnel under the road and onto a residential estate. I now needed to navigate my way through this estate into the centre of Mosfellsbaer, where hopefully I would find a café of some description. The estate consisted of blocks of two storey apartments, probably built in the 1990s. They would not have looked out of place in any British town or city, constructed of modern building materials. To think that, just a century earlier, people were still building their houses out of turf. Such is modernisation and progress.

I had to ask directions a couple of times to find my way to Mosfellsbaer's centre and here I found a sandwich bar next to a KFC. I piled in, placed my oversized rucksack propped up by a pillar and settled down for a breakfast of a baguette and several coffees, and boy, did I need that! The staff were very friendly and an assistant called Berglind, an exceptionally beautiful looking woman suggested how I continued my journey into Reykjavik. I knew there would be problems getting into the capital, because the roads were soon to develop into fast dual carriageways, that would become very unfriendly to pedestrian users too, lacking pavements beside them. I had to find a route that allowed me to walk safely into town. Berglind suggested I follow Route One and then head off onto R49. This sounded straight forward. It proved anything but.

The rain had stopped when I left the sandwich bar. I turned right to pick up Route One once more, and thankfully the pavement around here had re-emerged. I reckoned I had a walk of six miles to the centre of Reykjavik. As I crested a rise, I came to a sudden dramatic stop. There, for the first time, in the far distance, I could see the buildings of the Reykjavik I knew. Office blocks silhouetted against the skyline, but, most significantly I could see in the distance, Reykjavik's cathedral, the Hallgrimskirkja, the tall pointed arched structure that stood tall like a Saturn V Rocket.

Now, before I set off on my Iceland trek, I had always imagined what it would have been like to walk into Reykjavik after weeks of hard slog and endeavour. I had a clear picture in my mind of seeing Hallgrimskirkja, for the first time, and the emotional response it would draw from me.

Well, now I had arrived and I could see the Hallgrimskirkja and my emotional reaction was exactly as I had imagined. I was completely overwhelmed and almost dropped to my knees.

Hallgrimskirkja,

Day after day I had walked alone in the most difficult weather conditions along remote roads and tracks in places that were unfamiliar, intimidating and, indeed, frightening. But at all times, the one vision I had firmly implanted in my mind was this very one right now, the Hallgrimskirkja: bright, white, majestic, alluring, and it marked the concluding part of the most physical and mentally challenging assignment of my life. I stared at it, just a few miles further on, and choked back my tears. How I had longed for this moment, and this moment was now! Months and months of training, personal sacrifices for me and my family, loneliness and solitude – all for this one beautiful, cherished instant. I could not remove my eyes from it. I was entranced, almost bewitched. This tall, imperious building represented everything about my commitment to Iceland. As I stood there, visibly shaking, I was emotionally engulfed with a deep sense of veneration. I understood it, perhaps others might not, but I did not care. This was my moment, my reason for being here. I had proved something to myself and it felt good. It felt so good.

How long I waited there, I am not really sure. Ten minutes? Twenty? I took time to text family and friends with the words that simply said: "I can see Reykjavik. Ecstatic." These words understated the strength of my profound joy. Perhaps the words to express what I was feeling do not exist. It did not matter. I was there, gladdened, with an intense feeling of fulfilment. Other people have walked further, longer, higher. They have endured greater hardships, survived greater mishaps, accomplished far more. That did not matter. To me, this trek had been all about me. I had done it for me, nobody else, and standing here, I knew exactly what it meant. A purely selfish endeavour, the memory of which would stay with me for the rest of my life. As I stood on the outskirts of Mosfellsbaer, I knew what it meant and nobody could ever deprive me of that. I was proud, God I was proud.

Within seconds my phone was buzzing: "Can't express how proud we all are," said my niece, Katharine, echoing my sentiments. "Gosh, Mark, you've managed to do this against so many odds..." Katharine knew exactly how I felt, and through our texts, she shared my joy and my dream.

Unfortunately, I could not stand on the roadside in the suburbs of Reykjavik all day, so I heaved my pack onto my back as I had done a thousand times, and set off following Route One. I passed the Icelandic version of "Toys R Us" and this made me reflect on the incongruity of it all. Just that morning I had been standing in the middle of an isolated campsite, feeling ravenous, and now, an hour or two later, I was fully nourished, surrounded by all the trappings of a modern commercialised world. I struggled to get my head around it.

I came to the point where I had to turn right onto R49, but this is where it got difficult. I do not know whether modern town planners include pedestrians in their considerations, but following a major arterial route into Reykjavik was proving very tricky indeed. I had to leave the dual carriageway and negotiate a confused route through an anonymous industrial estate that seemed to be leading me *away* from downtown Reykjavik, not towards it. I spent a very frustrating hour trying to find a road alongside which I could walk without being mown down by speeding cars. When I did find a road with a walkway, it took me in the wrong direction. I did not realise Reykjavik was into labyrinths, but this was a pretty good one, to test even the mighty Theseus. I bumped into, metaphorically and thankfully, not literally, a cyclist who had stopped nearby and asked his advice in negotiating my way to the centre of Reykjavik. He laughed uproariously and said, in a Spanish accent, that he too was trying to find his way through the complex road system. He was cycling round Iceland and now he was completely baffled, unable to find a safe way in. We empathised at our situation, then he informed me he was headed for the campsite in Reykjavik, as was I, so we agreed to race each other there. With that he set off towards the harbour and I continued straight ahead. It was not long before I was totally lost again. Upon asking for advice, several Reykjavikers simply shrugged their shoulders as if to say, my task was all but impossible. I eventually found one kindly lady walking her dog, who helpfully gave me a set of quite complex instructions that would bring me out nearer the centre. I listened very carefully and followed her words exactly. This resulted in me in being completely lost in the middle of a quite attractive piece of parkland, next to a river in which several people were engaged in angling. I was now becoming rather infuriated and aggrieved. One angler, on seeing my bewildered countenance, stopped for a minute and directed me quite precisely. He even generously supplied me with a town map that he had stashed away in his car. This proved very useful, and a steady half hour uphill walk brought me eventually to the entrance of the campsite. It was at 3.20pm. I had finally arrived.

Of course, my trek was not over. The finish was at the Solfar, a contemporary stainless steel sculpture of a Viking boat designed by Jón Gunnar Árnason. It is said to contain within itself, the promise of undiscovered territory, a dream of hope, progress and freedom, and this truly reflected what my own individual trek had been about; a journey of discovery where I learned so much about myself, about Iceland and especially about people. I would come to realise in the coming days, how much the people I had met on my walk had affected me and changed my views on human nature and character.

Solfar

25. Reykjavik - a preamble to unity once more

Reykjavik campsite was a glorious place. A hive of activity, of transience, where people appeared and departed without fuss or noise, at all hours of the day and night, a bit like an airport really. Tents were clustered together, not in neat rows, but in a random higgledy-piggledy scatter-gun distribution. The reception area was a chaotic place where cooking and toileting took place rather too close together for my liking. A communal space, somewhere to gather when the weather was bad, basically all the time really, then. It was usually congested with backpackers, many sporting facial hair and all carrying electronic gizmos.

I sat in this place on my first night. It was heaving because the weather was being its usual miserable self, spoiling everybody's holiday. I managed to claim a space on the floor – all the seats being taken – and propped myself up against a pillar. I then took out my Psion word processor and started typing my thoughts on the day, when I looked up and absolutely everyone was engaged is some form of electronic discourse; not one person was speaking directly to anyone else. Fingers and thumbs were frantically operating mini keypads, screens were being swiped and tapped, but no one was saying anything. Cables criss-crossed the floor, connected to multi adaptors and around the wall were charging points for mobile phones into which everyone had plugged a device. I smiled. How the world has changed. Not many years ago you would have seen packs of cards being shuffled and dominoes being arranged. Now, it's the intense silent world of the internet that dominates. Apparently they don't call these people backpackers anymore. They are known as flashpackers, after the flash drives that store so many gigabytes of digital information. When a flashpacker arrives at a campsite, he asks two questions: firstly, "Can I charge my mobile phone here?" and secondly, "What is the password for the wi-fi?" A world that is, I'm afraid, leaving me far behind.

As I sat there, my backside becoming increasingly numb against an unremittingly hard floor, I happened to see the Spanish cyclist from earlier in the day. We greeted each other like long lost friends, which was nice. This is a situation that occurs regularly when you are on your own, participating in some physical challenge like trekking or long-distance cycling. You bond with your peers remarkably quickly. The intensity of empathy and friendship cannot be underrated. The cyclist was called Guillermo, that in English means William. He was a teacher back in Spain and he had spent a month cycling around Iceland. He too had really struggled to find his way to the centre of Reykjavik, but had arrived a little before me. We swapped stories about our unique Arctic adventures and got on really well with each other. In fact, after that evening, we met several times more. We should have formed our own Icelandic Travellers Club.

I also met a couple from Germany who I had run into at Thingvellir. For the past three weeks they had been cycling and camping around Iceland. They came from a place called Mainz, their names being Pascal, an IT networker and Claudia, a teacher. Once again, we were delighted to meet up again and we celebrated our reunion with a mug of tea. Very British. We swapped stories about our experiences battling the elements and we agreed that one of the benefits of travelling was the sheer diversity of people you met. People who really related to you. People who truly understood you.

Having arrived on the Friday, I now had to wait for the arrival of my wife and son on the Monday. They were coming to see me finish my walk at the Solfar, and for that reason, I was saving the final two miles between the campsite and the Solfar, until they arrived. In the meantime, I decided to explore Reykjavik for myself in the intervening period.

Saturday saw me catch a bus to the centre. From here I went to the bus station, BSI. It was here that I arrived three weeks earlier, frightened out of my wits, before catching an internal flight to Egilsstadir. I sat at exactly the same table in a café here, in exactly the same seat, drinking a coffee, exactly as I had done then. But what a difference! As I sat there this time, I felt a strong feeling of accomplishment, of conquest. I had risen to the challenge and tackled the terrain, the rivers and the weather. Whereas before, I had felt overwhelmed by the sheer scale of my task, I now felt changed, a different person to the one who had sat here quietly panicking.

A short walk to Hotel Natura, the place where my wife and son would be arriving on the Monday saw me introduced to Hrefna, the receptionist, there. The intention, upon my family's arrival, was for me to continue camping across town, while they luxuriated in the plush facilities that the Natura had to offer. All of a sudden this seemed absurd and pointless for I wanted instead, to join them in their hotel. Continuing to camp, especially with them residing a mere fifteen minutes away, would make me feel isolated and remote. Hrefna immediately understood my plight, as I told her of my walk across Iceland and my preference to stay at the hotel. Hrefna was a striking looking woman with good-natured, dark brown eyes. I looked at her almost pleading with her to allow me to stay here with my family. Would she go out of her way to help a rather smelly traveller stop in a swanky four star hotel? She gazed at me considering the situation, saw the hopeful look in my eyes and we connected. A few tricky phone calls and clarifying conversations later and the deal was done.

I was delighted! I smiled with delight and I think she felt she had carried out her charitable deed for the day. She knew too how grateful to her I was. The eyes said it all.

I walked to the Perlan, also known as the Pearl, a viewing point and restaurant over the airport and surveyed the scene, with light aircraft coming and going with great regularity into the clear sky. It felt good to be able to relax, not having to embark on a long walk into the unknown. I looked across at Hallgrimskirkja, a modern megalith in white, with a tower clad in vertical pillars based on the tall hexagonal basalt columns so prevalent throughout this volcanic country. I could see over to the harbour, a vastly developed area of cafés and restaurants while whale watching ships sat moored ready to take hopeful tourists to observe the elusive wanderers of the sea. Further round, Mount Esja posed with robust grandeur overlooking the city, and I screwed up my eyes scanning for the meandering route I had taken into the city, from Mosfellsbaer, the previous day. From my vantage point, high above the surrounding area, Reykjavik looked a very modern place, nestled in this south-western corner of Iceland on the edge of the Reykjanes Peninsular. Buildings dressed in a preponderance of white, many with red roofs, fitting neatly in the space between mountains and sea, swept by fresh breezes that originated way out over the water of the North

Atlantic. My 360 degree view was utterly splendid and I lingered here for an hour, just looking and thinking.

I then walked down to the harbour and the whale watching boats. I was hoping to catch up with Jonas, who I had met at the mountain hut at Helgaskáli, and who told me he worked here. Jonas who kept me awake all night with his thunderous snoring. I walked up to a kiosk and asked,

"Is Jonas around?"

"Do you mean Captain Jonas?" was the reply. Now I had no idea as to his status, so I just said,

"Jonas. He went on holiday up into the mountains recently. I met him there." The man in the kiosk smiled and said, "That's Captain Jonas. He's out on the boat at the moment but he'll be back at four." Now this surprised me to discover that snory old Jonas was in fact a captain of a ship, because seeing him stripped down to his off-white vest, lying in a bunk, snorting and dribbling right next to me, as I did a week earlier, did not give me an impression of a man who was actually of great status and authority. I assumed Jonas would have been a deckhand, a sort of midshipman, of lowly rank. Now I knew that he was almost an admiral, well in my eyes at least, I decided to grab some lunch and meet his boat when it arrived back in harbour, two hours later.

At four o' clock precisely, a boat displaying the name Andrea , drifted slowly into the harbour. I scanned the bridge of the boat and there, quite unmistakably, leaning out of a window was Jonas. He expertly moored the boat and a line of tourists disembarked. Jonas immediately saw me standing isolated on the jetty and grinned. I waved back and he shouted and beckoned me aboard.

Once on board, we shook hands firmly and looked at each other with a quiet respect. Strange to think that I had nearly throttled him in the middle of the night a week ago, anything to stop his glottal reverberations. But now, I appreciated his skill and his authority as a captain and he congratulated me upon learning I had finally reached the end of my trek. We shared tales of our evening together up in the mountains. I told him he snored like a trooper, and he smiled at me as if to say, "So what?" We shook hands again and shared a coffee. I was glad I had sought him out and his familiar face was a welcome sight in the sea of strangers around about. A short while later, I bade farewell, descended the gangplank and headed back to the campsite where I ate a basic tea of meatballs and noodles. The campsite had filled up and fortunately the weather remained dry. I spent the evening in the social area and caught up with Pascal, Claudia and Guillermo once more.

On the Sunday I went to the Lutheran Church at Háteigskirkja, a handsome building with Moorish towers standing high above the surrounding buildings. I had painted this building months previously at home, from a picture I had seen on the internet and now I had come to see it for myself in the flesh, so to speak. I discovered that a service was due to commence at eleven, so I attended the service along with a modest congregation of twelve others. Strange to think that quiet reflective place could affect me so much, but at this particular moment it really did. I needed time to appraise what I had done for the past month, to recognise that the endeavours and hardships were now over. Normal life could resume once more. I joined in with the Icelandic hymns, doing my best to pronounce the unpronounceable, in as tuneful as voice as I could muster. I could follow the rhythm of the service but the homily, delivered by the minister, left me mystified. The whole experience however provided me with a deeply spiritual sensation. I thanked God for helping me across the rivers, for providing me with support when I truly needed it, especially around Helgaskeli, Gullfoss and Tungufell. I thanked God for my guardians who had somehow kept me going. I am not especially religious, but on that Sunday, I felt a divine resonance that is now still hard to explain.

I waited at the end of the service and spoke with the minister at the entrance to the church. I thanked her for a lovely service and apologised for not quite understanding her sermon. She laughed and I then informed her about my solo Iceland trek. I recounted various events and I emphasised how surprised I had been at man's kindness throughout to me personally. She looked intently for a moment as I finished speaking, then she said, "This trek of yours across Iceland. I don't think it is really a trek, more a pilgrimage I think." I smiled at her.

Háteigskirkja

"You think so? I think it is more about me fulfilling an ambition that I have harboured for a long time. I've always wanted to walk across Iceland." Oh no," she insisted, "Yours is definitely a pilgrimage, I am absolutely certain about that." She smiled at me with her intent blue eyes.

This notion of "pilgrimage" interested me and, as I left the church, I wandered back into the centre of Reykjavik thinking quite deeply, immersed in a whole conglomeration of emotions, issues and ideas. Perhaps there was more to my journey than I had at first realised. Originally I considered the notion of walking from A to B in a remote country to be just that – a trek of physical exertion looking at the volcanic scenery and meeting a variety of folks along the way. However, the trek had quickly transcended that. I was having to confront emotions and situations that questioned quite specifically who I was, what I was about and who I wanted to be. I was learning that I had discovered another side to humanity that I did not realise existed – a compassionate, caring, interested side, and this shocked me greatly because I had been so used to a more indifferent world back home with me plodding along in a conventional, unemotional, almost blasé actuality. My trek was forcing me to into a kind of self-examination, as if I was pressing the pause button on my life and assessing where the heck I went from here. My trek had become, almost by stealth, an inner journey of self-appraisal; a taking stock of me, my family, my friends, my life.

I suddenly felt rather depressed at the size of the life task now facing me. My physical challenge was nearly ended, however my personal tilt still had a long way to run. I realised I had been away from home for over three weeks and this enforced solitude and introspective thinking was now making time pass so slowly, despite all the splendour and attractions of this thriving city. My wife and son were not due to arrive for another twenty four hours and that gave me rather too much time for self-analysis. It felt a bit like after the Lord Mayor's Show, so I did what most tourists do around Reykjavik and headed for the shops and museums. Shaking off an air of melancholy was somewhat of a struggle. Pilgrimages are meant to end in a sense of fulfilment, but I felt anything but fulfilled, and as I wandered round a couple of art exhibitions, I felt restless, heavy, distinctly un-me.

Monday was similar. I busied myself as best I could. I walked back into Reykjavik from the campsite and then ambled down to the harbour and site of the Hofdi House, the scene of the famous meeting between Ronald Reagan and Mikhail Gorbachev in the 1980s, that led to the end of the Cold War and a massive reduction in global nuclear armaments in the east and west. This was a fascinating place and my attention from my state of gloom was distracted for a short while, but generally this was a sorry time for me.

I knew my family were on their way to Iceland that very afternoon. I could imagine them excited to be airborne, as all holidaymakers are. I imagined them flying over Grindavik on the Reykjanes Peninsular, then landing at Keflavik, the international airport a mere hour's drive away.

I loitered back to the campsite once more, only to bump into Nina and Laura, the Dutch students I had encountered at Thingvellir. We were pleased to see each other and embraced like long lost friends. They were leaving that night, having completed their hitchhike around the country and I felt sorry to say goodbye to them. We had shared confidences and opinions and soon they would be gone. This did not really help my general sense of gloom.

I made my tea, two packets of asparagus soup with a baguette and a bar of chocolate. The campsite was busy as usual. My water for my coffee quickly boiled on my petrol stove. I was completely adept now at rustling up a drink in a trice, so well-practised was I. Suddenly my phone vibrated and I received a text from my son to say he and my wife had arrived at their hotel next to the airport. I texted back: "Is it ok?"

He replied, "Very nice. It's a big room." I was pleased he liked the room and switched my phone off. The intention was that I would set off the following morning from the campsite and they would meet me, as I completed the final two miles of my trek, at the Solfar. This is what we had

291

planned, what seemed an age ago. I finished my coffee and sat on my stool looking across at the other campers. Some were also busying themselves with their tea, with gas stoves roaring quietly, heating various versions of pasta and noodles. Others were washing up, others pitching tents. You could tell immediately which campers were seasoned veterans, sliding tent poles through nylon sleeves with confidence, whilst inexperienced rookies stood holding disjointed poles and armfuls of tent with a look of panic and consternation. I smiled and looked down at my feet. It was now seven o' clock. I had three hours to kill until I retired to my bed, then a long night, before I could finally be reunited with my family. But I could not stand it anymore. The loneliness was eating me up. I was all right whilst I had a purpose, trekking miles on a daily basis, but now that those miles had been achieved, the solitude was now just a terrible burden that was crippling my spirit and my soul.

Without a word, I washed up my cup and my cooking utensils. I zipped up my tent and with the emotion welling inside me, grabbed my jacket and headed for the bus.

Within twenty minutes I arrived at the hotel. Hrefna in reception informed me my family had arrived, gave me a key card to the room, smiled and pointed me in the right direction.

What followed was an emotional reunion at the Hotel Natura, by the airport. It had been twenty six days since I had left them on the driveway back at home in Lancashire. In between I had been petrified, excited, exhausted, traumatised, thrilled, soaked, supported and cared for to a greater and lesser degree. There had been a strong possibility that our reunion would never have occurred. The rivers could have put paid to that. But the rivers had been overcome and now we were back together. I hugged my wife and embraced my son then I shared the remainder of their meal with them. Words could not really express how I felt. I was emotionally wrung out, in desperate need for comfort and love and understanding. However, as I sat there, something was missing. The connection I so desired was incomplete. I was overjoyed to be there but I knew I had changed fundamentally. Did they realise it? If they did, no one was saying. That night, we walked up to the Pearl to look down over Reykjavik. I looked over in the direction of Mosfellsbaer, reliving my final day's trek to the centre of the city with a pang of regret that I had all but finished my solo trek, but not yet...

Tuesday morning saw me travel back to the campsite for the final time. I had arranged to be at the Solfar at midday, which would give me time to walk there, and for my wife and son, time to get across town from the hotel. It was a peculiar feeling dismantling my tent for the very last time, rolling up my sleeping bag and consigning my petrol stove to the side pocket of my rucksack. The patch of ground that I had laid claim to for the past few days was now going to be returned, no longer my territory. I was amazed at how small the flattened piece of ground actually was, an insignificant plot that had been so important to me, but now was part of my history. It was time to go.

The walk from the campsite situated in the Laugarás area of north-east Reykjavik, to the Solfar was quite simple. A short stroll along Sundlaugavegur, then turn right towards the coastal road called Saebraut. I had walked this way towards the Hofdi House the previous day, but I deliberately stopped short of the Solfar because that part was saved for today, the official end of my solo trek.

Now that I was actually completing the final leg of my walk, my mood and outlook felt slightly different to that of recent days walking around Reykjavik, because my agenda was now back on track; this was now the legitimate version of my walk; I was no longer wandering aimlessly. This short final section of road alongside the sea front was my bona fide solo trek and I was greatly pleased. I wore my baseball cap with my solo trek badge as always, strode out with my walking poles as always and treated this final part with the same attention as I had every other section, because, in many ways, this part was the most important of all.

Thankfully the weather was bright and the sea remarkably blue. I hoped that my wife and son had made it to the Solfar before me. Walking alongside the sea, I thought about the day I set out in the wind, rain and snow from Seydisfjordur. That now seemed a lifetime ago, another era. The road curved in a wide arc to the right. I passed the Hofdi House and waved. When I had visited there on Sunday, I told the guide inside that I would wave to him as I passed. Whether he saw me or not, I have no idea, but I really hoped he did and that he waved back to me. I could now discern the Solfar perhaps three hundred metres away, glistening in the sunlight. I squinted to see my wife and son, convinced myself I could, but in reality, they could have been any of the half a dozen figures gathered there. Two hundred metres and a slight quickening of pace. I swallowed hard, becoming increasingly emotional. One hundred metres and I could see my son, then my wife, standing on the steps behind the sculpture. Further gulps of air as I tried to retain my composure and then, all at once, I was upon the sleek Viking ship. I was there.

This beautiful shining work of art represented a fitting location to end my trek. As I approached it, I blinked back the tears and again swallowed deeply. I slapped my hand down hard onto its skeletal hull members with a triumphant outburst of achievement. My face creased and emotion took over. It is hard to describe the almost overpowering sense of euphoria, satisfaction, accomplishment and relief that is felt at the end of such a challenge as my Iceland solo trek. All I knew, was that it was a very private, intimate moment, as I grasped the stern of the Solfar and held it tight. It meant so much to me and I desperately blinked back my tears. My wife and son captured this triumphant moment with their cameras and then I turned, arms aloft to acknowledge them. Finality, at last.

Such was the emotion of the moment, I almost forgot that I had carried two stones in my pocket, collected from the waters of Seydisfjordur Harbour. They had remained in my jacket for the whole journey but now was the time to perform my final duty, to mark the official end of my trek. I took one of the stones from my pocket, and, holding it behind my head for a few seconds, hurled it high into the air, before it disappeared into the cold water of the bay with a gentle splash, as the surface of the water parted momentarily to allow this small, but significant piece of stone to sink. I turned round, and as I did so, a group of people, who had picked up on what was going on, burst into spontaneous applause. I bowed, doffed my cap and smiled a satisfied smile. I hugged my wife and my son. My trek was done.

There at last!

One pebble bound for the sea

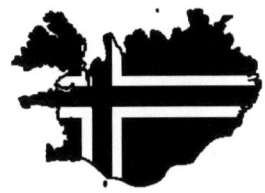

26. Home Landing

I have changed, of that there is no doubt. Life in Iceland and since has been a prolonged period of introspection, a period of reflection, analysis and an appreciation of the fact I am still around to talk about my journey.

Would I go again? Undoubtedly. I have some unfinished business to reconcile. I would still like to complete my disrupted walk along Sprengisadur, but not on my own. I do not think it is possible for me to walk it on my own anymore. I do not, unfortunately, have the physical capacity necessary to carry everything I would need for this extreme element of my walk, but I would certainly complete it with a companion.

I would also like to walk Landmannalaugar and Thorsmork, again not on my own. I am done, well and truly done, with extended walks, with only myself for company. I simply cannot cope with extreme remoteness for more than two days, as it tends to lead to severe despondency and anguish. I never realised that I was such a social animal. I am fine for a day, but then a cloak of isolation descends.

Iceland is a wonderful country, with breath-taking scenery. It draws you in unremittingly with its newness, its freshness, its intensity. It was a privilege to have been a part of its raw nature for several weeks in 2014. You cannot resist it.

I have come to appreciate people far more. Iceland taught me that there are so many people out there who are basically very kind and generous; in some cases, exceptionally so. I will never forget the considerable gestures of real benevolence and goodwill handed out to me. I will cherish always the strength of the bonds that developed between us, in such a short time. Connections made through our eyes, a look of perspicacity, of warmth, of genuine friendship with me, a mere stranger in another land!

The connections made with Margrét, Benedikta, Laura, Nonni and Hrefna will endure with me forever. Their eyes connected with me in a visceral way, beyond rational explanation. At the outset, my Iceland trek was fundamentally a physical challenge, with me testing my body to its limit, crossing hundreds of miles in a foreign territory.

It became far more than that. Not so much a feat of endurance, but instead a vehicle of relationships. The endless miles, day after day, connected the people, who came to mean so much to me. This walk was ultimately about people, connected by miles, whose eyes simply shone bright above absolutely everything else.

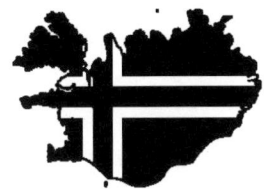

27. Finding my goal

Upon returning home I was almost shell-shocked by the normality of everything. To some extent it almost seemed like I had not been away and the mundane routine of home life resumed. The trouble was, I felt I was still in my own personal wilderness - the same wilderness that I had fretted about so much in my tent on the banks of Thingvallavatn and this now led to an increasing sense of unease and detachment. This was in sheer contrast to the Icelandic connections I had made on my journey. These had really impacted on me. I had been so humbled by the magnificent generosity of the people I had met. I simply was not used to such intense kindness.

But at times back in Lancashire, in the weeks and months afterwards, I felt lost, a spare part, unable to connect. I had, quite simply, lost my way and I desperately needed a map to get me back on track again. It's funny that now I had achieved my life's goal, I felt like this. This was not in the script at all but fundamentally I did not know where I fitted in. Strange that such a physical ordeal for me should turn into such an emotional and personal hiatus.

Now, a year later, I have not just reached a crossroads of self-examination, I have turned down a new path of discovery and enlightenment. What this fresh paseo will reveal to me, time will tell.

Do I regret my sub-Arctic foray? Not at all. Each day I feel distinctly enthralled, nay privileged, remembering my time there, with my sore, aching limbs and joints, the perpetual rain, my weighty rucksack, the damned flies and my acute sense of forlorn estrangement.

So I have moved on to face new personal challenges. But I know now, post-Iceland, I will cope. I can manage the humdrum of daily life once more, because I have finally met someone to share with me what the past eighteen months have been all about – a severe test mentally and physically, a discovery of myself as a person, a reflection of my life as it has been and a sense of renewal in anticipating what I wish my life to become.

She has a pastiche of light blue and cob brown eyes that look deep within me to reveal my soul, and that look transfixes me in an instant! A recognition that at last I have found someone who truly knows me; someone who can decipher the vital essence of my being; the quintessence of my psyche.

I now need a new purpose, a new aspiration, but, far from being simply a monthly foray into the chilly climes of a sub-Arctic landscape, it seems to lie within the elegant suburbs of a southern city for as long as I can possibly imagine.

Equipment List

Hilleberg Akto one man tent

Osprey Xenith 75 Rucksack

Osprey Hydraulics 3L Reservoir

Paramo Aspira Waterproof jacket

Rohan Spark Top super lightweight insulated pullover

Rohan Dry Explorers Waterproof Trekking trousers

Rohan Escapers lightweight trousers

Rohan Ultra Silver T Shirt

Rohan Microgrid Zip mid-layer

Cintamani Fleece

Cintamani midlayer

Rab Base layer

Icebreaker Merino Base Layer

Hi-tec v lite altitude ultra lux boots

Black Diamond Trail Shock Walking Poles

MSR WhisperLite Universal Stove + petrol fuel

Vango Venom 200 Sleeping bag

Thermarest Prolite Sleeping Mat

Spot Gen3 Tracker Satellite

Olympus XZ-2 Compact Camera

3 underpants

Hi-Tec Shore River shoes

Bridgedale Socks 2 pr

Bridgedale Undersock 2 pr

Trekmates Polyester longjohns

Garmin GPS 60

Sealskinz gloves

Bollé goggles

One plastic spoon/fork

Vango One person cook kit cooking pans

Third bar Dove soap

Microfibre towel

Toothbrush

Toothpaste small tube

Gillette Fusion Razor

Bog in a bag stool

Bog in a bag toilet bags

Small tarpaulin with lightweight pegs

Lowe Alpine Balaclava

Ron Hill Woollen hat

Sun glasses

Plastic mirror

Silva compass

6 Mal og Menning (Atlaskort) Maps 1:100000

Gorilla tripod

Coleman CHT7 Head torch

Spare AA batteries – 4

Spare AAA batteries - 4

Psion Word Processor

Passport

Travel Insurance, E111 Card

Grey metal water bottle

Trekmates Goretex Gaiters

Buck Polar bear knife

Sandwich bags

Lanacane Anti-chafing gel

About the Author

An enthusiastic and dedicated primary school teacher in north-east Lancashire, England for over thirty years with a passion for enthusing, educating and entertaining children. He has a son who taught him everything he knows about birds and planes. Mark likes to sing frenetic basso profundo, though he never fully knows the words of any of his songs, accompanying himself especially badly on acoustic guitar. He has a love of the outdoors, walking in the Pendle Hill area, The Forest of Bowland, the Ribble Valley and the Yorkshire Dales. He has cycled John O' Groats to Land's End, run the Windermere Marathon and enjoys travelling around Europe. He is obsessed with Iceland and reading about polar exploration - Ernest Shackleton is his all-time hero. He also likes plane spotting and reading funny books, with Bill Bryson and Michael Green being two of his favourite authors. He played league cricket in his youth and hopes one day to play rugby union at scrum half for England. He now lives in Hertfordshire and is trying to find a decent hill to climb.

19262119R00175

Printed in Great Britain
by Amazon